Date Due

BRODART, INC.   Cat. No. 23 233   Printed in U.S.A.

12.5°

SMALL GROUPS
AND POLITICAL RITUALS
IN CHINA

MICHIGAN STUDIES ON CHINA

Published for the Center for Chinese Studies of the University of Michigan

MICHIGAN STUDIES ON CHINA

THE RESEARCH ON WHICH THIS BOOK IS BASED WAS
SUPPORTED BY THE CENTER FOR CHINESE STUDIES
AT THE UNIVERSITY OF MICHIGAN.

MARTIN KING WHYTE

Small Groups
and
Political Rituals in
China

32644

UNIVERSITY OF CALIFORNIA PRESS
BERKELEY · LOS ANGELES · LONDON

University of California Press
Berkeley and Los Angeles, California
University of California Press, Ltd.
London, England

ISBN: 0-520-02499-0
Library of Congress Catalog Card Number: 73-80822
Printed in the United States of America

CONTENTS

ACKNOWLEDGMENTS

This study is the result of a long series of intellectual, emotional, and financial stimulations, without which the author would have been tempted at various points to move off into other pursuits. Many of the things learned along the way cannot, for reasons of brevity and focus, be included in the study itself, but my multiple debts of gratitude should be acknowledged here.

My interest in the distinctive ways communist regimes deal with primary group loyalties was first aroused by a seminar on the individual and society in the Soviet Union taught by Urie Bronfenbrenner at Cornell University, where I was an undergraduate. Further stimulation stemmed from discussions of group criticism and self-criticism rituals in courses on Soviet society (taught by Paul Hollander) and Chinese society (taught by Ezra Vogel) I took during my first year of graduate work at Harvard University. My first paper on the topic, which became my MA essay in Harvard's Soviet Union Area Studies Program, was completed that same year in a seminar on attitude change and social influence taught by Stanley Milgram. In this course I was able for the first time to start systematically comparing Soviet and Chinese strategies for dealing with primary groups, and relating those strategies to Western research on conformity and attitude change.

At that point I was "hooked" on what seemed to be a fascinating and important research topic, but uncertain about how to pursue it further. In particular, as my interest in China began to develop, I was plagued by doubts about whether a monographic study on Chinese small groups was needed (several articles on the topic had already appeared) and whether, in view of my late entry into the study of Chinese language and society, I would be capable of carrying such a study out. At this point the active encouragement of Ezra Vogel pushed me on in spite of my doubts. Quite clearly my major debt in this study goes to Ezra, who served for three years as the ideal combination of adviser, critic, rooting section, and friend.

Further opportunity to clarify my ideas just prior to conducting field research came in the way of an invitation to participate in a two month conference on change in Communist societies held in the summer of 1968 in Palo Alto, California, and sponsored by the American Council of Learned Societies. The financial support for the field research itself came mainly from a Foreign Area Fellowship, with supplementary research funds provided by the Comparative International Studies Program of the Social Relations Department at Harvard University. Office and interviewing space in Hong Kong were provided by the Universities Service Centre, and many of my associates at the Centre, but particularly Janet Salaff and M. H. Su, helped me get started in my research. Chou Tsui-ying and Luella Kam served me ably as both language tutors and sources of stimulating discussion about all aspects of contemporary Chinese society. I was aided in the actual interviews by three capable research assistants: Tang Wah, Yang Hsiu-lin, and Hung P'ing. These specifics aside, I found my year at the Universities Services Centre, with its intensive intellectual interchanges and abundance of information sources, an invaluable experience in broadening my general knowledge about China.

The first draft of this study was written under a research associateship at the Center for Chinese Studies at the University of Michigan, and support at the rewriting stage was provided by a summer faculty fellowship from the Rackham Graduate School of the University of Michigan. Helpful comments upon earlier versions of this study were provided by my dissertation committee (Ezra Vogel, Alex Inkeles, and John Pelzel) and by Ernest Young, Norma Diamond, William and Kathleen Whyte and Janet Salaff. The initial editing was performed by Janet Eckstein, whose comments on style and organization helped to modify the dissertational tone of the study. Typing at various stages was performed by Penny Greene and Dianne Gault, and the index was prepared by Ted Levine. As is always the case, I take full responsibility for the final product presented here.

Finally, special thanks are owed to my wife, Ronnie. Her patience and encouragement helped sustain me during the arduous interviewing stage. And she alone was subjected to listening to the manuscript at each successive revision. Her quizzical looks and occasional nods into somnolence helped improve the style of the finished product.

I

INTRODUCTION

In early 1924, in his lectures on the Three Principles of the People, Sun Yat-sen criticized Chinese society as a "sheet of loose sand":

The Chinese people have shown the greatest loyalty to family and clan with the result that in China there have been family-ism and clan-ism but no real nationalism. Foreign observers say that the Chinese are like a sheet of loose sand. Why? Simply because our people have shown loyalty to family and clan but not to the nation—there has been no nationalism. . . . The unity of the Chinese people has stopped short at the clan and has not extended to the nation.[1]

Chinese society was deficient in both vertical integration (ties and a sense of community between ruler and ruled) and horizontal integration (ties and a sense of community among people at the same level in society, for example among the broad masses of peasants).[2] This relatively low level of national integration is not unusual in peasant societies—Marx used a similar metaphor to describe the nineteenth century French peasantry as "a sackful of potatoes." The relative autonomy and non-involvement in national affairs of rural villages are in many ways assets in a traditional autocratic state, but they become liabilities

---

1. Sun Yat-sen, *San Min Chu Yi,* Frank W. Price, trans. (Shanghai, 1927), p. 5.
2. The importance of both horizontal and vertical integration for political development is stressed in Sydney Verba, "Comparative Political Culture," in Lucian Pye and Sidney Verba, eds., *Political Culture and Political Development* (Princeton: Princeton University Press, 1965), pp. 529–537.

when elites try to change a society to meet the challenge of modernization. In Japan, China's primary Asian rival, the feudalism of the Tokugawa period left a legacy of high vertical integration, of loyalty to superiors and reverence for the Emperor, which was manipulated by the Meiji reformers to hasten social change.[3] Sun Yat-sen and other Chinese modernizers, in contrast, were continually frustrated in their efforts to integrate and mobilize the nation. Chiang Kai-shek in 1945 continued to speak critically of the "sheet of loose sand." [4]

In recent years the "sheet of loose sand" has been replaced by metaphors of a different type, such as "the empire of the blue ants." News coming to us from China of massive political rallies in cities and isolated villages and of gigantic human efforts to eliminate sparrows, diseases, or counterrevolutionaries presents a vivid contrast to the earlier commentaries. While the "loose sand" image may have been an overstatement, and while foreign apprehension and lack of information may lead to exaggeration of the extent of organization and regimentation in China today, it is clear that a major change has occurred.

How this great social change was brought about is the central question underlying the research reported in this book. We will describe certain organizational innovations and activities that have played a major role in producing a relatively unified population, responsive to the demands of the elite. These innovations represent a model for organizing human action which departs in various ways from Western and Soviet experience. They must be understood on their own terms; mechanical efforts to apply Western or Soviet conceptions of organization to the Chinese scene can only lead to perplexity and disbelief.

The basic elements we will be concerned with are "small groups," "study," and "mutual criticism"—terms with a special meaning in the Chinese context.[5] Large parts of the Chinese population have been organized into small groups (hsiao-tsu) of between eight and fifteen

---

3. Much of the literature comparing modernization in China and Japan focuses on this difference. See the extended discussion of Chie Nakane, *Japanese Society* (Berkeley: University of California Press, 1970). See also Marion J. Levy, Jr., "Contrasting Factors in the Modernization of China and Japan," in Simon S. Kuznets, Wilbert E. Moore, and Joseph K. Spengler, eds., *Economic Growth: Brazil, India, Japan* (Durham: Duke University Press, 1955).

4. Chiang Kai-shek, *China's Destiny*, Wang Chung-hui, trans. (New York: Macmillan, 1947), p. 213.

5. For earlier discussions of small groups, see A. D. Barnett, *Communist China: The Early Years* (New York: Praeger, 1964), Chapter 8; H. F. Schurmann, "Organization and Response in Communist China," *Annals*, Vol. 321, January 1957; John W. Lewis, *Leadership in Communist China* (Ithaca: Cornell University Press, 1963), Chapter 5.

members. In some cases these *hsiao-tsu* are identical with the lowest administrative subdivision of a particular organization, such as the work group in a factory; in other cases *hsiao-tsu* have been organized where no formal groups would normally exist, such as groups within urban neighborhoods, or school classrooms. In all cases these *hsiao-tsu* are formed and supervised by higher authorities rather than emerging spontaneously. These groups seem to be a regular feature of schools, factories, mines, government offices, corrective labor camps, military units, and urban neighborhoods. Their existence and permanence among China's peasant population are less certain. Generally an individual belongs to only one such ordinary *hsiao-tsu*. However, Party or Youth League members also belong to a *hsiao-tsu* at the lowest level of these organizations.[6]

Hsiao-tsu members, in addition to carrying out organizational activities (such as work, military training, or academic study) together, also meet on a regular basis to engage in political study. During this study activity group members are expected to engage in regular mutual criticism, or criticism and self-criticism (*p'i-p'ing yü tzu-wo p'i-p'ing*). Each person is supposed to analyze his thoughts and actions, comparing them critically with the standards set in assigned study materials. He is expected to criticize his own shortcomings, to accept the criticisms of the rest of the group, and in turn to point out the failings of others. In this manner group social pressure is mobilized to encourage individuals to change their attitudes and conduct in order to conform more closely to the demands of higher authorities. In the pages to follow the term political rituals will be used to refer to organized political study, mutual criticism, and related activities carried on within *hsiao-tsu*.[7]

In Chapter 2 the significance of *hsiao-tsu* and political rituals in the attempt to unify and mobilize the Chinese population is outlined.

---

6. The lowest organizational level of both the Party and the Youth League in China is called a *hsiao-tsu*, not a cell. In the early post-1949 period the youth organization subordinate to the Chinese Communist Party was termed the New Democratic Youth League. Later it was renamed the Communist Youth League. In this study the term Youth League will be used throughout to refer to this organization.

7. The term political rituals is the author's, and the Chinese Communists do not refer to these activities in this way. The term is used both as a shorthand for a set of complex activities and in recognition of the fact that these activities are supposed to take place on a regular basis in prescribed and highly elaborated ways, which are described in Chapter 4. This is not to imply that these activities have no meaning to or effect upon participants. Sociologists have frequently stressed the great impact of rituals on social life, and Chinese Communist elites are constantly concerned with keeping these activities lively and meaningful.

Here the reader will learn what is distinctive about the organizational techniques represented by *hsiao-tsu* and political rituals. This is followed in Chapter 3 by a discussion of the historical origins of these practices and an explanation of how they diverge from similar practices in the Soviet Union.

The rest of the book describes the operation of *hsiao-tsu* in different kinds of organizations and assesses their effectiveness in changing the attitudes and behavior of their members. The logic of the analysis pursued is rather involved, in part because of the limited data available. Ideally to determine the effectiveness of group rituals one would spend time in different organizations in China, applying repeated interviews, attitude tests, and other instruments to their members over an interval of some time. Although China has "opened up" during the last few years, this ideal is still far from attainable. In the foreseeable future no foreigner is likely to have the access and freedom which would be necessary to conduct such an empirical research project in China. A collection of descriptions of *hsiao-tsu* and political rituals from the Chinese press over the span of years since 1949 would also be helpful, but here, too, there are problems. In the period immediately after 1949 detailed handbooks were published in China describing how political rituals were supposed to be carried out in *hsiao-tsu* and the problems that would be encountered. But after a few years concrete mention of *hsiao-tsu* virtually disappeared from the Chinese press, replaced by more abstract discussions of good and bad attitudes, good and bad organizational discipline, and good and bad mobilization. Only during the Cultural Revolution (1966–69) do concrete discussions of small group operations re-emerge, mostly in connection with the establishment of "Mao Tse-tung's thought study classes." For much of the period since 1949, then, the Chinese press contains only scattered and indirect information about the operation of *hsiao-tsu*.

Given these difficulties, the primary data used in this study are intensive interviews the author conducted in Hong Kong in 1968–69 with 101 refugees who had left China during the previous few years. Problems are inherent in any attempt to use information provided by people who have chosen to leave China for Hong Kong. The interviewing procedures, the types of individuals interviewed, and the way I have dealt with problems of bias are discussed in Appendixes I–III. I have not tried to quantify the results of the interviews or to generalize directly from my informants to the population left behind in China. In Chapters 5 through 9 case studies are presented of particular schools, factories and other organizations as they were perceived by individual informants. No assumption is made that the organizations described are in any exact sense typical. In fact, two separate case studies are presented in each of these chapters, and the differences between these cases are a focal point of the analysis. A lesser assumption is made, however, based upon internal comparisons of the numerous additional accounts from which the two case studies in each chapter were drawn. It is assumed that the features of the organizations described, such as their structure, personnel, and the round of daily activities, are not grossly atypical of other organizations of the same type in China. For example, the factory described in the first half of Chapter 8 is not necessarily a typical Chinese factory, but the case study should help the reader understand the general organization of factories in China and how they differ from factories in other societies and from other types of organizations in China.

The case studies presented concern organizations in China in the 1960's for the most part, up to and in some cases including the Cultural Revolution. Reforms that came in the wake of the Cultural Revolution have altered some of these organizations, particularly the schools, and some of these changes are noted in the pages that follow. Future research will have to determine more exactly in what ways organizations in China in the 1970's have been altered in basic ways from those described here.

How well can information supplied by refugees be used to judge the effectiveness of *hsiao-tsu* and political rituals in influencing their members? Clearly, direct judgments about the attitude changes experienced by the informants themselves or those around them cannot be taken at face value, since these are people who chose to leave China. However, this study uses a procedure that makes it possible to make indirect judgments about *hsiao-tsu* effectiveness in spite of the data problems. We have copies of the *hsiao-tsu* pamphlets from the early 1950's which explain how *hsiao-tsu* and political rituals have to operate, in the view of Chinese authorities, if they are to produce attitude change and behavioral compliance. In Chapter 4 some of these pamphlets, which define the ideal "strict political atmosphere," are analyzed in detail. This strict political atmosphere then serves as a standard against which to compare the accounts of actual *hsiao-tsu* activities provided by informants. The basic assumption underlying this study is that some organizations will be more successful than others in establishing a strict political atmosphere (and thus, according to the *hsiao-tsu* pamphlets, more able to change the attitudes and behavior of their members), and that the interview materials can be used to discover why.

How do we utilize the information gained by comparing informant accounts with *hsiao-tsu* ideals? The literature on Western organizational behavior, small groups, and attitude change could be used to provide hypotheses about under what conditions small groups would operate effectively, and then the interviews and comparisons could have been used to test these hypotheses. But the distinctiveness of the Chinese organizational context and the limited nature of the data available recommended another approach. Instead of testing previously derived hypotheses, the author has used the interview materials to inductively build toward generalizations about when and why *hsiao-tsu* operate well or poorly. The reader will find in Chapters 5 through 9 detailed case studies of *hsiao-tsu* operations in five different organizational settings: government offices, schools, rural communes, factories, and corrective labor camps.[8] As each case study is presented it is compared with the ideal strict political atmosphere described in Chapter 4 and with other case studies, and features of the organization and its environment which seem to help or hinder the operation of *hsiao-tsu* are highlighted. As more comparisons are added in these five chapters, the range of variables examined is increased. In Chapter 10 the conclusions of this analysis are summarized in the form of a series of generalizations about features of organizations and their environments which affect the functioning of *hsiao-tsu*, particularly in terms of the ability of these groups to change the attitudes of their members.

The final chapter presents a brief summary of what has been accomplished in this study, along with some concluding statements and speculation about the changing social structure in China in the 1960's. We hope to leave the reader with not only a greater knowledge of what organizations in China look like when viewed from within, but also an understanding of the changes which have taken place in Chinese society since 1949, and an appreciation of both the successes and the continuing obstacles in the Chinese Communist elite's ambitious drive to totally unify and mobilize their population.

---

8. The author was particularly interested in two other organizational settings: the army and the urban neighborhood. However, not enough informants from these settings were found to justify equal treatment with the other five.

II

THE SIGNIFICANCE OF SMALL GROUPS
AND POLITICAL RITUALS

Why are *hsiao-tsu* set up in so many organizations in China? What do these groups and the political rituals conducted within them accomplish for an organization? How do they make that organization different from organizations without these features? Where do these groups and rituals fit into what might be called the "Maoist line" on organization and modernization? [1]

These *hsiao-tsu* and political rituals are part of an organizational model developed by the Chinese Communists which differs in important ways from ideas adhered to in both the Soviet Union and the West. This model is meant to be applied generally throughout society in organizations of very different sorts. The Chinese Communists believe that by successfully implementing the model they will be able to organize and mobilize their population much more thoroughly than elites in other societies have been able to do. Therefore it is important that we try to understand the model and how *hsiao-tsu* and political rituals fit into it.

First let us consider some general problems facing elites interested in

---

1. A general discussion of the Maoist line on these issues is provided in the author's article, "Bureaucracy and Modernization in China: The Maoist Critique," in *American Sociological Review,* Vol. 38, April 1973. See also John G. Gurley, "Capitalist and Maoist Economic Development," in Edward Friedman and Mark Selden, eds., *America's Asia* (New York: Vintage, 1971).

changing the behavior of individuals. Discussions of the importance of communications in the modernization process often focus on the difficulties of getting "modern" ideas across to people and persuading and pressuring them to abandon parts of their "traditions" for these new ways. The targets of this persuasion are not isolated individuals, but are people tied into various social groups: families, extended kinship groups, neighborhood, friendship, and co-worker groups. To the modernizer these groups are often regarded as basic obstacles to his task, as reinforcers of traditional ways. Individuals who adopt the new ways may suffer criticism and social pressure for their deviance from local social norms. The first task of the modernizer may be to dislodge individuals from such ties, by rural-urban migration, by job changes, or by some other means, so that they will be more receptive to new ideas. But this leaves unsolved the problem of how to alter the attitudes of those who remain locked into traditional groups.[2]

There is a general problem for elites here, not just a problem for modernizers in developing societies. Consider the factory manager in America or some other industrialized society. Suppose he wants to increase production by offering special bonuses to workers who boost their output by a certain amount each month. There is no guarantee that such a policy will have the desired results and good reason to think that it might be counterproductive. The problem is that workers do not confront management as isolated individuals (even in the absence of trade unions); rather, they are embedded in social ties with their fellow workers, and individuals who try to produce much more than their fellows, or "rate-bust," will generally suffer criticism, ostracism, or even physical retaliation. Again, informal social groupings at the lowest level play a powerful mediating role between elites and individuals.[3]

The importance of such informal groupings, or primary groups, is one of the most thoroughly researched topics in Western social science. The term primary group was first introduced by the sociologist Charles Horton Cooley:

---

2. For a variety of discussions of freeing individuals from the inertia of their primary ties see Daniel Lerner, *The Passing of Traditional Society* (New York: Free Press, 1958); Karl Deutsch, "Social Mobilization and Political Development" in *American Political Science Review*, Vol. 55, September 1961; and Lucian W. Pye, ed., *Communications and Political Development* (Princeton: Princeton University Press, 1963).

3. The pioneering study of informal work groups is F. J. Roethlisberger and W. J. Dickson, *Management and the Worker* (Cambridge: Harvard University Press, 1939). Also see Henry A. Landsberger, *Hawthorne Revisited* (Ithaca: Cornell University Press, 1958).

By primary groups I mean those characterized by intimate face-to-face association and cooperation. They are primary in several senses, but chiefly in that
they are fundamental in forming the social nature and the ideas of the individual. The result of intimate association, psychologically, is a certain
fusion of individualities in a common whole, so that one's very self, for many
purposes at least, is the common life and purpose of the group.[4]

Examples of groups high in "primariness" are families, groups of
friends within a school, and streetcorner gangs. Primary groups can
exist on their own or within larger organizations, and an individual
may also have primary ties with individuals who do not form a group
(that is, with individuals who do not have primary ties with each
other). In this case we speak more accurately of a social network of
primary ties.[5] Research has illustrated the way primary groups in
American high schools contribute to an emphasis on athletics and con-
done cheating in spite of the efforts of school authorities to stress academics and to eliminate academic dishonesty.[6] Studies of the Nazi
Wehrmacht in the closing years of World War II noted that many
units kept fighting vigorously even when it was obvious that the Ger-
mans could not win. The explanation was found not in general fa-
natical devotion to the Nazi cause, but in the continuing strength of
primary ties to other soldiers in the same unit.[7]

As these examples and findings illustrate, in both developing and
developed societies individuals participate in primary groups and
informal social networks of various types. Individuals depend upon
these groups and ties for emotional support, cooperation, and self-
esteem. Social norms develop within these groups which exert an important influence on their members. Any appeal or demand for change
in the actions and thoughts of an individual will be mediated by these
informal primary groups and social networks, and whether these
groups will act to support or resist such demands depends upon a
variety of considerations. In the Wehrmacht, primary groups provided
firm support for higher authorities even in the face of rising personal

---

4. Charles Horton Cooley, *Social Organization* (New York: Scribner's, 1909), p. 23.
5. The primariness of primary groups, according to various definitions, refers to
frequent face-to-face contact, deep and extensive communications, relating to others
as entire persons rather than to specific roles, and gaining direct satisfactions from
the relationship (rather than using the relationship to pursue some other ends).
Thus a primary group can be as small as a dyad of two, and these dyads can inter-
connect to form a social network rather than a group. See the seminal discussion
in Elizabeth Bott, *Family and Social Network* (London: Tavistock, 1957).
6. James S. Coleman, *The Adolescent Society* (New York: Free Press, 1961).
7. Edward Shils and Morris Janowitz, "Cohesion and Disintegration in the Wehrmacht in World War II," in *Public Opinion Quarterly*, Summer 1948.

risk. In the factory rate-busting situation, primary group members may obstruct the demands of authorities. In other situations groups may react indifferently.

If elites, whether national or organizational, are bent on changing the attitudes and behavior of their followers and subordinates, as China's leaders certainly are, they must therefore come to terms in some way with the mediating influence of primary groups and informal group norms. Elites can act as if these informal groups did not exist and can try appealing directly to individuals. Or they can appeal directly to entire groups as autonomous units, urging and pressuring them to support new plans and programs. Elites can try to draw individuals away from their primary groups, or they can try to break up and disperse existing groups, thereby "atomizing" individuals and making them more susceptible to direct influence from above. Or they can try to penetrate and control existing groups and create new primary groups in which to encapsulate individuals, thereby gaining control over group norms and using them to reinforce higher demands. Much of the distinctiveness of the Chinese Communist organizational model results from the choice of this final and most ambitious strategy.

In China, *hsiao-tsu* and the political rituals carried on within them represent an attempt either to pre-empt or to co-opt the autonomous primary groups which would ordinarily exist in various organizations and throughout society. Individuals are not left on their own to develop social ties within an organization but are formed into *hsiao-tsu* under the direction of elites. Within these groups individuals who can be expected to support official demands are placed in leadership positions and encouraged to find other group members who will support them. Through political study and mutual criticism, group leaders and their supporters organize pressure on other group members to join them in enthusiastically supporting official policies. At least in theory, then, social groupings are provided for individuals, groupings with built-in obligations to develop support for organizational and national goals.

If this theory can be translated into practice, it should result in a much more effective mobilization of the population for social change than the other primary group strategies already mentioned.[8] Appealing directly to individuals or to primary groups as autonomous agents leaves these groups relatively free to continue competing for individ-

---

8. The term mobilization is used in varying technical senses by different authors. For our purposes it is sufficient to think of mobilization as the process in which individuals are uprooted from traditional habits and loyalties, get involved in new patterns of behavior, and provide loyalties to new collectivities.

ual loyalties. Drawing individuals away from primary ties may allow elites to mobilize those individuals, but it leaves the groups from which they came relatively unchanged and unmobilized. Breaking up primary groups and atomizing their members may destroy the competition, but the individuals involved may find their atomization so painful that they will comply with higher demands sullenly, rather than enthusiastically.[9] The Chinese Communist strategy involves encapsulating people in groups and then insuring that these groups do not compete for individual loyalties by mobilizing them as entire units.

The desired result, in other words, is a situation in which an individual finds himself surrounded by people who not only comply with higher demands, but also enthusiastically and creatively support those demands. The Chinese Communists do not expect such a situation to arise spontaneously within an organization or in society at large, no matter how wise or popular their programs are. Without proper organization only a minority of individuals within a unit can be expected to support official demands with the desired fervor. Mao Tse-tung makes this clear in his important 1943 statement "Concerning Methods of Leadership":

Wherever there are masses, there are in all probability three groups: those who are comparatively active, those who are average, and those who are backward. In comparing the three groups, the two extremes are in all probability small, while the middle group is large. As a result, leaders must be skillful at consolidating the minority activists to act as a leading nucleus, and must rely on this nucleus to elevate the middle group and capture the backward elements.[10]

One of the primary means by which a minority of activists can dominate an organization is through the *hsiao-tsu* network. By controlling social interaction within an organization and by developing social pressure within groups in support of official demands, this minority may be able to develop truly mass mobilization, rather than the separate mobilization of a few.

The ways in which this organizational model differs from both tra-

9. Discussions centered around the idea of the totalitarian society usually include the notion of the atomization of all individuals. However, it would seem to be difficult to generally atomize and then maintain in that state large portions of the population, given the assumed importance of primary groups for the emotional well-being of the individual. See David Reisman, "Some Observations on the Limits of Totalitarian Power," in *Antioch Review*, Vol. 12, 1952, pp. 155–168.

10. Translated in Boyd Compton, ed., *Mao's China* (Seattle: University of Washington Press, 1952), p. 178. This article is included in the third volume of Mao Tse-tung's selected works, but in recent editions the second sentence (concerning the size of the three groups) has been omitted.

ditional Chinese social structure and from Soviet ideas will be explored in greater detail in Chapter 3. In the remainder of this chapter we will specify the variety of other ways that *hsiao-tsu* are expected to play a role in Chinese organizations. So far we have focused on the role of these groups in mobilizing individuals for social change, and we have seen that the Chinese Communists place a strong emphasis on the use of organized group pressure as a way of influencing the behavior of individuals. It is generally agreed that the Chinese Communists, particularly in their recurring "Maoist" phases, have tried to de-emphasize material incentives in their efforts to influence behavior. However, they replace material incentives not merely with ideological exhortations, but with a heightened emphasis on group solidarity and political rituals. They hope, for example, that workers will work harder and produce more not simply in order to earn more, nor even simply to contribute to the socialist cause, but to earn the praise and escape the criticism of their *hsiao-tsu*. It is often said in the West that in activities like factory work no incentive can be used so effectively as material incentives, which not only are of great importance to the recipients but also can be calculated and manipulated more precisely than any other form of reward can. But Western factories lack the small group, and *hsiao-tsu* criticism rituals may give Chinese factory authorities much more precise control over group social approval than their Western counterparts could hope to have. So perhaps the de-emphasis on material incentives in China is not as utopian as it has often seemed to outsiders.

Hsiao-tsu are also important in the day-to-day process of communication within Chinese society. In a developing society with a high rate of illiteracy and various language and ethnic differences it is obviously difficult to get messages across from the elite to the population, much less to get the population to comply. If the *hsiao-tsu* network in China is functioning properly, messages about birth control, new agricultural techniques, or conflicts with foreign powers will reach groups as part of the regular study routine. There they will not only be communicated to individuals (orally, where group members are illiterate); they will also be the subject of prolonged discussion and debate. The communication is not solely one-way. In the course of group discussions individuals are supposed to reveal their attitudes, doubts, and misunderstandings about a given message. These are regularly reported by the *hsiao-tsu* leaders to higher authorities within an organization or locality. These authorities are then expected to modify their own methods and plans in order to achieve better popular response to such messages in the future. Thus in Chinese society communications down to the lowest level are formalized through *hsiao-tsu* rituals, so that much less is left to chance and informal communication networks than in other societies.

Hsiao-tsu and political rituals are not merely supposed to aid in getting messages across to the population and insuring mass compliance. In the process they are also supposed to help change the attitudes and thinking of their members. *Hsiao-tsu* are therefore an integral part of the "thought reform" effort in China. Thought reform involves much more than developing loyalty or devotion to China's leaders; it entails changing a broad spectrum of attitudes, habits, inclinations, and desires in order to produce "new men," individuals willing to work hard, to struggle creatively to overcome obstacles, and to devote themselves to broad organizational and national goals without concern for individual advancement or comfort. Thought reform takes place not only in intensive fashion in prisons and special training institutions, but also little by little in the everyday lives of individuals in all walks of life in China. In *hsiao-tsu* study and mutual criticism, individuals are pressured to change both their behavior and their ways of thinking. Group members constantly analyze their own attitudes, comparing them with models of correct attitudes presented in their study materials.

One important component of the effort to change attitudes is the drive to get individuals to be more analytical about their actions and the world around them. The underlying assumption is that much of the inertia in society stems from the way in which people go through life following habits and traditions and taking relatively little time to reflect upon the way things are. Through the process of organized group discussions people can learn to constantly analyze the world around them. They can begin to look at themselves and at those around them and ask what the consequences (for individuals, organizations, and the entire society) would be if one course of action were followed rather than another. Behavior will then be the result more of careful reflection and analysis than of impulse or habit. If *hsiao-tsu* discussions can successfully support this kind of analytical thinking, they can contribute to the members' feeling that they understand the world around them and are active and intelligent actors within it, rather than drifters in a sea of unpredictably changing circumstances.

Hsiao-tsu also play a role in social control, in detecting and punishing deviant behavior of various types. *Hsiao-tsu* discussion and mutual criticism do not have to start from political study materials. Poor work, laziness in study, disputes with fellow workers, constant complaining—a variety of undesirable acts can draw group attention and initiate discussion and criticism. The norms of mutual criticism demand that individuals be their brothers' keepers, that they encourage and push others to meet official standards of behavior. The group should not "protect its own" by shielding improper behavior from the notice of authorities. It should actively discourage deviance. In theory this should make it possible for leaders to de-emphasize penalties and threats of punishment, as well as material incentives, in their attempts to influence behavior. Authorities in Chinese organizations have a wide variety of sanctions at their disposal, including threats of demotion, expulsion, and even arrest. But it is considered desirable to keep such sanctions in the background insofar as possible, and to rely on persuasion and mobilized group pressure. If leaders do not follow this course they will have to devote much of their attention to checking for misbehavior and doling out sanctions, and this will tend to set them apart from their subordinates. If leaders do rely heavily on organizing group pressure, then in theory *hsiao-tsu* will take over much of the concern for checking up on the behavior of their members and correcting poor behavior. This should make it possible for the leaders to devote more of their attention to other concerns and perhaps to be regarded more favorably by their subordinates. To the outsider it may seem that the high demands and strict standards Chinese authorities set for their population could not be enforced without large-scale resort to physical coercion, but we can see that if *hsiao-tsu* are operating the way they are supposed to this will not be the case.

It has previously been noted that the single conception of organizational relationships which we have been discussing is intended to be used in organizations of widely varying types. In the West we are accustomed to thinking that organizations differ greatly in the ways they deal with their subordinates. When authorities can expect loyalty and fervent support (as in some religious sects and political parties), then they can rely primarily on persuasion and exhortation to get their objectives accomplished. When the expected orientation of subordinates shades into indifference (as in a factory) or into hostility and alienation (as in a prison), then they may have to rely more upon material rewards and finally on coercion in order to gain compliance.[11]

11. Broad empirical support for these generalizations is provided in Amitai Etzioni, *A Comparative Analysis of Complex Organizations* (New York: Free Press, 1961). Preliminary efforts have been made (in G. William Skinner and Edwin A. Winckler, "Compliance Succession in Rural Communist China: A Cyclical Theory,"

All of this assumes that relatively autonomous primary groups develop within these organizations; that in religious sects these groups actively support the leaders, while in a factory they obstruct the leaders, and in a prison they actively oppose them. But if the *hsiao-tsu* network can prevent the emergence of autonomous primary groups, then it may be possible to use a single approach to subordinates in different kinds of organizations and still retain effective compliance. This is what the Chinese Communists have tried to do.

Hsiao-tsu and political rituals are expected to contribute to organizations in still other ways. They are supposed to help prevent interpersonal hostilities and to deal with interpersonal conflict. The development of cliques, rivalries, favoritism, or spite should lead to group discussions and criticism sessions aimed at ironing out problems and restoring group unity. There is a slim parallel here with some group rituals in our own culture, with T-groups and sensitivity training groups. Both these groups and the Chinese *hsiao-tsu* are expected to develop in their members an awareness of how they affect others, a sensitivity for the feelings and reactions of others, and a desire to bring interpersonal conflict to the surface rather than let it smolder and develop into serious proportions. In the Chinese group individuals are expected to admit feelings of rivalry and enmity, and their fellows are supposed to pressure them to deal with and eliminate those feelings. Of course, the T-group is limited to this role, while the Chinese *hsiao-tsu* has a wide variety of other functions and is embedded in an authority structure which T-groups lack.

The *hsiao-tsu* can also play a role in discovering and training future leaders. The group structure enables leaders to delegate responsibilities, even if minor ones, to a very low level within an organization, and individuals who perform well in *hsiao-tsu* activities may be considered for more important tasks. The regular stream of information coming back to organizational authorities as a result of *hsiao-tsu* meetings and discussions can assist them in evaluating all of their personnel and in discovering individuals worthy of advancement.

Up to now we have been focusing on the role of *hsiao-tsu* and political rituals from the standpoint of organizational authorities, but

---

in Amitai Etzioni, ed., *A Sociological Reader on Complex Organizations,* 2nd edition [New York: Holt, Rinehart and Winston, 1969]) to apply Etzioni's organizational generalizations to the Chinese scene. In Chapter 10 we will return to this topic and conclude whether, on the basis of the case study materials, small groups and political rituals obviate the need for different "compliance strategies" in different types of organizations or not.

we should not overlook their significance for group members. If *hsiao-tsu* activities are carried out properly, a rewarding sense of solidarity and mutual concern should exist within the group. The *hsiao-tsu* network is meant to be applied in organizations of any size, and the organized solidarity of these groups may counteract the tendency toward depersonalization that occurs in large organizations in the West. In group activities each member should also gain a clear idea of how he is regarded by his peers (and indirectly by higher authorities). If this view is favorable the individual should gain a sense of security and well-being, but if it is unfavorable he will know what he has to do to gain approval. The group will provide encouragement and praise for acts which serve the organization and the nation, allowing an individual to gain in self-esteem (and maybe in position) through performing unselfish acts. In other words, an individual may be able to feel simultaneously that he is dong things for others or the nation and that he is advancing his own career. Through self-criticism before the group, an individual may also be able to unburden himself of feelings of guilt and insecurity and find comfort in reacceptance by the group once his self-criticism has been accepted.[12] *Hsiao-tsu* also provide ordinary citizens with opportunities to participate in national life, and a great effort is made to relate the most menial group activities to national goals.[13] This involvement in national affairs, though a break with tradition for most individuals, may be a highly invigorating experience. As people comment upon messages coming to them from higher authorities or suggest new ways of relating these messages

---

12. At least one Western commentator places extreme importance on institutionalized ways of relieving guilt for the health of a society. O. Hobart Mowrer feels that the move from group confessionals in early Christianity to individual confession in the Middle Ages weakened the Catholic Church and paved the way for the Protestant Reformation. The Reformers, however, did away with the confessional altogether, giving rise to still more serious problems for individuals who had no way to alleviate accumulating guilt feelings. O. Hobart Mowrer, *The New Group Therapy* (Princeton: Van Nostrand, 1964), Chapter 2.

13. An example comes from a recent pamphlet on political study for retail clerks. The clerks were told that if the job of getting pigs in from the countryside was done poorly not only would city residents not have enough pork to eat, but peasants wouldn't be able to sell their pigs. This would in turn affect the raising of pigs adversely, and with fewer pigs there would be a shortage of natural fertilizer, which would contribute to an overall food shortage, which would in turn adversely affect the progress of world revolution (presumably by making China look like a failure in agriculture to the rest of the world). Therefore the clerk's small part in this chain was extremely important and should be handled well. Ta kung pao, ed., *Tsai Mao Tse-tung ssu-hsiang pu-yü hsia ch'eng-chang* (Growing up under the nurture of Mao Tse-tung's thought) (Peking, 1966), pp. 58–59.

to their daily activities they may gain a new sense that their leaders are interested in their ideas and that they can have some impact on organizational life—and they may be correct. In theory, then, *hsiao-tsu* and political rituals should provide not only an effective way for elites to influence the behavior and attitudes of subordinates, but also a secure and rewarding organizational environment for participants.

In the previous pages we have been discussing *hsiao-tsu* and political rituals largely on a hypothetical level, as Chinese Communist leaders would like them to operate. How *hsiao-tsu* measure up to these expectations will be a primary concern in Chapters 5 through 9. But it should be clear by now that Chinese Communist ideas of organizational leadership are quite different from those we are familiar with in the West. *Hsiao-tsu* do imply a high degree of authoritarian regimentation, of pervasive scrutiny of and control over individual behavior by higher authorities. Yet they are also expected to facilitate a de-emphasis on commands, coercion, and material incentives and to lead to mass enthusiasm and involvement. To the Western mind regimentation and mass enthusiasm seem quite contradictory, or attainable only in very special organizations with highly selected participants (perhaps in a monastery). The Chinese Communists feel that the two can be combined effectively in one organizational conception, that this conception can be applied throughout society, and that the result will be a degree of mobilization of human wills unknown in previous societies.

III

THE ORIGINS OF SMALL GROUPS
AND POLITICAL RITUALS

We have seen in the previous chapter that *hsiao-tsu* and their political rituals are organizational innovations designed to penetrate and gain control over informal primary groups throughout society and to use that control to generate support and enthusiasm for the policies of the elite. How did the Chinese Communists arrive at these innovations? Are they rooted in traditional China? Were they borrowed from the Soviet Union? Since the historical materials on the Chinese Communist movement contain very few explicit and detailed references to *hsiao-tsu,* much of what follows is based primarily on analogy and parallels rather than firm historical evidence.

Many institutions and practices in traditional China bear some resemblance to *hsiao-tsu* in present-day China. In general in traditional China there were few efforts to penetrate, organize, or manipulate the lowest level of social groupings. Franz Schurmann summarizes this lack of emphasis:

But during most of Chinese history the state let society organize itself, confined its functions to exploitation and control, and acted managerially only for certain special purposes. . . . Villages developed various forms of cooperation based on kinship, work, religion, and other ties. Clan groups organized villages. Villages found links with the cities in the form of "native associations." Self-organization proved to be a more powerful and durable source of organization than the actions of the state.[1]

---

1. Franz Schurmann, *Ideology and Organization in Communist China,* Second Edition (Berkeley and Los Angeles: University of California Press, 1968), p. 407.

By and large the formal bureaucratic machinery of the state did not reach below the *hsien,* or county, level, and figures for the Ch'ing dynasty show that this meant on the average only one magistrate for 100,000 inhabitants in 1749, and one for 250,000 inhabitants in 1819.[2]

However, from the time of the Sung dynasty (960–1126 A.D.) there were efforts to supplement the formal bureaucratic structure with semi-official groupings of citizens. The most important of such efforts was the formation of the *pao-chia* system of social control. According to official Ch'ing dynasty (1644–1911) documents, throughout the empire inhabitants were to be organized into groups of ten households (termed a *p'ai*), ten of these groups were to be organized into a grouping called a *chia,* and ten of these would in turn form a *pao.* Each grouping would have a head chosen from its families, under the supervision of the *hsien* magistrate and his assistants. The primary purpose of the *pao-chia* system was to keep track of the population and to control crime and disorder. If crimes were committed the entire group, and particularly its head, could be held responsible if they failed to report those crimes to the authorities. In certain periods *pao* heads were even required to make regular trips to the office of the *hsien* magistrate to report on local social order. The *pao-chia* system shows some parallels with Chinese Communist *hsiao-tsu,* both in augmenting formal organizational structures with semi-official groupings of ordinary citizens and in assigning collective responsibility for reporting deviance to higher authorities. The *pao-chia* groupings were supposed to cut across kinship and village lines in order to prevent local elites from gaining control of them. For similar reasons commoners rather than members of the gentry were supposed to serve as the group heads. In practice these rules were not strictly followed.[3]

A somewhat similar network, called the *li-chia* system, was supposed to assist in tax assessment and collection. One hundred and ten households were to be grouped into a *li,* within which the ten households with the largest number of taxpaying adult males would serve as heads of groupings of the remaining households, each of which was called a *chia.* The heads were to assist in tax registration and in informing residents of the taxes they had to pay each year.[4] These groupings were supposed to differ from both *pao-chia* groupings and natural village

---

2. Kung-chuan Hsiao, *Rural China: Imperial Control in the Nineteenth Century* (Seattle: University of Washington Press, 1967), p. 5.

3. *Ibid.,* Chaps. 2–3.

4. *Ibid.,* Chaps. 2, 4.

patterns and thus to crosscut natural social patterns in still another
way.

Neither the *pao-chia* nor the *li-chia* system entailed meetings or the
indoctrination of members. However, another traditional institution
dating back to the Sung dynasty, the *hsiang yüeh* lecture system, played
this role to some extent. Lecturers and assistants were appointed to give
bi-monthly speeches to the populace throughout the empire stressing
conformity with Confucian virtues and advocating an orderly, indus-
trious life. In some places special lecture halls were set up, often with
notice boards on which the names of good and bad citizens were posted
for all to see. Sometimes the lecturer would mention the names of good
and bad citizens in his oration, urging his listeners to emulate the former and criticize the latter.[5] There were no obligatory meetings or organized study and discussion connected with the *hsiang yüeh* system,
but there was an underlying notion that regular moral education and
exhortation of the population should be carried on.

None of these groupings emerged naturally from the local villages.
They were all imposed by the imperial bureaucracy as part of the apparatus for maintaining social, economic, and ideological control over
a vast empire. They never effectively took root in the villages, and
many imperial decisions over the centuries were devoted to trying to
revive and strengthen the basic level groupings. They were not able to
prevent major disorders—for example, the Taiping Rebellion of 1850–
1865—during periods of dynastic decline. Nevertheless, the potenti-
alities of small groupings of residents with mutual responsibility for
maintaining social order have fascinated Chinese rulers for centuries.
Indeed, Chiang Kai-shek revived the *pao-chia* system after 1930 in his
struggle to eliminate communist influence from rural areas.[6]

There are many contrasts between these traditional institutions and
the Chinese Communist *hsiao-tsu* as well. The Chinese Communist bureaucracy extends much further down into society and is able to maintain closer supervision over basic level groups. *Hsiao-tsu* are organized
primarily on the basis of units of work or study, although there are
also residential groups. The elements of systematic ideological study
and group criticism are largely missing from the traditional scheme.
The range and intensity of activities required of *hsiao-tsu* members
under the Communist system is much greater. The peasant in traditional times could carry out his daily activities with little contact with

---

5. *Ibid.*, Chap. 6.
6. Franz Schurmann, *op. cit.*, pp. 409–412.

the semi-official control and indoctrination institutions. All these contrasts reflect, of course, the basic difference between China's dynastic rulers and her present elite: traditional officials were primarily concerned with the maintenance of the status quo, while the current rulers have embarked upon a vast social, economic, and political revolution in which *hsiao-tsu* are expected to play a significant role.

When the Chinese Communists came to power in 1949 they did not directly adopt the *pao-chia* system; in fact, they denounced and set about destroying it. (This was understandable, since Chiang Kai-shek had revived the *pao-chia* system primarily as a means to check the spread of communist influence.) It seems doubtful, then, that these traditional institutions served in any conscious way as a model for Chinese Communist *hsiao-tsu*.[7] However, it is clear that a precedent existed for extending the power of the state over the populace by creating semi-official groupings of citizens under the supervision of the state.

Some elements of Chinese Communist *hsiao-tsu* rituals can also be seen in more general practices, inclinations, and philosophical themes of traditional China. There is a substantial literature on these parallels and we will only mention several briefly here.[8] The notion that an individual's nature is not set, and that he can reform himself through diligent study of prescribed texts, has a long history. There is also a stress in traditional Chinese culture on the importance of a unified ideological perspective for achieving national unity and avoiding chaos. The use of force or even reliance on rules, laws, and commands

---

7. Franz Schurmann notes some evidence of carry-over specifically for the urban *pao-chia* groupings. These had been established by the Japanese in areas of occupied China and then maintained by the Nationalists after 1945. When the Chinese Communists came to power they abolished both urban and rural *pao-chia* institutions. But in 1951, when they began to introduce urban residents committee groupings, the most frequent press accounts concerned Tientsin and Shanghai, cities where the earlier Japanese-sponsored *pao-chia* had been most successful. Schurmann also notes, however, that compared with the earlier urban *pao-chia*, which was devoted to social control, the role of these residents groups was much broader, including also dispute mediation, sanitation and health work, literacy training, and a variety of other tasks. Cf. Franz Schurmann, *Ideology and Organization in Communist China*, 2nd edition (Berkeley and Los Angeles; University of California Press, 1968), pp. 368–377.

8. See David Nivison, "Communist Ethics and Chinese Tradition," in *Journal of Asian Studies*, Vol. 16, no. 1, 1956; Arthur F. Wright, "Struggle vs. Harmony: Symbols of Competing Values in Modern China," in *World Politics*, Vol. 6, no. 1, 1953; Benjamin Schwartz, "On Attitudes toward Law in China," in M. Katz, ed., *Government under Law and the Individual* (Washington, D.C.: American Council of Learned Societies, 1957); Hu Hsien-chin, "The Chinese Concepts of Face," in *American Anthropologist*, Vol. 46, no. 1, 1944; and Richard W. Wilson, *Learning to be Chinese* (Cambridge: MIT Press, 1970), Chap. 1.

to gain compliance was viewed as a sign of moral weakness in traditional China, and persuasion and the force of example were preferable.

In the Confucian tradition, loyalties to family, extended kin, and other primary groups were inculcated from early childhood. An individual was led to believe he could not become a complete person outside of the group context. Both childhood and adult socialization included a strong reliance on "shaming" techniques, and individuals were warned that "loss of face" was not an individual matter because poor behavior brought dishonor to the entire group. With the weight of his group's honor riding on all his acts, the properly socialized individual would look upon a loss of face with "a real dread affecting the nervous system . . . more strongly than physical fear." [9]

On the other hand, there are several ways in which *hsiao-tsu* and political rituals fly in the face of traditional inclinations and practices. The Confucian emphasis on maintaining harmony and avoiding conflict in interpersonal relationships had to be broached in order to get mutual criticism aired. Also, the universalistic spirit of Chinese Communist mutual criticism conflicts with the traditional emphasis on favoritism toward primary group members. Now individuals may have to publicly denounce friends and relatives and accept criticism from those to whom they feel no special ties. *Hsiao-tsu* are not the primary groups of traditional China, working on their own to deal with internal problems while maintaining the appearance of unity to outsiders. Instead, the tie of the *hsiao-tsu* to higher authorities breaks the isolation of the group and brings its internal affairs into the public domain. Thus, whatever security a *hsiao-tsu* may afford an individual, it is not the security of knowing that the group will solidly support him in any conflict with outsiders. Often precisely the reverse will happen: the group will isolate and criticize the individual until he admits the error of his ways. While the traditional emphasis on group-rootedness and fear of loss of face may make public criticism and self-criticism more effective in influencing individuals than they might be in a more individualistic culture, these activities would not be easily adapted to by individuals socialized in traditional ways of thinking. Finally, *hsiao-tsu* entail a much greater involvement in public and national affairs than existed in traditional China.

Thus, despite certain parallels and continuities with past forms, contemporary small-group practices represent a sharp break with the past. Any simple view that traditional institutions "paved the way" for Chi-

---

9. Hu Hsien-chin, *op. cit.,* p. 50.

nese Communist practices must be rejected. Individuals experiencing *hsiao-tsu* rituals for the first time might find them either exciting or agonizingly painful, but all could agree that these activities were quite unlike anything they had experienced in the old society.[10]

A second set of precedents comes from Soviet experience. The basic ideas behind *hsiao-tsu* and political rituals stem directly from activities in Bolshevik Party cells, which seem in turn to have evolved out of similar activities among the earlier Russian narodnik revolutionaries.[11] Thus many of the specific norms surrounding Chinese small group activities, which are discussed in Chapter 4, have direct counterparts in the internal rituals of the Bolshevik Party. In the Soviet Union, however, these political rituals were never extended to the ordinary population as systematically as they have been in China. This difference represents a divergence in strategy for dealing with primary group loyalties in the two countries.

Lenin's most significant additions to Marxist theory were his ideas about the party: his advocacy of a disciplined, conspiratorial, hierarchically organized party of full-time revolutionaries. Lenin introduced a variety of organizational practices designed to promote unity and discipline within the ranks of the Bolsheviks. Careful screening and then probation of candidates for Party membership were instituted. Party members had to pledge to submit to Party authority in the form of the regulations of "democratic centralism." [12] Each Party member and each cell of members were expected to carry out regular study of political texts and Party programs designed to raise the general level

---

10. One piece of evidence for *hsiao-tsu* study as a novel and uncomfortable experience is the mention in Chinese psychological journals in the 1950's of "study" as a common contributor to a type of mental disorder called neurasthenia (*shen-ching shuai-jo cheng*), essentially a form of neurosis for which out-patient treatment is generally suitable. See the summary in Robert & Ai-li S. Chin, *Psychological Research in Communist China: 1949–1966* (Cambridge: MIT Press, 1969), Chap. 3, especially pp. 69–78.

11. James H. Billington, "The Intelligentsia and the Religion of Humanity," in *American Historical Review*, Vol. 65, no. 4, 1960.

12. Democratic centralism is defined in the 1961 Rules of the Communist Party of the Soviet Union as including:

a. election of all Party executive bodies from bottom to top.

b. periodic accountability of Party bodies to their Party organizations and to higher bodies.

c. strict Party discipline and subordination of the minority to the majority.

d. the absolute, binding character of the decisions of higher bodies upon lower bodies.

For a discussion of the relative balance of democracy and centralism, see Merle Fainsod, *How Russia is Ruled*, Rev. Ed. (Cambridge: Harvard University Press, 1963), Chap. 7.

of political consciousness and to create a unified political outlook within the Party. Members also were expected regularly to reveal their shortcomings in cell meetings and to accept the criticism of others. Thus the activities with which we are primarily concerned, political study and mutual criticism, were present in their basic forms in what came to be known as Bolshevik "Party life" (*partinaia zhizn'*), the regular political rituals required of all Party members. These rituals were extended to other elites in Soviet society, such as the Party's youth auxiliary, the Komsomol. And in certain highly structured organizational situations, such as the army and the schools, it was possible to institute a high degree of penetration and control over primary groups. But political rituals were never extended even to the ordinary membership of the Party-controlled mass organizations, such as the trade unions, much less to the rest of the population. These rituals remained part of the discipline of the elite in Soviet society, and were one of the many things which distinguished that elite from ordinary citizens.

The Bolsheviks came to power in 1917 in effect by a coup d'état without having developed a broad national base of support. In subsequent years the weakness of Bolshevik support in many sectors of society contributed to a continued emphasis on the key role played by the Party elite. After Stalin came to power the hierarchical and autocratic aspects of Marxism-Leninism were emphasized still further, and centralism came more and more to dominate the "democratic centralism" formula. Increasingly, demands for strict obedience replaced efforts to develop a spirit of initiative and enthusiasm even within the elite, and the intra-Party political rituals atrophied. The term "criticism and self criticism" came to refer to a vertical communication process rather than to the horizontal criticism among comrades within a Party cell; superiors pointed out the mistakes of subordinates, and subordinates revealed the deviations and abuses of power of superiors. In 1939 Stalin denounced "the fetishism of study circles," and in subsequent years the emphasis in indoctrination within the elite shifted from group discussion to individual study of the "Short Course," the history of the Soviet Communist Party written under the personal supervision of Stalin himself.[13]

While within the elite the emphasis was changing from active involvement in political rituals to unquestioning obedience, in the Party's relationship with the rest of the population the tendency to

___

13. See the discussion in Robert Conquest, *The Politics of Ideas in the USSR* (New York: Praeger, 1967), pp. 101–102; also Alex Inkeles, *Public Opinion in Soviet Russia* (Cambridge: Harvard University Press, 1951).

centralize all authority and manipulate or fragment social groups became more pronounced. A prime example of these tendencies is the forced collectivization of agriculture carried out after 1929. Party strength in the countryside remained weak throughout the 1920's and was weakened further by a membership purge on the eve of the collectivization drive. Little was done to prepare the rural population for collectivization or to mobilize and train supporters within the villages. Instead teams of urban organizers, aided by the secret police and in some cases the army, swept into the villages, expropriated and exiled the village elite, the kulaks, and announced to the remaining villagers the program of collectivization.[14] Even after collectivization the Party remained weak within the collective farms, with only 5 per cent of the farms having Party units in 1939, and still only 15 per cent in 1949.[15] In most periods since collectivization, outsiders have been recruited to go into farms to assume top leadership and technical positions, and control over farm activities and decisions have been largely in the hands of outside agencies. Only since the amalgamation of collective farms after 1950 into units roughly five times their original size has Party leadership within individual collective farms been consolidated. In the rural events of the Stalin years we can see both the fragmentation of existing social groups (the exile of the kulaks, leaving a local leadership vacuum) and the extensive manipulation and control of social groups from outside.

In the factories there was a brief experiment in 1918 with workers' control, and even after that was abandoned there were efforts to promote individual initiative and collective volunteer efforts, as in the *subbotnik* campaigns initiated in 1920 in which workers pledged to spend certain Saturdays working without pay. However, the emphasis soon shifted more and more to a hierarchical one. The concept of "one man management" emerged, with decision-making power and responsibility centralized in the factory manager (and in one subordinate at each lower level). Material incentives came to be espoused more and more, and earlier egalitarian wage schemes were denounced. During the 1930's a wide variety of forms of "socialist competition" (including the famous Stakhanovite campaign) were initiated, in which workers competed among themselves to see who could produce the most, with honors and bonuses going to the winners. At the same time, the prac-

---

14. Moshe Lewin, *Russian Peasants and Soviet Power* (Evanston, Ill.: Northwestern University Press, 1968).

15. R. Laird, *Collective Farming in Russia* (Lawrence, Kansas: University of Kansas Press, 1958), p. 138.

tice of using secret police informers to check for sabotage in any work slowdown or machine failure added to interpersonal tensions. In the industrial production drive, then, Soviet authorities stressed central-ized decision-making and pitting worker against worker to prevent in-formal work groups from resisting the demands for higher produc-tion.[16]

Similar illustrations come from other spheres of Soviet life. Political education for the masses was carried out mainly by agitators who de-livered speeches and organized other forms of communication to largely passive audiences. In the educational system the innovations and "pro-gressive" experiments of the 1920's gave way to a re-establishment of strong school authority over students, teaching in the traditional lec-ture format, and a strong emphasis on examinations, grades, and com-petition for placement into higher schools.[17] In corrective labor camps the ideology of re-educating prisoners was abondoned in the 1930's and prisoners were pitted against each other, particularly ordinary crimi-nals against political offenders, in a brutal struggle for survival. Within many sectors of society, but particularly among the educated and the elite, the purges of these years and the heavy reliance on secret police informers led to increasing fear of confiding in any but the closest of relatives and friends, and to the need to toe the line obediently in public.

Thus, the Soviet model of modernization as it developed under Stalin came to mean the centralization of decision-making in a few hands, the manipulation of social groups from outside by propaganda, material incentives, orders and sanctions, and the fragmentation of many primary groups through individual competition and secret police terror. This combination made it possible for the leadership to formu-late plans and get them implemented with minimal overt opposition (except in cases like collectivization, where basic level organizational strength was missing). In the process, the face of Soviet society was radi-cally altered. However, these tactics also tended to produce a lack of initiative and a low level of enthusiasm on the part of ordinary citi-zens, a legacy which Soviet leaders since Stalin have acknowledged. Khrushchev in particular denounced Stalin's reliance on "administra-tive measures" (a euphemism for commands imposed on unwilling sub-

---

16. S. M. Schwarz, *Labor in the Soviet Union* (New York: Praeger, 1952); Alex-ander Vucinich, *Soviet Economic Institutions* (Stanford: Stanford University Press, 1952).

17. Ruth Widmayer, "The Evolution of Soviet Educational Policy," in *Harvard Educational Review*, Vol. 24, 1954, pp. 159–175.

ordinates and for the use of secret police terror). Khrushchev introduced some measures designed to bring about more participation at the lowest levels of society and to correct the partial atomization of previous years, both within the Party and without. Political study circles were revived, and efforts were made to get more of the public enrolled in them. A variety of organizations were formed to get ordinary citizens more actively involved in law enforcement.[18] The secret police were purged and placed under firmer Party control, thus becoming less important in manipulating the lives of ordinary citizens. Rural Party strength was built up and efforts were made to put some life into "kolkhoz democracy" by getting more ordinary farmers involved in meetings and decision-making. The intense competition among workers was replaced by milder forms of competition, some of which emphasized group efforts and solidarity.[19]

These measures were accompanied by a renewed emphasis on collectivism and horizontal criticism and self-criticism. The individual's "collective" was supposed to take on increased responsibility not only for his work or study, but for encouraging his general conformity with "communist morality." However, the Soviet collective is considerably broader and vaguer than the Chinese hsiao-tsu; it refers, for example, to anything from an immediate work group to an entire factory. And the "brigades of communist labor" which were supposed to lead the way in displaying group work spirit and being their members' keepers do not seem to have engaged in anything like the regular, intensive political study and mutual criticism meetings of the Chinese hsiao-tsu. Thus even in the period of Khrushchev's attempt to revive the spirit of the 1920's, regular political rituals were not significantly extended outward from the Party to the ordinary population.[20]

---

18. See Robert Conquest, *op. cit.*, pp. 103–107; L. Lipson, "Law: The Function of Extra-Judicial Mechanisms," in Donald Treadgold, ed., *Soviet and Chinese Communism* (Seattle: University of Washington Press, 1967); and R. Osborn, "The Withering Away of the State: The Role of Social Institutions," in *Survey*, October 1961.

19. In line with this shift the former miner Alexei Stakhanov criticized the production movement he had initiated in 1935 because it tended to shower glory on one man while causing resentment among fellow workers. Cf. *Komsomolskaia Pravda*, May 30, 1967; translated in *Current Digest of the Soviet Press*, Vol. 19, no. 24, p. 11.

20. Details on this new emphasis on collective responsibility and the brigades of communist labor are provided in D. Chesnokov, ed., *Kommunism i Lichnost'* (Communism and the individual) (Moscow, 1964). For a general discussion see the author's unpublished MA thesis, *Criticism and Self-criticism in the Soviet Collective*, Harvard University Soviet Union Program, 1966. One commentator who feels political rituals were more successfully developed during this period than implied

Some of these measures and others like them have been undermined or de-emphasized by Khrushchev's successors, but nonetheless the general trend has been away from command and manipulation from above and toward developing general support and initiative from below. However, the main result has not been the creation throughout society of solidary primary groups firmly tied to and actively supporting the demands of the elite. Rather, fairly autonomous peer groups of a type we are familiar with in the West are emerging, groups which may support some of the elite's demands and reject others, according to how these demands match group norms. For instance, a recent study of factory work groups found that powerful informal norms developed within them which, contrary to the desires of the leadership, opposed "rate-busting" and condoned the drinking of alcohol provided for industrial uses.[21]

Much of the foregoing discussion is based on impressionistic evidence, but the examples given illustrate the contention that Chinese and Soviet authorities have differed over the proper way to lead the masses and to deal with the potential inertia represented by primary groups at the lowest level in society. Soviet leaders have been unable or unwilling to penetrate and mobilize primary groups throughout their society and instead have generally stressed the external manipulation of primary groups (through orders, sanctions, etc.) or have attempted to weaken and fragment existing groups. (It should be clear that this is a difference in relative emphasis between these two countries. Compared with the United States, for example, penetration and control over primary groups does appear to be stressed in the Soviet Union. The argument is that this tactic has not been stressed as much, nor pursued as successfully, in Russia as in China.)

How and why did the Chinese Communists modify Soviet leadership conceptions in the manner they did? Again the historical evidence is sketchy and we must rely primarily on inference and analogy. In the first years following the founding of the Chinese Communist Party in 1921 the young Party was advised and guided by representatives of the Cominterm and other Soviet sponsored organizations. In 1923 the Chinese Communists were particularly active in organizing labor unions

---

here is Joseph Novak (a pseudonym for Jerzy Kosinski). See his *No Third Path* (Garden City: Doubleday, 1962).

21. V. B. Ol'shanskii, "The Individual and Social Values" from *Sotsiologia v SSSR* (Moscow, 1966), Vol. 1; translated in *Soviet Sociology*, Fall 1966. It should be noted that the work groups which showed improper behavior were at that time competing for the title "brigades of communist labor."

and peasant organizations.[22] During this period the Cominterm advisors worked to make both the Chinese Communist Party and the Kuomintang into disciplined parties on the Leninist model. Efforts to screen membership, to build up strong Party branches and Party small groups at the basic levels, and to introduce regular Party life rituals were all undertaken.[23] Ideas about the proper organizational form for trade unions and peasant associations varied over time, and the Chinese Communists often made use of existing organizations (such as secret societies and workingmen's associations). Generally only the members of these organizations who joined the Party or the Youth League were subjected to regular political rituals.

The difficulties of cooperating with the Nationalists and the debacle of 1927 provided important lessons for the Chinese Communists. In some sense they had failed because of organizational weaknesses at the top and bottom. At the top the alliance had subjected Communist activity to the shifting whims of their Nationalist allies, and the frequent withdrawal of military support by local commanders often wiped out long months of organizational efforts among peasants and workers. At the bottom, when military support was provided, the Chinese Communists often moved too fast in establishing peasant and worker organizations in the quest for statistical shows of success. Much of their organizational strength existed only on paper or was unreliable. When the Communists tried to mobilize workers and peasants to fight by their side against the Nationalists in 1927 they found their support much smaller than they had counted upon.[24]

In the years after 1927 the Chinese Communists gradually worked out strategies for developing firm mass support, and in the process they laid the groundwork for important divergences from Soviet organizational strategies. Mao Tse-tung led a group of his followers to establish a base area in what was to become the Kiangsi Soviet and developed a new military force, the Red Army, to defend that base area. The Nationalists' military and economic blockade around the Communist base area and the constant fighting forced the Chinese Commu-

---

22. Jean Chesneaux, *The Chinese Labor Movement, 1919–1927* (Stanford: Stanford University Press, 1968); Roy Mark Hofheinz, Jr., "The Peasant Movement and Rural Revolution: Chinese Communists in the Countryside (1923–1927)." Unpublished Ph.D. dissertation, Harvard University, 1966.

23. C. Martin Wilbur and Julie Lien-ying How, *Documents on Communism, Nationalism, and Soviet Advisers in China, 1918–1927* (New York: Columbia University Press, 1956).

24. See the discussion of the Autumn Harvest Insurrection in Roy Hofheinz, *op. cit.*, Chap. 7.

nists to search for ways to develop popular support and a high level of morale and initiative. During the 1927–1934 period the primary innovations took place within the military.[25] While the reforms introduced into the Soviet Army by Trotsky during the Soviet civil war had tended to reinforce the hierarchical nature of military authority,[26] in the Fourth Red Army after 1927 there developed an emphasis on decreasing the gap between officers and men, involving ordinary soldiers in political study and in discussion and evaluation of battle plans and results, and on the Party penetrating down to the lowest levels of the military hierarchy. Political study, discussion meetings, "Lenin Clubs," and similar activities were designed to give the ordinary soldier a clear idea of what he was fighting for. At the same time soldiers became actively involved, through army-run propaganda teams, in carrying propaganda to the civilian population and in trying to organize the peasants to support the Communists. Through measures such as these, and through building up a strong political commissar system and political core in the army (an estimated one in three soldiers was a Party member), the Chinese Communists felt they were developing an army very different from traditional Chinse armies, an army which relied more upon ideological training and the development of solidarity to motivate soldiers than on threats of punishment or promises of plunder.[27]

During the Kiangsi Soviet period (1930–34) there was also a great concern to penetrate and organize villages, and to use village support to push through land reform in the rural areas. However, to a certain extent the peasant villages of the Kiangsi Soviet remained "outsiders" to be manipulated, rather than disciplined organizational supports of

---

25. Doak Barnett asked Chang Kuo-t'ao, a former member of the Chinese Communist Politburo who broke with Mao Tse-tung in the 1930's, about the origins of regular political study routines. Chang replied, "It started in the army. The rank and file of soldiers were uneducated peasants. We experimented in explaining commands and then seeing what they understood and remembered. It was difficult to teach them, and we had to teach them all sorts of things—how to work a rifle, how to live together, why they should not steal. The idea of teaching them through group discussion slowly developed." Quoted in Doak Barnett, *Communist China: The Early Years* (New York: Praeger, 1964), p. 102.

26. Roman Kolkowicz, "Heresy Enshrined: Idea and Reality of the Red Army," in Kurt London, ed., *The Soviet Union: A Half Century of Communism* (Baltimore: Johns Hopkins University Press, 1968).

27. Extensive documentation on these events is contained in the Ch'en Ch'eng Microfilm Collection available at major libraries. For a brief discussion see John Gittings, *The Role of the Chinese Army* (London: Oxford University Press, 1967), pp. 106–116. For more extensive comparative comments on the Soviet and Chinese Armies see Alexander George, *The Chinese Communist Army in Action* (New York: Columbia University Press, 1967).

the Party and Army. Propaganda teams and organizers came to the villages and organized various meetings to proclaim the goals of the new government. Poor peasants were urged to "speak bitterness" (*su k'u*). This meant publicly voicing their grievances at the poverty and hardships they had suffered in recent years, and then, aided by the outsiders, connecting this suffering with the system of class exploitation dominated by the landlords and rich peasants. With the support engendered within villages by measures such as these, the organizers moved to establish new rural organizations: rural soviets, poor peasant corps, farm labor unions, and special bodies to confiscate and redistribute land. Strenuous efforts were made to recruit local support, to form local organizations, and to stay in close communication with the populace, but they were less than fully successful. Organizations based in the natural villages (i.e., the actual settlements) sometimes fell under the control of traditional village elites, and subsequent organizational efforts centered on the township or administrative village level (the *hsiang*, encompassing several natural villages), where leadership could be more effectively supervised from above. Subunits and small groups of organizations were built up within the villages below the *hsiang*, but these often were poorly organized and disciplined. The result was village organizations of more substance than those of the 1920's, but still not firm parts of the "organizational weapon." [28] There is also evidence, particularly from factional disputes within the Party, that rural leadership without firm roots in the villages was acting in a dictatorial manner and was pushing through programs of expropriation and terror against class enemies, thus alienating large parts of the rural population.[29]

Thus, during the period prior to being driven out of their base and off on the Long March of 1934, the Chinese Communists had developed new notions of leadership and mass relations, but still had difficulty in applying them successfully and in creating the close relations between leaders and led that they felt were desirable. Under different conditions in bases in Northwest China after 1935, these ideas were further developed and applied. During the years known as the "Yenan period," (1935–1946) the Chinese Communist leaders had more oppor-

28. Franz Schurmann, *op. cit.*, Chapter 7. The term "organizational weapon" was used by Philip Selznick to refer to the Leninist conceptions of leadership and mass mobilization embodied in the Party. See Philip Selznick, *The Organizational Weapon* (New York: McGraw-Hill, 1952).

29. This criticism was voiced by Chang Wen-t'ien in 1934. Tso-liang Hsiao, *The Land Revolution in China 1930–1934* (Seattle: University of Washington Press, 1969), pp. 285–287.

tunity to read Soviet and other materials on leadership and organization and to reflect upon their own past experiences and mistakes. During these years the "mass line" concept of leadership was fully elaborated, a concept which specifies ways of maintaining close ties and communications between leader and led in order to overcome the traditional arrogance of leaders and hostility and passivity of subordinates.[30]

The difficulty of carrying out a guerrilla war against the Japanese while blockaded (particularly after 1941) by the Nationalists provided the Communists with both a great need to develop the support and initiative of the population and new opportunities for creating that support. Stalinist style command and obedience were not suitable for dispersed guerrilla bands and poor communications; instead, emphasis was placed on combining firm indoctrination and general policy guidelines with local initiative and enthusiasm. The Chinese Communists also had to find ways to combine personnel of very disparate backgrounds (nationalistic students, intellectuals, retained local officials, new cadres from poor peasant backgrounds, etc.), many with little exposure to Marxism-Leninism, into a unified leadership corps. One of the major responses to these problems was the indoctrination and study campaigns staged in 1939-40 and 1942-44.[31] The first campaign was limited to about 4,000 cadres and students in the immediate vicinity of Yenan, but the latter, known as the *Cheng Feng* campaign, was much more extensive. Party members, cadres, students, and intellectuals throughout the base areas spent several months undergoing intensive group study of assigned documents, mutual criticism of past attitudes and activities, and professions of renewed dedication to official policies and styles of leadership. Where possible, regular work and other activities were suspended for a period of weeks for this activity, and even after regular activities were resumed a daily period of political study was advocated.

---

30. The mass line refers to the general conception of how to organize the masses, of which *hsiao-tsu* and political rituals are an important part. For extended discussions of this concept see John W. Lewis, *Leadership in Communist China* (Ithaca: Cornell University Press, 1963); and James R. Townsend, *Political Participation in Communist China* (Berkeley and Los Angeles; University of California Press, 1967).

31. A good summary of these campaigns is contained in Mark Selden, *The Yenan Way in Revolutionary China* (Cambridge: Harvard University Press, 1971), pp. 188–200. Cf. also Boyd Compton, *Mao's China: Party Reform Documents, 1942–1944* (Seattle: University of Washington Press, 1966).

In the Yenan period, then, regular political rituals were extended further outside of the Party and army to embrace all cadres (including non-Party members) and students and some intellectuals as well. Peasants were not uniformly involved in these rituals in the same way, but the Communists did manage to penetrate and organize villages much more effectively than in the Kiangsi period. The goals became not management of village affairs from outside, but the development of organizations and local leadership within the natural village. With the aid and initiative of outside organizers and propagandists a myriad of new village organizations was established, all linked in various ways with the war effort: national salvation associations, village militias, women's organizations, mutual aid teams, and village cooperatives. Some of the local leaders were drawn off for special leadership and ideological training, and the more responsive villagers were enrolled in study and discussion activities: winter schools, evening literacy classes, and mass meetings of various village organizations. As Franz Schurmann summarizes the results of these efforts, "The Chinese Communists were finally able to achieve what no state power in Chinese history had been able to do: to create an organization loyal to the state which was also solidly embedded in the natural village." [32]

Further research is needed to determine exactly how various parts of the base area population took part in organizations and in political rituals during the Yenan period. But it is clear that the *hsiao-tsu* and political rituals we are concerned with were extended further out from the Party during this period, and that the basic idea underlying that extension—the notion of penetrating to the basic levels of society and organizing social groups so that they would actively support governmental programs—was further elaborated and put into practice in these years. The historical record gives ample evidence of the success of these efforts in mobilizing the population for production and war despite the difficult military and economic situation in the base areas.

The extension of *hsiao-tsu* and political rituals to other parts of the population seems to have been largely a post-1949 phenomenon, connected with the shift from appealing for popular support against the enemy to consolidating control over the total society. Apparently only after 1949 were all workers, intellectuals, urban residents, and miscellaneous employees exposed to these activities in a regular and systematic fashion. The clearest official statement of the process by which

---

32. Franz Schurmann, *op. cit.*, p. 416.

these political rituals (specifically mutual criticism) were extended to various parts of the population comes from Mao Tse-tung's 1957 speech "On the Correct Handling of Contradictions among the People":

In 1942 we worked out the formula "unity—criticism—unity" to describe this democratic method of resolving contradictions among the people. To elaborate, this means to start off with a desire for unity and resolve contradictions through criticism or struggle so as to achieve a new unity on a new basis. Our experience shows that this is a proper method to resolve contradictions inside the Communist Party, namely, contradictions between the doctrinaires and the rank-and-file membership, between doctrinairism and Marxism. . . . A few years later in 1945 when the Chinese Communist Party held its Seventh National Congress, unity was thus achieved throughout the Party and the great victory of the people's revolution was assured. . . . We extended this method beyond our Party. During the war it was used very successfully in the anti-Japanese bases to deal with relations between those in positions of leadership and the masses, between the army and the civilian population, between officers and men, between different units of the army, and between various groups of cadres. The use of this method can be traced back to still earlier times in the history of our Party. We began to build our revolutionary armed forces and bases in the south in 1927 and ever since then we have used this method to deal with relations between the Party and the masses, between the army and the civilian population, between officers and men, and in general with relations among the people. The only difference is that during the Anti-Japanese War, this method was used more purposefully. After the liberation of the country we used this same method—"unity-criticism-unity"—in our relations with other democratic parties and industrial and commercial circles. Now our task is to continue to extend and make still better use of this method throughout the ranks of the people; we want all our factories, co-operatives, business establishments, schools, government offices, public bodies, in a word, all the six hundred million of our people, to use it in resolving contradictions among themselves.[33]

We have described the gradual process by which the Chinese Communists extended the activities and rituals of "Party life" outward into broader and broader segments of the population as part of an overall attempt to get the population fully involved in national life and solidly in support of the goals of the Chinese Communist elite. The road to power taken by the Chinese Communists thus gave them both the necessity and the opportunity to develop a genuine mass base of support and techniques for maintaining leadership over the masses with

---

33. Translated in Robert Bowie and John Fairbank, eds., *Communist China 1955–1959: Policy Documents with Analysis* (Cambridge: Harvard University Press, 1962), p. 278.

less reliance on hierarchical command and external manipulation than had been the case in Stalinist Russia.[34]

What can we conclude about the origins of the Chinese Communist use of *hsiao-tsu* and political rituals? Clearly there are some precedents from traditional China, but these are weak and ambiguous at best. The Chinese Communists do not seem consciously to have tried to incorporate these traditional precedents in their own political system, and the population did not find *hsiao-tsu* either very familiar or easy to adapt to. The direct precedents for *hsiao-tsu* activities stem from Bolshevik Party rituals. But in the Soviet Union these activities served to set the Party and its auxiliaries off from the rest of society, as an "organizational weapon" designed to be the motive force behind social change. In China during the decades of struggle for power the Chinese Communists by trial and error created a closer and more symbiotic relationship between the Party and the masses and extended Party rituals outward until they were applied to many ordinary citizens. Through such innovations as *hsiao-tsu* and political rituals, increasing parts of the population were to become not passive objects to be manipulated by the Party, but integral parts of a much larger and more ambitious organizational weapon.

---

34. After 1949 some Soviet political study handbooks were translated into Chinese, but without exception they reveal a level of organization and sophistication far below what the Chinese were already practicing at this time. See, for instance, Soviet Youth Guard, *Kuan-yü ch'u-chi cheng-chih hsüeh-hsi hsiao-tsu hsüan-ch'uan-yüan ti kung-tso,* (On the work of a propaganda officer of a lower level political study *hsiao-tsu*) Ch'en Chiang, trans., Canton, 1950.

IV

SMALL GROUPS AND POLITICAL RITUALS: THE IDEAL FORMS

The terms *hsiao-tsu*, political study, and mutual criticism stand for activities of considerable complexity which we hope to clarify in this chapter. Our information comes primarily from party directives, manuals, and pamphlets which describe how *hsiao-tsu* are to be organized and how political rituals are to be carried out within them. Most of these were published in the period right after 1949, when organizational control over Chinese society was being consolidated and when citizens in various walks of life were being exposed for the first time to *hsiao-tsu* activities. Rarely before or since that time have the desires of the leadership regarding *hsiao-tsu* operations been discussed in such detail.[1]

The discussion presented here serves two major purposes. First, by studying the "ideal" form of political rituals we can get some idea of the thinking of the Chinese elite about leadership methods and relations with the masses—of how the "mass line" is to be implemented within organizations. Second, we can establish a standard of comparison

---

1. The sources consulted were Tsou Shu-min, *Tsen-yang kao-hao chi-t'i hsüeh-hsi* (How to run collective study well) (Peking, 1951); Chou Yüan-ping, *Hsüeh-hsi kuan-tien yü hsüeh-hsi fang-fa* (Study outlook and study methods) (Hong Kong, 1950); T'ang Ti, ed., *Hsüeh-hsi yü hsüeh-hsi hsiao-tsu,* (Study and the study small group) (Shanghai, 1950); and Hung Fu-ch'uan, ed., *Hsüeh-hsi ching-yen yü fang-fa* (Study experience and methods) (Hong Kong, 1952). Issues of the Party ideological journal *Hsüeh-hsi* (Study) were also consulted.

against which to evaluate the case studies presented in later chapters. By comparing our accounts of how *hsiao-tsu* were organized and run in schools, offices, and other organizations in the 1960's with the ideal form presented in these manuals we can develop hypotheses about what circumstances and organizational conditions contribute to or detract from approaching this ideal.

The formal structure of political study activity established throughout China after 1949 represented an elaboration on study routines of earlier years, particularly those of the *Cheng Feng* campaign (1942–44). During both periods the general direction of study activities originated from study committees established within each organization, led by committees at higher administrative levels. These study committees, at least at lower levels, contained both Party members and non-members. A leading role was generally played by representatives of the Party Propaganda Department (or Party propaganda officers at lower levels), whose primary responsibility was political indoctrination. The committees drafted plans for how political study should be organized, how study groups would be set up, what materials would be discussed and how, what kinds of meetings would be held, and how much time would be spent in each stage of study. Under the leadership of the study committee in a locality or organization, individuals were assigned to various study groups according to their levels of education, revolutionary experience, and a number of other factors. The study committee then adapted its plans to the various levels of groups; generally, higher level groups relied heavily on individual study of complicated texts, middle level groups relied mainly on group study and discussion of less difficult texts, and lower level groups combined listening to lecturers with group discussion and literacy training. This, then, was the formal structure: Party Central Committee and Propaganda Department at the top, study committees at territorial and organizational levels down to the individual unit, and study *hsiao-tsu* divided into different grades under the local study committee. Thus, before the Chinese Communists came to power the activities and norms of *hsiao-tsu* operation had been worked out in considerable detail. The main difference in the post-1949 period in comparison with the earlier *Cheng Feng* campaign was that study activities were extended to wider segments of the population; not only cadres, students, and the military were included, but also ordinary workers, urban residents, and others increasingly participated.

Study manuals from the post-1949 period presented detailed "dos and don'ts" concerning every phase of study activity within this structure, from the initial establishment of study groups to "final examinations" at the end of a study period. The pamphlets followed a standard form: first readers were advised how properly to carry out some aspect of the study routine, and then they were alerted to various "deviations" which might detract from this routine. The presentation of "deviations" is a common way in which "don'ts" are presented in Communist media, and we should point out that is difficult to say how common these deviations were.

It is clear from these early study manuals that *hsiao-tsu* activities were supposed to be closely supervised. Although immediate supervision over day-to-day study was generally entrusted to study committees or Party propaganda officers within a unit, all leading cadres were supposed to help set the tone. They were expected to emphasize to their subordinates the importance of study and mutual criticism, while the study committee worked out the specifics on what to study, how to organize each stage, and how much time to spend in various activities. Organizational leaders and all Party members were expected to set an example for others by their own enthusiastic study and vigorous self-criticism. Leaders were to scrutinize the regular reports of study group heads, examine individual study notes, and check the results of examinations; any de-emphasis on mass political study, or any deviations in the study process, were supposed to be quickly rectified. However, the pamphlets tell us that leaders often failed to meet these high standards. Some complained that work burdens were too heavy and that political study had to be skipped in order to concentrate on getting the work done. Some felt that their subordinates did not need political study, while others felt that the political study routine was not effective in changing attitudes and behavior, and was thus a waste of time. Some leading cadres set a poor example by engaging in little study themselves and by refusing to accept criticism from others. Some leaders made all the decisions about the study process themselves, leaving no room for "mass initiative," while others left study leadership entirely in the hands of lower level cadres and did not concern themselves with the results. The outcome was that "backward elements" gained control of some *hsiao-tsu*. Some leading cadres paid to much attention to external results (study reports, quiz results) and were unconcerned with whether the members' thoughts were really being reformed. All of these deviations in leadership were said to lead to lowered motivation and enthusiasm in study.[2]

The first practical responsibility of leading cadres (and of the study

---

2. Tsou Shu-min, *op. cit.*, Chap. 3.

committee in particular) was to divide subordinates into *hsiao-tsu*. Most of the study pamphlets give the ideal group size as around ten, although peculiar organizational circumstances could justify variations. If a group was too small, it might not have strong leadership or enough conflicting views in discussions. Too large a group would lower the extent of each person's participation and could make it difficult to keep discussions under control. Individuals in a locality or organization had to be divided into various levels of *hsiao-tsu*, with specific study plans tailored to each level. When people of too widely differing backgrounds were placed in one group, the results were generally negative. For this reason, from two to five different levels of groups were formed, with several small groups in each level and with relative homogeneity within each group. However, too much homogeneity was not desired, because similarity of views would not promote debate and mutual criticism. Ideally, a group should contain enough heterogeneity to permit "trade-offs" in ideas between those with more knowledge of Marxist theory and those with little grasp of Marxism but more practical or revolutionary experience. The exchange of information among levels was also provided for in some organizations by having individuals in higher level study groups serve as "study advisers" or "instructors" to individuals and groups at lower levels.

Leaders in an organization were supposed to consider primarily education, contact with Marxist ideas, and past revolutionary experience in forming *hsiao-tsu*. In practice, however, there were deviations. Using such criteria it should have been possible, and indeed common, for leading cadres to be placed in a *hsiao-tsu* together with janitors or other service personnel. However, leaders sometimes formed people into groups according to their rank within an organization, a practice which interfered with feelings of equality and with "mass line" methods of leadership by reinforcing the hierarchical aspect of organizational life. In some other places individuals were allowed freely to choose their own *hsiao-tsu*, and this method also created problems. Friendship and similarity of backgrounds were generally the basis for such choices, and the resulting groups did not develop good debate and criticism and contributed to cleavages and rivalries within an organization. Another method was for a study committee or leading cadres arbitrarily to divide people into various groups based on their educational and ideological levels (perhaps using some sort of quiz to sort people out). However, this method was only to be used in units where the individuals were new and did not know each other (e.g., students entering a school), and even then it was to be only temporary. Too much dictation from above would harm the leadership's "democratic style" (*min-chu tso-feng*) and lead to dissatisfaction and poor study by subordinates.

The ideal procedure was to combine leadership with mass participation. Authorities would announce the criteria to be used in dividing people into groups—emphasizing education and revolutionary experience rather than rank or friendship. They would examine information they had about subordinates in order to get a preliminary idea about how many levels would be needed and who should be in each. Then meetings of subordinates would be called in which the criteria would be discussed until everyone knew how to apply them—a process referred to as fermentation (*yün-niang*). Then in a large meeting each individual would say what level group he thought he qualified for according to these criteria, and others who disagreed with his judgment could raise objections—a procedure known as self-report and mutual evaluation (*tzu-pao kung-yi*). Then the leading cadres would do the actual division of the groups, relying on the views expressed in the meeting, but making sure that each group had some backbone elements (*ku-kan fen-tzu*) and potential activists (*chi-chi fen-tzu*) to provide leadership.[3] Then the group compositions would be announced to all.[4] Certain common organizational practices are apparent in this description of the ideal way to form study *hsiao-tsu*. Natural primary groups and friendship ties were to be cross-cut, as in the traditional *pao-chia* groups, but this should not be done simply by an order from on high. Rather, the masses (i.e., all members of the organization) were to be involved in discussing and implementing the demands of the leadership so that they would uderstand and come to accept these demands.

Each *hsiao-tsu* had a head and generally an assistant head, and these posts, we are told, were to be filled in a similar manner. If the personnel were new the leaders could appoint group heads, but this should be only temporary. In most cases a group should elect its own head. But, as in the case of dividing up the groups, this election should be

---

3. Backbone elements are people who can always be relied upon to support official policies energetically. Most Party and Youth League members will be considered backbone elements, as will some individuals outside of these organizations. The term activist has similar connotations, but it has more of a temporary quality. An activist may offer enthusiastic support today but may fall back into the ranks tomorrow. The term activist may also refer to more specialized support and enthusiasm, as in the case of a work activist or a study activist, while backbone elements are expected to offer support in all kinds of activities. Both terms are generally informal designations rather than formal titles, although from time to time there are selections for work or other types of activists.

4. Tsou Shu-min, *op. cit.*, Chap. 4; T'ang Ti, *op. cit.*, pp. 59–64.

preceded by the leadership's announcing the criteria and procedure for the election. The general criteria for a *hsiao-tsu* head included the following: he should possess a firm revolutionary standpoint (i.e., total support for the policies of the Chinese Communist Party); he should set a good example for others both by diligent study and a good life style; [5] he should be willing to help others in study; and he should be able to serve as an effective bridge between the leadership and group members, obeying the former and reflecting and reporting the views of the latter. Before holding the elections leading cadres should warn subordinates against letting personal ties and feelings affect their votes. A good leader they did not like was preferable to a poor leader they liked.[6] In some circumstances the leaders might continue to nominate individuals to run in *hsiao-tsu* elections.

In this period *hsiao-tsu* were often subdivided into mutual help small groups (*hu-chu hsiao-tsu*), each with three or four members. The methods of forming these groups and picking their leaders were supposed to parallel the "directed mass participation" format already outlined. Much of the preliminary discussion of study materials was supposed to take place within these mutual help *hsiao-tsu*, and the heads of these groups were supposed to aid the *hsiao-tsu* head in organizing the meetings of the larger group.

Once this basic structure had been established, regular political study could be initiated.[7] However, there remained the problem of dealing with individuals who did not want to participate at all, or who approached group study with improper attitudes. Participation in *hsiao-tsu* and political study was never stated to be compulsory, but leading cadres were expected to make sure that everyone took part. What was desired was not mere presence in meetings, but active involvement accompanied by the desire to reform oneself and others. But many individuals approached these activities with quite different attitudes. Intellectuals, particularly, disliked the discipline and lack of per-

---

5. A good life style essentially means self-discipline and asceticism in free time activities—not drinking too much, gambling, spending a lot of money, wasting time in frivolous activities, and so forth.

6. For a similar, but more recent list of criteria for picking small group heads see Ta kung pao, ed., *Tsai Mao Tse-tung ssu-hsiang pu-yü hsia ch'eng-chang* (Growing up under the nurture of Mao Tse-tung's thought) (Peking, 1966), pp. 95–96.

7. This discussion assumes that basic political control of an organization had been established. Of course in the period 1948–1951 there was a long and involved process of establishing control over organizations throughout the country which had to be basically completed before a regular study routine could be initiated.

sonal privacy of group rituals. Old revolutionaries sometimes thought their thoughts needed no further reforming. Individuals with some knowledge of Marxism often disliked having to plod along beside beginning students of the doctrine. Other individuals claimed they were too busy to find time to study, or tried to memorize new terms and jargon simply to impress their superiors.

Leading cadres in an organization were advised to employ a variety of techniques to involve hostile individuals and to correct harmful attitudes. Before full scale study got going (or before the start of a new study topic) leaders were advised to conduct "thought mobilization" (ssu-hsiang tung-yüan) meetings, at which all the members of an organization would hear speeches on the importance of hsiao-tsu political study and the proper ways to conduct this activity. These speeches should stress that every person in the organization, no matter what his background or rank, needed to engage in intensive political study in order to change his attitudes and raise his level of political consciousness. Each person should approach political study with the idea of "demanding progress" (yao-ch'iu chin-pu) in his own political attitudes. Only intensive political study as prescribed by the leadership would bring about such "progress." Individual study was not enough, since one person was limited in what he could learn by his own experience, background, and knowledge. Only by group discussion and criticism could he realize and begin to overcome his own personal biases and shortcomings. Group members had to rid themselves of their anxieties about political study and plunge themselves enthusiastically into this activity if they were not to be left behind in the onrushing tide of revolutionary change in China. Only when mistaken attitudes toward study itself were eliminated could study be effective in changing other attitudes of participants.

Organizational leaders and hsiao-tsu heads were advised to use a variety of other techniques to deal with poor attitudes toward study. Group heads could assign special tasks to some individuals (for example, preparing an oral report on a particular topic) as a way of getting them involved. Individuals who displayed negative attitudes toward study could be criticized by the group. Private talks could be held in which the group head would ask a member what was troubling him or why he was listless and uncooperative in study. Hsiao-tsu heads were advised to use their ingenuity to make group study and group life more attractive to members. Study could be varied with debates, inspection trips, and competition between groups. Joint recreation could be organized so that group ties would be strengthened by common activities.

If group spirit and solidarity were built up, the resistance to group study activities would melt away. The *hsiao-tsu* was supposed to cut across lines of friendship within an organization, but once formed it had to build up its own internal solidarity in order to be effective in influencing attitudes.[8]

Political study was divided into distinct stages: individual study, mutual help *hsiao-tsu* meetings, *hsiao-tsu* discussion, mutual criticism, larger meetings, and summations. Study committees assigned particular articles, essays or texts to be read individually. Lectures or oral readings were provided for illiterates. The success of later group study depended to a considerable extent on the diligence of individuals in this first stage, and detailed *do's and don'ts* were specified. The individual should proceed in an organized manner, reading the assigned materials carefully, perhaps several times, in order to grasp the main ideas and their implications, Neither memorization nor the learning of obscure phrases was desired. Rather, the individual should as he went along consider his family origin, his past activities, his state of mind—all through the prism of the new ideas he was absorbing. He was also supposed to think about how he could apply these new ideas in his daily work and other activities. He should reflect upon what he was reading rather than regarding his task as a requirement to be completed as soon as possible. Skepticism was even advocated in limited ways—an individual should read unorthodox material from his new Marxist-Leninist perspective and treat that material skeptically. However, doubting everything one read was condemned as a deviation, and leaders were urged not to assign texts containing unorthodox views until orthodox ones had been firmly implanted.[9] Often the study committee would provide a study outline which contained questions to which individuals were supposed to seek answers through their reading. Individuals were also supposed to take notes as an aid to comprehension. The notes also played a role in the supervision of study, since individuals might be asked to hand in their reading notes for inspection.

Individual study was generally followed by mutual help *hsiao-tsu* meetings. In these meetings people were expected to explain their understanding of what they had read and to raise questions about points they didn't understand. Members were also expected to express boldly

---

8. See the discussion in T'ang Ti, *op. cit.*, pp. 57–66; Ai Ssu-ch'i, "Ts'ung-t'ou hsüeh-ch'i", (Start studying from the head), in *Hsüeh-hsi*, Vol. 1, no. 1, September 15, 1949.

9. Chou Yüan-ping, *op. cit.*, pp. 84–88; *Hsüeh-hsi*, Vol. 1, no. 3, November 1949, pp. 30–31; *Hsüeh-hsi*, Vol. 1, no. 1, September 1949, pp. 29–30.

their own views even when (or especially when) these conflicted with
the line taken in the study materials. Through these meetings misunderstandings could be cleared up and major doubts and conflicting
views could be aired and then referred to *hsiao-tsu* heads, study advisers, study committee members, and other leaders. A variety of deviations interfered with the proper operation of the mutual help *hsiao-
tsu*. Sometimes these groups were based on friendship ties and failed to
develop lively discussion of the texts assigned. Sometimes activists did
not like the burden of helping their slower or more backward compan-
ions. Individuals often refrained from boldly stating their views for fear
of later criticism. And sometimes the caliber of mutual help *hsiao-tsu*
heads was low and the sessions were poorly supervised.[10]

The reports from mutual help *hsiao-tsu* heads were to be used by
study committees and *hsiao-tsu* heads in planning the discussion sessions to follow. Leaders would examine the kinds of questions and
doubts which had been aired in the earlier meetings and use them in
drafting a discussion outline for the *hsiao-tsu* meetings to follow. More
preparation was involved before a *hsiao-tsu* meeting could be convened,
however, in order to avoid poorly run meetings or discussions which
ground to a halt because nobody was willing to speak (a situation referred to as a "cold floor"—*leng-ch'ang*). The first step was to check
whether individual and mutual help *hsiao-tsu* study had been conducted well. Then a new study outline based on these previous stages
would be distributed to *hsiao-tsu,* and fermentation would begin again.
The group head would rely upon activists within the group to try to
develop general enthusiasm for the discussion to come, to convey the
leadership's plans and demands, and to allay any anxieties about participating in the discussion. Some of these preliminary sessions were
devoted to what is called *man-t'an* (literally, spreading talk), a kind of
unstructured discussion in which individuals were expected to express
their feelings, comprehensions, and doubts. After such a session each
group member was supposed to write an individual speaking outline of
his views on the questions posed in the discussion outline. This task
facilitated review of the material studied and also forced everyone to
prepare something to say in the discussion.

Hsiao-tsu discussions were in some ways the key link in the study
routine. The *hsiao-tsu* head was provided with detailed guidelines for
leading these discussions. He should not act like the family patriarch,
dominating the floor and lecturing the members. He should not act like

---

10. Tsou Shu-min, *op. cit.,* pp. 66–69; Chou Yüan-ping, *op. cit.,* pp. 128–135;
T'ang Ti, *op. cit.,* pp. 73–80, *Hsüeh-hsi,* Vol. 1, no. 1, September 1949, pp. 42–43.

a teacher who knows all the answers or in any other way try to set him-self apart from the rest of the group. He should not spout jargon all the time. He should set an example for others by studying diligently, but he should not try to progress too far ahead of the rest of the group, thus destroying the force of his example by its inaccessibility. He should not tell his group one thing while reporting another to the study committee. He had to realize the importance of political study and use his ingenuity to create enthusiasm within the group. His suc-cess as a *hsiao-tsu* head could be judged by the extent to which he made his own role unimportant, i.e., by the degree to which the others in the group participated eagerly and actively without pressure and criticism from him. The *hsiao-tsu* head should obey the leadership's study plans and instill discipline into his group. He should never hesitate to criti-cize deviations from orthodox views. But at the same time he should be considerate of all group members. He should familiarize himself with the thinking and problems of each member and report these accurately to higher authorities. He should make special efforts to help those in the group who were having difficulty understanding the material. He should often chat with group members during their free time and so-licit their suggestions on how to improve study. In sum, the *hsiao-tsu* head had to play a balancing act between being a friend of the group and an agent of the leadership, and too much emphasis on either side of the relationship would be harmful to group study.[11]

The pamphlets describe a number of reasons why people partici-pated poorly in discussion meetings. Individuals who felt they did not understand the study materials, who harbored unorthodox views, or who were simply lazy often kept silent during group meetings. On the other hand, in many groups there were activists or people trying to compensate for past errors who sought to monopolize discussions. It was the responsibility of the meeting chairman to see both that the talkers were kept in check and that the silent ones were drawn into the discussion. The latter was the more difficult problem, and a number of tactics were recommended. First, as we have mentioned, the leadership could require everyone to prepare speaking outlines, which might have to be turned in for inspection after the discussion. If anyone persis-tently refused to participate, the *hsiao-tsu* head should have an individ-ual chat with him to find out the reason and to try to convince him to voice his opinions more often. Criticism and the use of threats were to

---

11. See Chou Yüan-ping, *op. cit.*, pp. 123–124. The demand that the *hsiao-tsu* head not make himself too important has been missed in much of the Western writing on *hsiao-tsu*.

be avoided. Other *hsiao-tsu* members should be instructed not to laugh at things said by the less educated and not to immediately bombard the views of the backward with criticism. The meeting chairman should also hold back in expressing his own views in order not to permaturely cut off discussion.

Several other tactics were available. The chairman could simply ask a non-speaker to say something, but this could lead to the attitude that speaking in meetings was a burdensome task one should only do when called upon. If a "cold floor" developed, however, this tactic was acceptable. The group could also try having each person speak in turn. This would force everyone to prepare, but if this tactic was used too often it could lead to excessive formality and a listless, compliant attitude. The *hsiao-tsu* head could pick people in advance to give talks on individual topics. But this method also lacked spontaneity, and might lead those not chosen to stop preparing. Another tactic was to rotate the chairmanship of discussions so that each member of the group, especially the habitual non-speakers, would have the experience of organizing a discussion, and would thereby begin to appreciate the problems of getting others to speak, and might not be so silent himself in the future. However, not everyone in the group was capable of running group meetings well, and the negative effects on others of a badly run meeting would outweigh the positive influence of this experience on the temporary chairman. So it was recommended that in general the *hsiao-tsu* head should serve as chairman, although from time to time he could pick a temporary chairman. No sure-fire way to get everyone to participate actively was available, and the *hsiao-tsu* head was supposed to use his ingenuity and persuasive powers to deal with the problem of listless discussions.[12]

A discussion for which everyone had prepared and in which everyone had something to say would still be a failure if no conflicts of views or criticism developed. So the meeting chairman also had to try to encourage debate and criticism. He could encourage those in the group who had doubts about orthodox views to state their feelings boldly. He could sometimes voice unorthodox opinions himself as a way of stimulating discussion, although he had to be careful not to laugh and reveal his deception (and not to confuse other group members). The *hsiao-tsu* head often had difficulty provoking debate since group members, hav-

---

12. Tsou Shu-min, *op. cit.*, Chap. 7; Chou Yüan-ping, *op. cit.*, pp. 136–140; Hung Fu-ch'uan, *op. cit.*, pp. 25–33, 46; T'ang Ti, *op. cit.*, pp. 99–105; *Hsüeh-hsi*, Vol. 1, no. 1, September 1949, pp. 40–41, *Hsüeh-hsi*, Vol. 1, no. 5, January 1950, p. 39.

ing read the orthodox texts and having heard amplifying speeches, were often only too clear about what the "safe" opinions were.

Generally, no specific meeting was called to carry out mutual criticism within the group. Rather, criticism and self-criticism were to go hand in hand with the discussion and were viewed as indispensable to it. What is more, mutual criticism was supposed to take place whenever the thoughts or actions of any group member deviated from the official standards contained in political study materials. Not only poor study performance, but also poor work habits, marital disputes, and unorthodox comments to friends were supposed to come to the attention of the group and result in criticism. And in each such case every other member of the group should display his own ideological progress by vigorously criticizing individuals who had committed errors. However, mutual criticism is the element in these political rituals which is most alien to Chinese traditions, and for this reason attitudes of resistance to participation in mutual criticism were formidable. The sections on how to conduct mutual criticism are perhaps the most detailed parts of these pamphlets, and the views of Mao Tse-tung and other top Chinese Communists are marshaled behind the advice given.[13] Again one had both left and right deviations: attitudes which hindered criticism (right) and attitudes which fostered excessive or unfair criticism (left). Some individuals were reluctant to criticize their friends or their kin, and others resisted criticizing anyone for fear of retaliation in the future. Some people simply liked to say nice things and be polite to everyone, while others were unconcerned about whether their peers harbored improper attitudes. Some were willing to criticize others but resisted self-criticism, finding excuses for their own shortcomings. Some individuals harbored grudges against those who had criticized them. Others developed skills in self-criticism which made them appear very repentant about their errors, but in practice their behavior did not change at all. On the other hand, there were those who loved to criticize others, who could see only defects and no merits in those around them, and who were skilled at using ideological jargon to magnify the errors of their peers out of all proportion. In some cases personal animosities and grudges were vented in meetings under the guise of principled criticism, and at times criticism was reinforced by gossip and rumors spread outside of meetings.

---

13. Mao Tse-tung's most important statement of deviations in mutual criticism is contained in his 1937 essay "In Opposition to Liberalism" translated in Boyd Compton, ed., *Mao's China* (Seattle: University of Washington Press, 1966), pp. 184–187.

The *hsiao-tsu* head and organizational leaders were expected to find ways to avoid such deviations. Criticism should be focused on the points under discussion, it should be based on ideological principles and the correct class standpoint, it should not be too severe or too moderate, and it should be constructive, designed, in Mao's terms, "to cure the illness to save the man." Criticism should be accompanied by efforts to look for the source of deviant views and to help the recipient find ways to correct his error. Criticism should be accompanied by moderating praise in order not to devastate its target. The recipient of criticism was asked to realize that his critics were really trying to help him. He should think over their criticisms and engage in thoughtful self-criticism. He could refute criticism he felt was unfair or incorrect, but in these pamphlets the better attitude was for the target of criticism to resolve "to change my ways if criticism is correct, and to avoid that error in the future if it is incorrect." (There is a traditional couplet here—*yu-tse kai-chih, wu-tse chia mien*.)[14] The individual should be more critical of himself than of others, and he should not wait for others to criticize him before pointing out his own failings to the group. He should realize that admitting errors is not condemning oneself totally, and that by such an admission he can rid himself of an emotional burden and can begin to progress ideologically.[15]

The *hsiao-tsu* head bore the main responsibility for developing proper mutual critcism. It was advised that he not take the lead in criticizing others; rather he should set an example by engaging in thorough and sincere self-criticism. As with the problem of developing discussion, the *hsiao-tsu* head should use a variety of tactics in the effort to get everyone participating in mutual criticism fairly equally. Activists should be encouraged to engage enthusiastically in criticism and self-criticism, but not be overly critical or monopolize the floor. Reluctant group members could be the target of individual talks outside the meetings, and of course they could also be criticized publicly for not engaging in criticism!

---

14. For a recent example showing the continued advocacy of this sort of attitude toward criticism see Jan Myrdal and Gun Kessle, *China: The Revolution Continued* (New York: Pantheon Books, 1970), p. 129.

15. Deviations and correct procedures in criticism meetings are discussed in Tsou Shu-min, *op. cit.*, Chap. 10, China Democratic League Southern General Branch Propaganda Committee, ed., *Chih-shih fen-tzu ti ssu-hsiang kai-tsao wen-t'i* (The problem of the thought reform of intellectuals) (Canton, 1952), pp. 1–31, 173–180; Hung Fu-ch'uan, *op. cit.*, pp. 20–25; Ta-ch'un shu-tien, *Tsen-yang chin-hsing p'i-p'ing yü tzu-wo p'i-p'ing* (How to carry out criticism and self-criticism) (Peking, 1950); Mao Tse-tung, et. al., *Ssu-hsiang chih-nan* (Ideological primer) (Peking, 1949), pp. 103–114.

Mutual criticism in a sense is the prime motive force behind attitude change in *hsiao-tsu;* as such it was extremely important that mutual criticism and the atmosphere surrounding it be correct. The desired atmosphere was one quite different from that valued in traditional Chinese primary groups. The terms used convey this point. What was desired was a "happy, tense, lively atmosphere" (*yü-k'uai chin-chang, huo-p'o ti ch'i-fen*),[16] a "happy and strict atmosphere" (*yü-k'uai er yen-su ti ch'i-fen*),[17] "solidarity but not harmony," (*t'uan-chieh. . . . pu tan pu shih yi-t'uan ho-ch'i*).[18] Thus a new kind of unity was to develop, one based on rigorous group criticism rather than on the smoothing over of conflict in order to preserve harmony (the traditional emphasis). On the other hand, *hsiao-tsu* were not supposed to be the scene of relentless and merciless criticism, which would serve only to alienate members. Solidarity and criticism were to be combined, with criticism leading not to disharmony but to improved unity. The procedure was signified by the sequence "unity—criticism—unity." The idea was for a group to start with a certain degree of unity and mutual respect, but with various defects in the thinking and behavior of members. This unity would be disrupted as unanimous criticism of these defects became the center of group life. As those criticized acknowledged their defects and resolved to change their ways, unity was restored, but at a higher level (i.e., with the defects corrected). Only if criticism was properly balanced with group solidarity could it be effective in changing the attitudes of members.

Discussion and criticism sessions could be continued in larger groups (often created by merging several *hsiao-tsu*), especially if there were problems left unresolved in *hsiao-tsu* meetings.[19] At the close of each discussion meeting of whatever size, the chairman was expected to summarize the main views expressed, what had been accomplished, and what problems remained. At the close of a study "unit" or a set of related topics a number of different kinds of summation were to take place. Each member of the group was to prepare an individual summary (*ko-jen tsung-chieh*) of his views on the questions that had been discussed, how these views had changed during the course of

---

16. Tsou Shu-min, *op. cit.,* p. 96.
17. *Ibid.,* p. 164.
18. T'ang Ti, *op. cit.,* p. 77.
19. Serious unresolved problems could result in the convening of intense "struggle meetings" (*tou-cheng-hui*). These were not included in the routine described in the pamphlets we have been discussing, but we will mention them at times in Chapters 5–9.

study, and the kinds of bad attitudes he still retained.[20] These summaries were then discussed one at a time in the mutual help *hsiao-tsu* or the *hsiao-tsu* or both. Here the most systematic mutual criticism was necessary, and the fact that everyone had to prepare a summary insured participation. The group could demand revisions if a summation was not sufficiently frank or thorough. Then the entire group would pass on each summary. The *hsiao-tsu* head would rely in part upon these summaries in giving a report to the group of his estimate of the results of the past study unit and the goals for the future. In this report he should try to raise issues and problems to the level of ideological principle, so that group members could relate their day-to-day disputes to overall national goals. The *hsiao-tsu* head's report and the individual summaries were then passed along to the study committee or Party propaganda officer. There might follow an overall report from one of the cadres in charge of study to all of those in an organization about what had been accomplished in the previous study unit, and what problems remained.[21]

The process described here might take several weeks or even months, and then was repeated for the next study unit. There were often variations in this routine. Sometimes a written quiz was given at the end of each study unit, and sometimes individuals and groups competed with each other for recognition as praiseworthy in political study. Sometimes study advisers were attached to *hsiao-tsu,* and sometimes *hsiao-tsu* sent representatives to other groups to search out ways to improve their own results. Sometimes study committees assigned people to man bulletin boards and wall newspapers which publicized the results of study activity. Variations such as these were encouraged, but the routine we have described was the basic study ritual advocated during the early post-1949 period.

The reader should note that these rituals were meant to be carried out, with modifications, among cadres, workers, students, soldiers, and many other kinds of personnel, rather than being aimed solely at some defined elite. In some circumstances (in prison, in political training classes) virtually the entire day could be spent in activities such as these, but for most individuals political study had to be fitted in

---

20. These self-examinations and summaries were much more thorough in settings where individuals were engaged in full-time thought reform. See Robert J. Lifton, "Thought reform of Chinese intellectuals: a psychiatric evaluation," in *Journal of Social Issues,* Vol. 13, no. 3, 1957. For a detailed handbook on thought summaries see Li Ming-ch'u, ed., *Tsen-yang tso ssu-hsiang tsung-chieh* (How to make a thought summary) (Shanghai, 1950).
21. Tsou Shu-min, *op. cit.,* Chap. 10.

around regular work, academic study or military training, and therefore occupied less time (anywhere from two to four hours a day to only two to four hours a week).

Over the years since 1949 there have been some modifications in the study routine. By the late 1950's much of the population had received a basic exposure to Marxist concepts and to political study, so perhaps it was not necessary to have such an elaborate study routine. By this time also the Chinese leaders were increasingly trying to move away from the Soviet model, and this entailed attacking "formalism" and bureaucracy within political institutions. Generally since the late 1950's the division of individuals into various levels of groups has been abandoned, and hsiao-tsu have been formed within natural administrative subdivisions (e.g., a factory work group, an office section or subsection). Study committees also dropped from sight by this time, and Party propaganda officers took over direct leadership of political study. Some techniques used in earlier periods, such as the mutual help hsiao-tsu and the study quizzes, also fell into disfavor. Recently there have been other modifications and new wrinkles, such as the organization of "Mao Tse-tung's thought study classes." However, the core elements of this ritual—the formation of hsiao-tsu engaged in regular political study and mutual criticism—seem constant over the years. The purposes this activity is to serve, and the atmosphere which is supposed to accompany it, also seem to have remained constant.[22]

We have presented here the "ideal form" for hsiao-tsu rituals, the form authorities say these rituals should take if they are successfully to influence behavior, change attitudes, and mobilize enthusiasm. When our case studies from organizations in China in the 1960's are presented (in Chapters 5 through 9) we will try to compare political rituals as they are actually carried out with the ideal forms authorities are striving for. Before we can do this we must extract out from under the procedural complexities the kind of group situation and atmosphere which are desired, and how these are supposed to be achieved. In other words these later comparisons will not be with the specific steps and stages of hsiao-tsu study which, as noted, have changed somewhat over the years, but with the underlying ideal group atmosphere.

---

22. For more recent group study advice consult Ta kung pao ed., op. cit.,; San-lien shu-tien, Hsüeh-hsi Mao chu-hsi chu-tso fu-tao ts'ai-liao (Materials for advisers in the study of Chairman Mao's thoughts) (Hong Kong, 1966); San-lien shu-tien, Yi-ting yao pa ch'uan-kuo pan-ch'eng Mao Tse-tung ssu-hsiang ti ta hsüeh-hsiao (Definitely turn the entire country into a big school for the study of Mao Tse-tung's thought) (Hong Kong, 1967); San-lien shu-tien, Ch'uan-kuo tou lai pan Mao Tse-tung ssu-hsiang hsüeh-hsi-pan (The entire country should set up Mao Tse-tung's thought study classes) (Hong Kong, 1967).

The pamphlets consulted seem to be saying that any individual who displays deviant or unorthodox attitudes or actions should find himself in the following situation if group rituals are to be fully effective in changing his ways:

Official standards of thought and behavior must be applied to all an individual's activities (i.e., not just to his conduct in political study, but to his work, he relations with others, and even to some extent to his private life). Compartmentalization, either through activities beyond the attention of members of the organization or through activities within the organization not subject to rigorous scrutiny, should not be possible. Effective group pressure must then be mobilized in support of official norms and in opposition to the deviation in question. The other members of the group should be unanimous in publicly criticizing the deviant, thus isolating him. The individual should not be able to find social support for continued deviance, either from within the group or from without. The individual should not be able to interpret this criticism as something other than what it is supposed to be—an ideologically principled defense of political standards designed to pressure and encourage him to reform his views and ways. He should not be able to feel that the criticism is incorrect, that his critics are insincere, that they are merely complying with official demands to criticize him, or that they are motivated by rivalry and personal spite. The individual should be made to feel that the only way he can regain group favor is sincerely and thoroughly to change his attitudes and behavior in the ways indicated by his critics. The individual should feel close ties toward the group and a desire to avoid its criticism. These ties may have a variety of origins, including affective ties to other members, respect for the views of others, and identification with the larger organization. These ties should make it psychologically painful for the individual to continue suffering group criticism and should lead him to resolve to change.

The ideal group situation just described may be called a "strict political atmosphere." [23] Many of the specific *do's and dont's* in the pamphlets reviewed here concern the preconditions for such an atmosphere: how to instill the proper attitudes toward criticism and how to develop ties with other group members. The assumption is that when the prescribed procedures are followed and the desired

---

23. The Chinese press sometimes uses a very similar term: a "dense political atmosphere" (*nung-hou ti cheng-chih k'ung-ch'i*). This refers not only to political standards being applied to all activities, but also to the particular group setting in which this occurs.

atmosphere is achieved, conditions will be optimal for pursuing all the goals which *hsiao-tsu* are assigned. When the desired atmosphere is not created, it will be impossible to achieve some or all of these goals, and political rituals may even become counterproductive.

Are Chinese authorities correct when they say that the atmosphere described above, if successfully maintained within an organization, will be the optimal one for changing the attitudes and values of participants? On what do they base this judgment? We will briefly mention here some of the findings of Western research on attitude change and group conformity to see how effective we should expect this ideal strict political atmosphere to be. Much of the reasoning presented in the Chinese pamphlets parallels closely the findings of Western social psychologists. "Cognitive dissonance" theorists note that expressing an attitude contrary to one's true beliefs (for example in role playing) can result in some attitude change in the direction of the view expressed, but that the more the subject perceives that he is being forced to express such a view the less his attitudes will change.[24] Other social scientists, arguing from the perspective of "incentive theory"[25] or compliance structure analysis[26] draw similar conclusions. The pamphlets reviewed do not cite Western social science and do not discuss the matter in such terms, but the conclusion is substantially the same: the more controlled and coerced are the study sessions and the less they are engaged in willingly, then the less effective this activity will be in changing attitudes. Therefore indirect pressure, persuasion, and the force of example should be emphasized and commands and threats deemphasized. Experiments in the West have shown that active discussion of views generally results in more attitude change than passive listening to a lecture,[27] and that efforts to think of arguments in favor of a position one does not support result in more attitude change than reading a prepared statement in favor of that position.[28] The Chinese Com-

---

24. L. Festinger and J. M. Carlsmith, "Cognitive consequences of forced compliance," in *Journal of Abnormal and Social Psychology*, Vol. 58, 1959, pp. 203–210; Jack Brehm and A. R. Cohen, *Explorations in Cognitive Dissonance* (New York: John Wiley, 1962), pp. 84–88.

25. C. I. Hovland, I. L. Janis and H. H. Kelley, *Communication and Persuasion* (New Haven: Yale University Press, 1953), pp. 223–231.

26. The basic source here is Amitai Etzioni, *A Comparative Analysis of Complex Organizations* (New York: Free Press, 1961).

27. I. L. Janis and B. T. King, "The influence of role-playing on opinion change," in *Journal of Abnormal and Social Psychology*, Vol. 49, 1954, pp. 211–218.

28. B. T. King and I. L. Janis, "Comparison of the effectiveness of improvised versus non-improvised role-playing in producing opinion changes," in *Human Relations*, Vol. 9, 1956, pp. 177–186.

munists, without consulting these findings,[29] have arrived at similar conclusions and have built active discussion and demands for reasoned public support of orthodox views into their study ritual.

Other Western experiments have shown that group social pressure exerts a powerful influence on the attitudes of group members, and that the more cohesive a group is and the more attractive it is to its members the greater will be its ability to influence individual attitudes.[30] We have already seen that the Chinese Communists place special emphasis on building up solidarity within *hsiao-tsu*. It should be clear, however, that their desire to produce attitude change is limited by other considerations. The group should not be too solidary or it might be difficult to control and might resist the demands of higher authorities. The potentially most solidary groups, composed of friends, or relatives, should be cross-cut and replaced by new groups with a different kind of solidarity. Control and other considerations cause the Chinese Communists to deviate from other possible arrangements which might promote attitude change. Western experiments make it clear that an authoritative and influential leader can influence the attitudes of his subordinates.[31] However, in the Chinese setting the *hsiao-tsu* head is not to be too authoritative, because this would hamper the development of group social pressure (and perhaps also for control reasons, to prevent the *hsiao-tsu* head from gaining too much independent control over his subordinates).

Unfortunately, the full range of *hsiao-tsu* activities has not been tested in the Western social science laboratory and probably could not be tested because of professional canons limiting the use of human sub-

---

29. Many of the relevant Western social psychological experiments were of course conducted after the Chinese Communists had fully elaborated their *hsiao-tsu* ideals (roughly in 1948–1951). Robert Lifton concluded in his study of thought reform that Western psychology had not influenced Chinese techniques, and that even the Chinese psychologists trained in Soviet Pavlovian psychology had no direct role in formulating thought reform procedures. See Robert J. Lifton, *Thought Reform and the Psychology of Totalism* (New York: Norton, 1961), Chap. 20.

30. See for example, Stanley Schacter, "Deviation, rejection and communications," in *Journal of Abnormal and Social Psychology*, Vol. 46, 1951, pp. 190–207; J. W. Thibaut and L. H. Strickland, "Psychological set and social conformity," in *Journal of Personality*, Vol. 24, 1956, pp. 115–129; Arthur R. Cohen, *Attitude Change and Social Influence* (New York: Basic Books, 1964).

31. J. Allyn and L. Festinger, "The effectiveness of unanticipated persuasive communications," in *Journal of Abnormal and Social Psychology*, Vol. 62, 1961, pp. 35–40; C. I. Hovland and W. Weiss, "The influence of source credibility on communication effectiveness," in *Public Opinion Quarterly*, Vol, 15, 1952, pp. 635–650.

jects.[32] However, some aspects of *hsiao-tsu* rituals could be submitted to more systematic Western experimentation. For instance, the notion that venting criticism within the group will result in a new and somehow better unity is a constant theme in *hsiao-tsu* pamphlets (and, as we mentioned in Chapter 2, forms part of the ideology behind Western T-groups and sensitivity training). On the other hand, there is the traditional Chinese notion, reflected in other strands of Western thought, that the venting of emotions and animosities inevitably has a corrosive effect on organizational unity, and that emotions have to be kept inside in order to sustain cooperative relationships with others.[33] It would seem that there are certain conditions in which the venting of criticism would lead to greater solidarity and other situations in which would lead to greater conflict, and that these varying conditions remain to be specified.

To sum up, there are many parallels between the Chinese *hsiao-tsu* ideal and the findings of Western social psychologists. The *hsiao-tsu* ritual should be readily understandable to social scientists as an effort to combine vigorous peer group pressure with tight hierarchical control. Western experiments do not permit us to examine every aspect of Chinese group rituals, but the parallels that exist suggest that, if the ideal form of the rituals can be established, these rituals should be fairly effective in influencing attitudes. If the individual can be successfully isolated from social support for unorthodox views and confronted with unanimous social pressure from valued peers in support of orthodox views, the pressure for change in his attitudes and values should be great.[34]

---

32. There has been one experiment using Chinese subjects in Hong Kong which tried to investigate the *hsiao-tsu*–attitude change situation. However, even this attempt fell far short of including all of the elements of *hsiao-tsu* rituals. See Paul J. Hiniker, "Chinese reactions to forced compliance: Dissonance reduction or national character" in *Journal of Social Psychology*, Vol. 77, 1969.

33. William F. Whyte, "Leadership and Group Participation" in *New York State School of Industrial and Labor Relations Bulletin* no. 24, Ithaca, New York, May 1953.

34. Even when the ideal strict political atmosphere is present, attitude and value change is by no means automatic. The accumulated habits and ways of thinking an individual has developed over the years may be exceedingly resistant to change, even when an individual truly wishes to transform himself. In this study we are primarily concerned with social structural obstacles to the creation of a strict political atmosphere rather than with the individual psychology of attitude change. Interested readers should consult Edgar H. Schein, *Coercive Persuasion* (New York: Norton), 1961; Robert J. Lifton, *Thought Reform and the Psychology of Totalism* (New York: Norton, 1961).

Therefore, the ideal form of the rituals described should, as the Chinese authorities claim, be an effective arrangement for producing attitude change in the desired direction. But can this ideal form be achieved in ordinary factories, schools, prisons, and other organizations? What factors determine whether it can be achieved? And if something less than this ideal form is achieved, how will the participants in political rituals be affected? The pamphlets consulted make it clear that it is not an easy matter to achieve this ideal atmosphere. Many "deviations" and harmful attitudes can undermine *hsiao-tsu* rituals and there are many fine balances to be struck (for example, group solidarity balanced by a willingness to criticize others; diligent reporting by the *hsiao-tsu* head to higher authorities, but without being viewed primarily as an agent of those authorities). The pamphlets do not present enough information about what other factors might affect the atmosphere in *hsiao-tsu,* and in the case studies that follow we will be looking for the ways the external environment of an organization, personnel recruitment policies, the quality of leadership, and other social structural factors affect the achievement of the ideal strict political atmosphere.

With a less than strict atmosphere the consequences may be quite different. Not only can we expect less effective pressure for attitude change, but also, if the departure from the ideal is sufficiently great, we can expect *hsiao-tsu* and political rituals to lead to increasing alienation and hostility. If, for instance, a member feels that others in the group are constantly spying on him and criticizing his slightest error, thereby hoping to earn the praise of superiors and gain promotions and favors, he is not likely to "progress" under the influence of that criticism. The ways in which *hsiao-tsu a*nd organizations can depart from a strict political atmosphere will also be examined in more detail in the case studies. The organizational innovations described in this chapter were conceived as a way of combining leadership from above with enthusiasm from below, of maintaining initiative and dedication on the part of subordinates even in large, complex, bureaucratic organizations. Organizational leaders who are more concerned with controlling the actions of their subordinates than with whipping up mass enthusiasm from below or changing attitudes may be able to use these group rituals as well, and the result will be regimentation without the desired "thought reform." If the primary concern is control and manipulation, then the *hsiao-tsu* network provides a way for superiors to get detailed information about the behavior of subordinates and, through activists within *hsiao-tsu,* to institute mutual surveillance and criticism for the slightest misbehavior. It is important, therefore, to try to specify the conditions under which a strict political atmosphere can be achieved and the conditions in which some other atmosphere will emerge which will have quite different effects on participants. The case study materials should help throw light on just what the critical conditions are.

V

CADRES AND POLITICAL
STUDY RITUALS

In traditional China the unity of society was preserved in part by subjecting the potential governing elite to a long course of study of orthodox philosophical texts. Unified in outlook by this rigid indoctrination, the elite could then give unity to the state bureaucracy and the entire society. A similar practice exists in China today, although the nature of both the texts and the elite has changed. Now it is the writings of Marx and Lenin and the thoughts of Mao Tse-tung which are studied, and the most rigorous study of these materials is prescribed for cadres, the leaders high and low in every sector of society.[1]

The term cadre (*kan-pu*) is an ambiguous one, with at least two separate, though overlapping, usages.[2] It is used to refer to anyone with a formal position of leadership, from Mao Tse-tung down to the rural production team head. The term also refers to state employees above a certain rank, a usage which includes many white-collar positions in the state and Party bureaucracy which lack leadership roles (e.g., accountants and clerks), and excludes positions of leadership which fall outside the state civil service network (e.g., the rural production team

1. This parallel is discussed in J. W. Lewis, "Party Cadres in Communist China," in James S. Coleman, ed., *Education and Political Development* (Princeton: Princeton University Press, 1965).

2. See the discussion in E. Vogel, "From Revolutionary to Semi-Bureaucrat: The 'regularization' of Cadres," in *China Quarterly*, No. 29, January–March 1967.

head). Cadres may be Party members, but many, especially those of lesser rank, are not. Some work organizations are made up almost entirely of cadres, while others have only a few cadres in leadership positions.

The Chinese leadership has made a continual effort to blur the leader-led distinction and to get the ordinary population involved in discussing policies. However, since cadres do provide the basic leadership at all levels in society, their ideological training remains crucial, and much of the political study ritual applied to the rest of the population was worked out first in the study life of cadres. Thus the indoctrination of these leading personnel remains a central pillar in the political system.

As we noted in Chapter 3, the systematization of political study took place in the Yenan period, particularly during the 1942–1944 *Cheng Feng* campaign. While *Cheng Feng*, or "rectification" (literally rectify work style), was the rough equivalent of the Soviet Party purge, the emphasis was on intensive study and thought reform as a way of correcting problems and deviations; demotions and more severe sanctions were rarely used. The central activity in this campaign was full-time study of eighteen (later twenty-two) prescribed documents (both Chinese Communist and Soviet materials), accompanied by mutual criticism, summations, etc.[3] The complex study organization described earlier, with study committees at various levels supervising several ranks of study groups, with activities gauged to the rank of the group, emerged at this time.

Chinese documents from the 1940's and subsequent years reveal the variety of types of cadre study stressed. Regular (generally daily) study by cadres as individuals and in groups is consistently advocated, but with a variety of goals. The primary study activity of the *Cheng Feng* campaign is classified as political theory study (*cheng-chih li-lun hsüeh-hsi*), designed to raise the general ideological level of cadres and to deal with deviations from the current orthodoxy. Even during non-campaign periods regular political theory study (often one or two hours a day) has been advocated. Political study of a more topical sort is termed current events study (*shih-shih hsüeh-hsi*), consisting of organized study of articles in the press and similar materials. Policy study (*cheng-ts'e hsüeh-hsi*) involves study of current policy proclamations and how to apply them in daily work. In addition, many cadres are

---

3. See Boyd Compton, ed., *Mao's China: Party Reform Documents, 1942–1944* (Seattle: University of Washington Press, 1966); also Mark Selden, *The Yenan Way in Revolutionary China* (Cambridge: Harvard University Press, 1971), pp. 188–200.

supposed to engage in regular professional study (*ye-wu hsüeh-hsi*) of technical journals and the experience of other organizations in solving technical problems. These kinds of regular study activity may be supplemented by general literacy training and cultural study. All these activities are supposed to be part of the regular in-service study of all cadres, and the cadres' work units are supposed to determine schedules so that they get the proper dose of each type on a regular basis.

In addition to these normal study activities cadres or potential cadres may be sent to training classes or to the network of cadre and Party schools which provide special, more intensive study and training.[4] And periodically campaigns requiring more intensive political study and mutual criticism occur. For instance a rectification campaign in 1947–48 dealt with deviations in land reform in North China, and another in 1950 dealt with the problems of absorbing many new people into the Party and the ranks of cadres.[5] Since that time, of course, many other campaigns have burdened the lives of cadres with new demands. The periodic rectification campaigns would seem to indicate that the regular routine of study for cadres is not sufficient to deal with all the problems and deviations which arise and must be supplemented from time to time by more intensive efforts.

After 1949 the system of cadre study became increasingly formalized. Central, regional, provincial, and local Party authorities regularly issued directives on the content, organization, and methods of cadre and employee political study.[6] In 1949–50 there was a selection of translations of the important writings of Marx, Engels, Lenin, and Stalin called the twelve cadre-must-read books (*kan-pu pi-tu-shu*) which formed the core of cadre theoretical study. Then more intensive reading of Stalin's "Short Course" in Soviet Party history was prescribed, supplemented by Mao's major theoretical writings ("On Practice" and "On Contradiction") and materials on the history of the Chinese Com-

---

4. This network of cadre and Party schools, which had specialized in political and professional training, was attacked during the Cultural Revolution as bourgeois and elitist. After 1968 a new network of "May 7th cadre schools" was set up in the countryside, where the emphasis was on manual labor and political study. See Martin K. Whyte, "Red vs. Expert: Peking's Changing Policy," in *Problems of Communism*, Vol. 21, no. 6, November–December 1972.

5. "Notes on Party cheng-feng campaigns," in *Hsüeh-hsi*, August 1, 1952.

6. Documents consulted include *T'ienchin Jih-pao*, October 3, 1949; *Tung-pei Jih-pao*, December 31, 1949 and January 1, 1950; *Hsin-hua Yüeh-pao*, Vol. 1, no. 5, 1950; *Ch'ang-chiang Jih-pao*, January 26, 1950; *Ch'un-chung Jih-pao*, February 1, 1950; *Ch'ingtao Jih-pao*, June 14, 1952; *Ch'ang-chiang Jih-pao*, October 19, 1952; *Hsin-hua Yüeh-pao*, February 1950; *Jen-min Jih-pao*, August 9, 1952; *Ta kung pao* (Tientsin), April 26, 1953; *Kuangchou Jih-pao*, March 15, 1954; and *Nan-fang Jih-pao*, September 13, 1954.

munist Party. With the inauguration of the first five-year plan Soviet writings were given greater emphasis; a national directive on cadre study for 1953–54 listed twenty-six documents, mostly writings by Lenin and Stalin on economic matters.[7] In this directive four to six hours a week of theoretical study supplemented by two hours of policy study were prescribed for cadres.

In these early years the complex study organization of the *Cheng Feng* period was retained, with various levels of study committees, study groups, mutual help small groups, study advisers, quizzes, and study competitions. Study committees within individual units were expected to specify in detail for each level of study group how much time would be spent and what methods would be used in each stage of the process: individual study, mutual help *hsiao-tsu* study, *hsiao-tsu* discussions, self-examination and mutual criticism, and summation. If cadres were called away on work assignments or were ill they were expected to make special arrangements to carry out the required study while away, or to catch up after they returned.

In practice this elaborate routine did not always work out well. Some units de-emphasized political study because of pressing work needs, or conducted it in a "bookish" atmosphere, with no relationship to current work and problems. Sometimes study committees placed people from different subdivisions of a unit into one group, and their lack of common interests and problems led to pro forma study. In rural areas it was often difficult to assemble enough cadres to support such an elaborate system, and simpler procedures were devised. Long term study plans were often disrupted by the national political campaigns which erupted so often in these years. And some organizations were not organized well enough to establish such a study routine until after 1953. Often individuals in low-level study groups resented the patronizing manner of the study advisors assigned to them for higher level groups. In sum, the evidence we have suggests that political study for cadres in the early 1950's was not always run as well as desired.[8]

From the late 1950's on, the study routine was increasingly modified. The early system seems to have been recognized as too formal and

7. *Ta kung pao* (Tientsin) April 26, 1953.
8. Some of the problems in these early cadre study efforts are described in *Jen-min Jih-pao*, February 10, 1950, March 11, 1950 and May 10, 1950; *Hsin-hua Jih-pao*, October 7, 1952; *Jen-min Jih-pao*, February 21, 1953; *T'ienchin Jih-pao*, February 4, 1953; *Jen-min Jih-pao*, May 22, 1953; *Yünnan Jih-pao*, January 24, 1953; *Jen-min Jih-pao*, November 21, 1953, April 14, 1954, and May 9, 1954; *Kuangchou Jih-pao*, July 30, 1954; *Kansu Jih-pao*, January 21, 1955; *Hsinchiang Jih-pao*, February 22, 1955; *Nan-fang Jih-pao*, February 20, 1955, March 9, 1955, and April 12, 1955; *Chianghsi Jih-pao*, May 13, 1955, and June 12, 1955.

structured, suitable for teaching new concepts and imposing discipline but unsuitable for arousing enthusiasm and initiative. By that time, of course, cadres new and old had already had some exposure to political study and new concepts, so that such an elaborate routine was perhaps no longer so necessary. No further national study directives are available for the period after 1954. In December 1957, in the wake of the anti-rightist campaign, a detailed reading list on socialist education was published, with Soviet and Chinese documents keyed to topics in Mao's 1957 speech "On the Correct Handling of Contradictions among the People." [9] Although cadres were directed to study these materials where appropriate, the main focus seems to have been on schools, especially universities and Party schools.

In 1957–1960 the hectic events of the *Hsia Fang* campaign and the Great Leap Forward disrupted the study routine. In this period sedentary study lost favor to mass rallies and participation in social action. After the failure of the Great Leap Forward a simpler study routine emerged. The various levels of study groups, the study committees, advisors, quizzes, etc., are all missing from cadre study in the 1960's. Long term study plans were replaced by sort term study themes adapted to current work tasks and campaigns. Time spent studying the ideological classics decreased in relation to time spent in policy and current events study (study of the classics was still encouraged, but more on an individual basis, outside the organized study routine). The basic administrative subdivisions of the work unit became in most instances the study group as well. However, the regular study by cadres of political texts, with group discussion, mutual criticism, and reports to higher authorities continued in spite of these changes.

Increasingly after 1963 cadres were presented with demands from higher authorities for more intensive political study and for study of new themes. Cadres were urged to study the experiences of the People's Liberation Army, exemplary cadres, and the writings of Chairman Mao. During the Cultural Revolution Mao's opponents were charged with trying to undermine and sabotage such study. The debates of the Cultural Revolution reveal that Mao Tse-tung and his supporters were not satisfied with the attitudes of cadres during the early 1960's. Perhaps the de-emphasis on the study of ideological classics and the concentration on topics close to immediate work problems made such

9. This curriculum is published, with commentary, in Arthur H. Steiner, "The Curriculum in Chinese Socialist Education: An Official Bibliography of 'Maoism'" in *Pacific Affairs*, Vol. 31, no. 3, September 1958.

study ineffective in counteracting the growing bureaucratization which Mao saw developing within cadre ranks. Political study rituals had helped to mold individuals from widely varying backgrounds into a relatively unified, disciplined leadership corps, but their ability to sustain revolutionary élan among administrators and officials remained in question.

MA KAN-PU: A PROVINCIAL ECONOMIC CADRE

At this point we turn from the examination of trends in cadre political study to the first of two concrete cases describing the way political rituals were experienced by cadres during the 1960's.[10] Ma Kan-pu was 36 at the time of my interviews in 1969, and altogether I talked with him eight times, for a total of twenty-four hours. As a result of the land reform campaign in Kwangtung province (1951–1953), his family had been classified as "overseas landlords." This meant that Ma's family had excess land taken away and that his father, who had only recently returned to China from Southeast Asia, was subjected to struggle meetings.[11] However, in other respects their treatment was more lenient, and the stigma passed on to the children was less serious than was the case for non-overseas landlords. Ma enrolled in a university shortly before the Communist victory in the South in late 1949. He states that prior to this time he had not been very concerned with politics and had concentrated his energies simply on being a good student. He was urged by some relatives to leave China before the victory of the Communists, but he felt he had no reason to fear the new government, and he decided to stay.

Soon after the Communist victory, students in Ma's university were organized to participate in campaigns for the restoration of social order. Ma joined campaigns to combat the black market and currency speculation and to sell bonds to the populace, measures designed to

10. During my fieldwork I interviewed twenty-two individuals about their former work as cadres. Their work units varied: six had worked in government and Party offices, five as staff members in production units, six as teachers, and five in other miscellaneous jobs. Four had served in units under national control, three in provincial units, three in special district units (between province and county levels), ten in city or county level units, and two in commune level units. None of the cadres included was engaged in the direct leadership of production.

11. Struggle meetings are in some sense criticism meetings carried to an extreme. They are generally large meetings in which individuals picked as struggle "targets" are presented to an audience to be shouted at and vilified. Examples of struggle meetings will be noted in subsequent chapters.

bring the ruinous inflation under control. Ma was impressed by the success of the new government in checking inflation, and he found personal participation in this effort exhilarating. He began to get more deeply involved in political activities, and in 1950, on the strength of his new activism, he was admitted to the New Democratic Youth League. These activities also inspired him to major in economics as the best way to contribute to building the new society.

In 1953 Ma graduated and was assigned to work in an economic agency subordinate to a regional government.[12] The following year his unit was reorganized and became an economic office under the Kwangtung provincial government, and in 1955 Ma was appointed to the post of assistant head of his section (k'o) within that office and was also accepted into the Communist Party. Later that same year he was transferred to work in another administrative system [13] and only returned to his original unit late in 1957. Soon after his return he was promoted to the position of section head, a position he held continuously until his departure from China in 1968.[14]

About three-quarters of the twenty-five or so cadres in Ma's section had backgrounds similar to his own. They were youths from the middle and upper classes of pre-1949 society who graduated from middle schools and universities in the early 1950's. All but eight came, like Ma, from Kwangtung province. Most of them also combined political reliability with their high educational level. Ma states that his unit was viewed as an important agency of the provincial government, and most "white experts" and "retained personnel" [15] with questionable political pasts were weeded out in the early 1950's. After about 1955 the reorganizations and transfers subsided, and there was little change in personnel in later years. Ma recalls that of the members of his section there were seven Party members, fourteen Youth League members, and

---

12. Prior to 1954 China was divided into six large administrative regions which were an intermediate level between the center and the provinces.

13. The major administrative systems in China are the finance and trade system; the industry and communications system; the agriculture, forestry and water conservation system; the cultural and educational system; the political and legal system; and the foreign affairs system. See the discussion in A. Doak Barnett with Ezra Vogel, *Cadres, Bureaucracy and Political Power in Communist China* (New York: Columbia University Press, 1967).

14. Ma started work as a rank 21 cadre (out of 30 ranks, with rank 1 the highest) and by 1960 had been promoted to rank 17, which gave him an income of about 110 yüan per month (U.S. $44 at the official exchange rate).

15. White experts are individuals employed for their technical skills in spite of their apolitical or anti-communist attitudes. Retained personnel are individuals kept on in the posts they held in the Kuomintang bureaucracy. See the discussion of types of cadres in Ezra Vogel, *op. cit.*

only three or four who did not belong to either organization. Important exceptions to this general pattern of young educated activists were the four or five old revolutionary cadres assigned to Ma's section. Their educational level was low, but they had joined the Communist cause at an early date.

Prior to 1957, Ma's unit had a political study routine roughly similar to that described at the beginning of this chapter, with cadres divided into four levels, and each level in turn divided into *hsiao-tsu* which followed study routines set by the unit's study committee. In the period 1953–1955 Ma felt that this political study routine, while occasionally a bother, was generally interesting, since much of what was studied concerned issues of economic development strategy with which the cadres were all concerned in their work.

After 1957 this arrangement was criticized as too formal, and in later years political study took place in the work section itself, with Ma in charge as section head, or in two *hsiao-tsu* formed from section members. The membership and leadership of these groups tended to vary, due to the frequent absence of cadres on outside work assignments. Study conducted within the section made it easier to relate study themes to work problems, and during the 1960's most of this activity was concrete. A two-hour daily study session was no longer required, as had been the case during the early 1950's. Rather, the study schedule was adapted to work demands and campaign pressures, with from one to three evenings a week spent in political study. In group discussions there was little mutual criticism, and section members were not constantly examining their thoughts and defects before the group. Criticism of those who did not prepare or who studied poorly did occur, however. Ma regularly reported to the Party branch officers about these political study meetings.

Ma states that during the 1950's there had been a rule that there should be two sessions of professional study a week, mostly the study of economic journals, but sometimes lectures by the section head on technical topics. However, this schedule was adhered to much less strictly than the political study schedule.

There were no regular section meetings to discuss past work and future tasks. Section meetings (called administrative meetings by Ma) were convened whenever it was necessary to formally discuss work problems or new work directives. Most minor problems and work assignments were handled informally through consultation between Ma and the other members of his section. Ma states that there was little organized study of current events per se, since it was taken for granted that cadres at this level were keeping themselves fully informed about national and world events through the press and other media. The cadres were, however, subjected to fairly frequent reports and speeches from their superiors and outside officials, many of which dealt with current affairs.

Although individual defects and poor behavior could to some extent be brought up in any forum—in study *hsiao-tsu*, in professional study sessions, or in administrative meetings—in fact, mutual criticism was fairly rare in such meetings. The cadres in Ma's unit generally responded readily and willingly to new directives and advice from superiors, and little social pressure was needed for reinforcement. However, there was an additional type of meeting specially designed for the airing of group criticism. At irregular intervals, often once or twice a month, Ma convened his section for a livelihood self-examination meeting (*sheng-huo chien-t'ao hui*).[16] In these meetings any problem in the thought or behavior of any section member could be brought up for public scrutiny. Sometimes such a meeting would be called especially to deal with a particular problem—cadres who were constantly getting into disputes, lateness in arriving at work, or lack of diligence in daily work. At other times there would be no specific problem to be criticized, and everyone would sit around informally and talk about whatever was bothering him.

Ma gives an example of the way one particularly serious problem arose and was dealt with. In his section there was a female cadre named Ch'en whose father and elder brother had been minor Kuomintang officials. Ch'en's family had been separated during the War, and she claimed that she wasn't really aware of the political activities of her father and brother. She graduated from middle school in 1949 and was recruited to take part in a land reform work team. During training for this work she did not mention any Kuomintang activities within her family. Ch'en was enthusiastic in land reform activities, and the head of her work team asked that she be assigned to work with him when he was transferred back to his original job in the courts. She joined the Youth League at this time and also fell in love with a Party member in her new unit. Then in 1956, during the cadre investigation campaign which followed the *"su-fan"* campaign, her past was uncovered and, in spite of her pleas of ignorance, it was decided that continued work in the courts would be too sensitive for her. Because there were no problems in her own past activities Ch'en's penalty was rather leni-

---

16. In some other units these meetings are referred to as "democratic life" (*min-chu sheng-huo*), a term which emphasizes the parallel with Party life meetings.

ent: she was transferred to Ma's unit and was allowed to retain her Youth League membership. But her boyfriend was forbidden by his Party unit to marry her (or rather was told that if he married her he would have to give up his Party membership). After some complaining he accepted this verdict, but when Ch'en arrived in Ma's unit she was still resentful, particularly about the Party's interference in her love life.[17] She often complained, worked listlessly, and interfered with the work of others.

Ch'en began to receive criticism while Ma was still away in another job, but when he returned he took charge, as head of Ch'en's section, of handling her "thought problem." Ma had many private talks with Ch'en about her behavior and the way she had been treated. He sympathized with her claim that the breakup of her romance had been unfair, since her own record was good. Still, she *was* disrupting the work of his section, and he decided to call a livelihood self-examination meeting to discuss the problem. In fact, several long and tense meetings were held. Other cadres in Ma's section criticized Ch'en severely for putting her own feelings above the demands of the Party as well as for disrupting work. They demanded that she cease causing trouble and that she admit that she had been selfish in criticizing the Party's judgment. Ch'en replied that she was sorry she had disrupted work and would try to avoid this in the future, but that she could not so easily stop feeling that she had been treated unfairly. For several sessions the arguments went back and forth, with nobody budging from his original opinion. Ma saw that they were getting nowhere and he decided to leave further discussion of Ch'en's problem to her Youth League organization, which had been simultaneously holding criticism meetings. Youth League criticism did not resolve Ch'en's problem in any final way, and only over time did she gradually forget her bitterness. However, Ch'en immediately began to work more diligently and stop publicly complaining. Ma felt that, although criticism sessions were not always able fully to solve problems, as this case illustrates, they provided a useful way of airing problems and grievances so that improvements could be made.

Another forum for mutual criticism was the annual summation. Each cadre was expected to write an annual report on his work, his

---

17. As Ma explains it, Ch'en felt that her own record was clean and that, since she was allowed to remain a cadre and a Youth League member, she should also have been permitted to marry a Party member. This interference in her love life would have been easier for her to understand if she had been sanctioned in other ways.

political activities, his thoughts, and his defects. These summations were discussed in section meetings, accompanied by comments and criticism from others, and then were forwarded with revisions and a summary of group comments to the Party branch. The Party branch used these summaries along with other materials in arriving at its own annual evaluation (*chien-ting*) of each cadre, which was recorded in his personnel dossier. These summaries were viewed as very important to the future of each cadre, and the investigation of all aspects of behavior and thoughts during the preceding year was thorough. A similar process of summation accompanied by group criticism and higher level final evaluations took place at the conclusion of many political campaigns. Connected with the annual summation was the selection of "advanced workers" (*hsien-chin kung-tso-che*). On the basis of the individual summaries and group discussion each section nominated a few of its members as advanced workers, an honorary title with no cash or other material rewards. These nominations were revised and approved by the Party unit and then announced. Generally this title was a way of singling out for public attention ordinary cadres (rather than leading cadres) who had performed especially well during the year. Ma felt that in the discussion of these summaries in his section, most cadres were fairly open about their defects and fair in criticizing others. The general atmosphere of group solidarity and trust kept the criticism on a constructive level and avoided both empty formality and personal spite.

Thus, regular self-examinations and mutual criticism were built into the organizational routine for all cadres, although they tended to be somewhat separate from the political study meetings. Even more rigorous mutual criticism took place within the Party and the Youth League, organizations to which the majority of cadres belonged. In Ma's unit there was a Party general branch corresponding to the entire office (*pan-kung-shih*), a Party branch corresponding to his division (*ch'u*), and a Party *hsiao-tsu* within his section. Party meetings were held at least once a week, generally on Friday after work for one or two hours. Most of these weekly meetings were held in the Party *hsiao-tsu*, with branch or larger meetings called only for such things as disciplining or admitting members, transmitting higher Party directives, and discussing major problems. For Ma and other Party members the discussion and criticism of "Party life" were more important than the meetings in study groups or in work sections. The format of these sessions varied. If no special topic or problem was assigned the members of the *hsiao-tsu* would sit around and discuss their thoughts and problems as in livelihood self-examination meetings, only more rigorously (i.e., with more pressure on each individual to speak, and more detailed criticism). At times work problems were discussed as well, or the group would discuss Party study materials, the experience of model Party units elsewhere, or the content of directives which had been presented in larger meetings. The Party *hsiao-tsu* head planned the meetings in consultation with the Party branch secretary and other officers, and he regularly reported to them on what transpired in *hsiao-tsu* sessions, using notes taken during the meeting.

These meetings were not devoted merely to imposing strict Party discipline, and Ma notes that Party members could raise some kinds of personal problems and grievances which they probably would not raise in meetings with non-Party cadres present.[18] He mentions one case in which a middle-aged unmarried Party member was lamenting his poor prospects for finding a wife, since there were few eligible women in their unit. The Party *hsiao-tsu* head showed concern for his problem and was able to arrange to get some women from another organization invited to a party in Ma's unit. Unfortunately the fellow did not find a wife at the party, but Ma felt this incident was indicative of the kind of concern and assistance that the Party was supposed to show for its members. The frequent criticism of individual defects was thus balanced to some extent by displays of solidarity and mutual concern.

Ma notes that status within the Party did not correspond to job status. Ma was outranked in influence within the Party by the old revolutionary cadres although some of these individuals were his subordinates in daily work.[19] Because of this status inconsistency there was a certain amount of friction between the young intellectuals and the old revolutionary cadres in Ma's section. Ma and others took particular dislike to an arrogant older cadre named Pai. The younger cadres described Pai, formerly a poor shepherd from Inner Mongolia, as "relying on history to eat" (*k'ao li-shih ch'ih-fan*), i.e., lording it over others on the basis of past exploits. Ma's low status within the Party did interfere somewhat with his work authority, but he generally accepted this and felt that the reversals and mixing of status were positive features of the new society. Until the Cultural Revolution, open conflict with Pai was avoided.

18. In general, matters discussed in Party meetings were not supposed to be mentioned to other cadres unless these were matters they could know about from public sources, or unless Party authorities declared that comments to outsiders were permitted.

19. The clear divisions in status within the Party according to the length of Party membership are discussed in Ezra Vogel, *op. cit.*

There were two Youth League *hsiao-tsu* within Ma's section, and he feels that Youth League life tended to be similar to Party life, except probably not as strict. There were few non-League non-Party cadres within the unit, so the Youth League had little in the way of "masses" to lead and confined its attentions mostly to assisting the Party and tending to the problems of its members.

The picture Ma paints of his unit is one of a relatively strict political atmosphere. In spite of some cleavages and tensions his section worked fairly well together, and higher cadres were for the most part capable, fair, and understanding. There was confidence in the loyalty and dedication of all the cadres and faith that individual errors could be dealt with in an orderly and constructive fashion. The cadres, according to Ma, did not live in constant fear of making a mistake or a slip of the tongue, and the atmosphere of trust enabled them to be fairly open about admitting errors and doubts.

Still, despite this overall picture of organizational health there were certain ways Ma's unit departed from the ideals set forth by China's elite. First, there was not complete openness by each cadre about his inner thoughts and feelings. There was a general frankness, but small secrets and privacies remained concealed. Ma, for example, developed close relationships with a few of the cadres in his section (particularly Ch'en) and with his roommates in the office dormitory (he roomed with two heads of other sections and a cadre from another division) to whom he would express privately some thoughts he would not mention publicly, such as doubts about official policies, rumors he had heard about China's leaders, and expressions of his dislike for Pai. Another departure from the ideal was the conflict between the young cadres and the old revolutionaries, exemplified by Ma and Pai. There was also the practice, considered deviant by the higher authorities, of low level cadres cultivating the friendship of individual leading cadres in the hope of gaining patronage or protection. Ma himself endeavored to cultivate such close relations with the head of his division. Also, there was a clear sense of rank and of who the leaders were and who were the led. While leading cadres within Ma's unit were not arrogant or distant in their dealings with subordinates, they kept tight control in their own hands and did not go out of their way to develop the autonomy and initiative of subordinates. All of these deviations, however, qualify only in minor ways the general picture of solidarity and the strict political atmosphere which had been built up through years of joint activities.

In spite of this generally healthy picture, Ma's unit was in no way exempt from the periodic rectification campaigns which swept the cadre ranks. Ma was away doing other work during the tense 1955–56 campaigns to clean out counterrevolutionaries and to investigate cadres (the campaigns referred to earlier in the case of Ch'en). He also participated in the 1957 anti-rightist campaign in another unit. Ma notes that the changes in personnel in his unit as a result of these campaigns were relatively minor.

Late in 1959 a campaign was launched to counter rightist sympathies in society (dubbed *Fan Yu Ch'ing*). This campaign was basically aimed at combating growing doubts about the wisdom of the Party's policies during the Great Leap Forward launched the previous year, particularly in regard to the rural people's communes. The campaign lasted for over a year (not in each organization, but in society generally), and its focus gradually shifted more toward dealing with the discontent arising out of the growing food shortage of this period. This campaign was not generally as severe as the 1955 and 1957 rectification campaigns and was designed to deal with a variety of "thought problems" through propaganda, study, and group pressure. In Ma's unit cadres were organized to read articles supporting the main policy line of the period, the "three red flags" (*san-mien hung-ch'i,* referring to support for the Great Leap Forward, the people's communes, and the Party's general line for the construction of socialism). The focus was particularly on the difficulties of the people's communes, and cadres read explanations that the food shortages stemmed from bad weather and natural disasters, rather than from basic defects in the communes themselves. In Ma's section each cadre was expected to give his views on each "red flag" in turn. Ma had earlier commented to other cadres that the mass involvement in steelmaking of the Great Leap Forward was perhaps a good thing, but that the small scale and poor preparation of many of the "backyard steel furnaces" resulted in too much waste. During the *Fan Yu Ch'ing* campaign Ma was criticized for this view, but the criticism was not too severe, since the other cadres knew Ma supported the basic features of the Party's policies. In the end each cadre in turn reaffirmed publicly his support for the official policies. But Ma feels that many cadres, particularly the young intellectuals, continued to harbor doubts about the wisdom of specific aspects of these policies and about the official explanation for the economic downturn. Nevertheless, there were no severe morale problems, and at the conclusion of the campaign work resumed as before, with perhaps a little more discretion exercised by Ma and others in criticizing official policies.

In the spring of 1960 a new campaign was initiated which over-lapped to some extent with the *Fan Yu Ch'ing* activities. This was called the New Three-anti campaign (*hsin san-fan*), after a similar campaign of 1951–52. The object was to check abuses of cadres, partic-ularly graft and waste. While there were no organizational changes introduced in Ma's unit during the *Fan Yu Ch'ing* campaign, in the New Three-anti campaign a core leadership small group was formed (*ling-tao ho-hsin hsiao-tsu*) composed of the leading cadres in the staff office—in other words, the same superiors as before, only with new titles. This core small group planned the amount of time to be allotted to various activities in the campaign and composed a black list of those cadres suspected of errors. Then speeches called mobilization reports were made to all cadres about the goals and activities of the new cam-paign. The cadres on the black list were assigned to separate study groups together with specially picked, reliable activists, whose task it was to criticize the suspected cadres until they confessed any wrong-doing.[20] Meanwhile the rest of the cadres studied the documents of the campaign in their regular offices and held examination meetings in which they were expected to reveal any evidence of graft. Not being assigned to a special study group meant some assurance that a cadre would not become a "target" in the campaign, but each was still ex-pected fully to reveal his own errors and any knowledge he might have of graft or waste committed by others. Cadres were organized to write big character posters (*ta-tzu-pao*) containing accusations against others. Most of the posters concerned the cadres chosen for the special study group, but some concerned other cadres in the unit or even individuals outside, perhaps someone a cadre met while out on a work assignment. The core small group assigned certain cadres to collect and organize the charges made in the posters for use in later criticism or struggle meetings.[21]

In the end only one person in the entire office was found to have made a serious error. Nobody in Ma's section had engaged in graft or was called upon to participate in the special study group, either as target or critic. Although they engaged in economic work they did not

---

20. In some units these special groups are called battle groups. Rectification campaigns with preselected targets use them. In some units when there are no specific targets the organization of meetings will still be changed at the beginning of a campaign to stimulate activity, perhaps only by merging two *hsiao-tsu* together.

21. In some other units the core leadership small group is called the campaign office (*yün-tung pan-kung-shih*). Sometimes during a campaign a special investiga-tion group is organized as well, to go out into the field to check into the charges made against various cadres.

handle money directly, and they joked among themselves about how difficult it would be to embezzle funds even if they wanted to. The cadre who became a target worked in the division which handled the office's operating expenses. He was subjected to two large struggle meetings before the entire office staff.[22] In the first he admitted he had embezzled some funds, and in the second he acknowledged that in his first confession he had understated the amount embezzled. He was ordered to pay back over time the entire amount embezzled (Ma forgets the exact amount, but thinks it was a few hundred yüan—one yüan = $.40 U.S. at the official exchange rate), and he was demoted in rank, but he received no further penalties. The entire campaign lasted for about four months in Ma's unit.

The following period was relatively free from campaigns. In early 1962 there was a period of concentrated study and debate connected with the reopening of rural free markets and the restoration of private plots, measures taken to try to restore agricultural incentives and production. This was not considered a campaign, however, and was mainly concerned with preparing the cadres for new work connected with these policy changes. Everyone in the unit realized that these concessions to "capitalism" constituted an admission of serious defects in the communes, defects which were strenuously denied in the *Fan Yu Ch'ing* campaign just two years earlier. However, for the most part this realization went unspoken as cadres unquestioningly adapted to the changed line.

In 1963 the Socialist Education campaign was initiated in Ma's unit, and from that time on political activities and pressures began to mount. Again a core small group was formed to lead the activities of this campaign, with membership more or less the same as in the New Three-anti campaign. However, no special study groups were formed. At first the main emphasis was simply on reinvigorating class sentiments. Workers and peasants were invited to go to Ma's unit to tell bitter stories about their pre-1949 suffering, and cadres within the unit with similar pasts, such as the former shepherd Pai, also spoke of early

22. A struggle meeting is in a sense an escalation of a mutual criticism session. Although the term struggle may be used loosely to refer to ordinary criticism, there is a clear distinction between criticism and struggle meetings. In a struggle meeting preselected targets are placed before an audience and presented with accusations, often accompanied by shouted slogans in a tense emotional atmosphere. Struggle meetings may take place within *hsiao-tsu*, but usually the forum is a large meeting. These meetings tend to be well planned in advance, with accusers specially selected and briefed. They are usually the climax of a long series of preliminary discussions and criticism meetings.

hardships. At about this time some cadres were selected to leave the unit to participate in Socialist Education campaign work teams then being formed.[23] In early 1964 the cadres were organized in their offices to criticize their own pasts and to confess their own failings. After listening to workers and peasants "speak bitterness" about the past, cadres of intellectual origin were expected to criticize their own bourgeois backgrounds and tell of the ways they had underestimated the suffering of others. Ma says that most of his fellow cadres were deeply moved by the tales of past suffering. However, they had little other than generalities about forgetting the class struggle to confess, and after a few weeks of discussion and individual self-examinations, the core small group declared the campaign was basically concluded and initiated the final "thought construction" stage (*ssu-hsiang chien-she*) —the idea being that bad thoughts had been removed, and that further political study should be undertaken to implant and consolidate correct thoughts.

In the fall of 1964, however, higher authorities stated that this activity had been superficial, and that a more rigorous examination of all cadres was needed.[24] The core small group was reactivated, the campaign was rechristened the Four Cleanups campaign, and cadres were directed to write two lengthy documents—the first a detailed family history going back three generations [25] and the other a written examination of how clean the cadre was in four matters: economics, organizational affiliations, politics, and thought.[26] The searching self-examination and group criticism went on for six months and was more of an ordeal for cadres than the earlier Socialist Education campaign activities. Ma did not know much about his grandfather, and he had to spend much of his free time visiting relatives to try to fill in the details of his family history. After each cadre had prepared his written

---

23. Six members of Ma's section were drawn off for this campaign. They were trained and then sent to direct campaign activities in rural villages (see Chap. 7).

24. The shifts in campaign goals seem to be connected with the conflict in policies between Mao Tse-tung and Liu Shao-ch'i. See R. Baum and F. Teiwes, *Ssu-ch'ing: The Socialist Education Movement of 1962–1966* (Berkeley and Los Angeles: University of California Press, 1968).

25. In earlier periods Ma had been required to fill out many forms with information about his family, but never in as much detail for as far back as was required in 1964.

26. "Economic uncleanliness" means graft and waste. "Organizational affiliation" refers to unrevealed facts about ties with the Kuomintang or other political groups as well as illegitimate means used to join the Communist Party or the Youth League. "Politics" refers to political action and participation generally, while "thought" concerns attitudinal problems which may not be directly expressed in behavior.

materials he had to read them to his section and try to get them accepted, a procedure referred to as trying to "pass the gate" (*kuo-kuan*). At one stage work was called off for about ten days to concentrate on these activities.

Ma set an example for his subordinates by trying to "pass the gate" first. He admitted to having two problems, both of which fit into the "thought" category of the four uncleans. He said he still harbored some resentment over the fact that his father, who had only returned from overseas in 1947 after years of strenuous labor and sending money home to his family, was nonetheless struggled during the land reform campaign as a landlord and an exploiter. This confession was largely a matter of form, a way in which Ma could admit that his class standpoint needed firming up. The cadres knew that Ma understood the reasons why his father was subjected to struggle, and that he accepted those reasons and harbored no great resentment. Ma also said he was bitter that his fiancée had been treated unfairly by the Party. Like many other unfortunates during the 1957 Anti-rightist campaign, she had been reluctant to criticize the Party until pressured to do so by local authorities. When she did finally post a *ta-tzu-pao* concerning unfair treatment of her father in the past it got her branded as a minor rightist. She was subjected to a great deal of criticism and humiliation in the following years, and finally in 1963 she was sent to work in an isolated rural area. She was assured that she could return after a year, but almost two years later she still had not been given permission to return. Ma felt that she had been misled and mistreated throughout this period, and he was resentful of the enforced separation. This issue was also not a new one, since Ma had made his discontent known and had been criticized in Party and section meetings previously, particularly in 1963. As in the similar case of his section-mate Ch'en, this earlier criticism had not completely eliminated Ma's resentment, and so it was natural for him to bring up this issue for criticism again in the Four Cleanups campaign.

After Ma read his self-examination and family history the other section members subjected him to sustained criticism, particularly on the issue of his romantic disappointment. The criticism was severe, but Ma felt that to some extent it was pro forma and that he continued to be liked and respected by others, many of whom sympathized with or at least understood his feelings. Ch'en in particular, who had suffered from similar Party interference in her love life, had over the years developed a close friendship with Ma and privately expressed her sympathy to him. In the end Ma simply promised to continue to struggle with his defects, and the attentions of the group turned to the other section members one by one. Each individual read out his written materials in turn and then received group criticism. The individual essays, with group comments appended, were then turned over to the core small group for possible further action.[27] In fact there were no serious individual errors turned up during the Four Cleanups campaign, and the grueling weeks of self-examination and group criticism served mainly to put each cadre on his best behavior. Ma thinks that grumbling about his fiancée's fate might have gotten him into serious trouble in another organization, but that the high degree of mutual trust and the close relationships he had with co-workers and superiors protected him from such a fate.

In early 1965 the Four Cleanups campaign reached a conclusion as the cadres moved on to a new thought construction stage. This involved studying documents and criticizing the views of the ideologues Yang Hsien-chen and Feng Ting and launching a systematic study of Mao's writings.[28] Some time was also spent studying military heroes such as Wang Chieh and exemplary cadres, particularly Chiao Yü-lu.[29] Ma feels that his fellow cadres could not easily identify with the lives of the military heroes, but were impressed by the deeds and self-sacrifice of the various model individuals studied during this period. Ma found the new, more intensive study of Mao's works somewhat boring, since the cadres had all read Mao's writings many times in the past. However, he found this activity a welcome change from the hectic meetings and self-examinations of the previous period.

In sum, during the early 1960's Ma's unit was continuously buffeted by campaigns designed to deal with cadre "problems." Generally the cadres "passed the gate" successfully each time, though. The success in these repeated ordeals reinforced the general feeling of mutual trust and persuaded the cadres that they could be relatively frank in

---

27. By this stage a cadre could be relatively certain of having "passed the gate," since the core leadership group had been directing campaign activities throughout and would not have let problems get past work group consideration. It should be noted that the Soviet notion of the purge originally denoted a similar process, with the records of cadres being reviewed one by one with a purging commission in charge. Only later did arrest and imprisonment form a basic part of the procedure. See the discussion in Z. Brzezinski, *The Permanent Purge* (Cambridge: Harvard University Press, 1956).

28. Yang Hsien-chien was the head of the Higher Party School in Peking. He was criticized for the view that "two merge into one," which was interpreted to mean that the class struggle was dying away. The philosopher Feng Ting was criticized for his book, *The Communist Philosophy of Life*, which was said to encourage elitism and the desire to climb up into official positions.

29. Chiao Yü-lu's exploits are detailed in *Jen-min Jih-pao*, February 7, 1966.

admitting their errors in each new campaign and still remain in good favor. With each succeeding campaign the familiarity with the rhythm of campaigns gave the cadres confidence that they could adapt to future ordeals. In spite of this past experience and basic confidence, however, Ma says that each new campaign produced a great deal of anxiety, at least among the ordinary cadres (those outside the leadership core small group). Partly campaign activities were simply a grueling physical ordeal, with extra meetings, wall posters to be written, difficulties in finding time to do regular work, and in some cases lengthy self-examination materials to be prepared. But more important, the cadres still found facing prolonged and concentrated group criticism painful, and they possessed a lingering fear that a new campaign might not hold true to past patterns but would unexpectedly change direction and find them as a target. The staging of campaigns increased this anxiety, since there was often a long period of mobilization and study before the goals and targets of campaigns became clear, and still longer before the cadres were permitted to "pass the gate." Ma's lingering fear of becoming a target became a reality during the Cultural Revolution.

In early 1966 the cadres in Ma's unit began to sense a major new rectification campaign in the offing, as national figures in the cultural and propaganda fields began to be criticized. At this time meetings began to be held every evening to study the flood of articles criticizing these officials, and sometimes additional study sessions had to be arranged during the mornings. With the fall of the Peking Party Committee in June 1966, Ma's office was filled with rumors and debates, as the cadres tried to fathom the meaning of these events and the impact they might have on their own lives. The lack of clear information about what was going on led to a sense of foreboding perhaps stronger than in past campaigns. In July of 1966 the cadres began spending half of each day in work and the other half studying the mushrooming documents of the Cultural Revolution. At this stage the campaign was focused within educational institutions, and Ma and his fellow cadres were not sure whether they would be involved eventually or not. In the fall of 1966 student Red Guard organizations were formed and began to shake fear into their teachers and to search private homes for "four old articles" (see the account in Chapter 7). Ma was bothered by what he felt were the excesses of the Red Guards, but he still did not see where these events were leading. Some Red Guards came into Ma's unit and conducted propaganda about the Cultural Revolution, but they stayed only briefly. Then in December

1966, in line with the national propaganda in favor of establishing rebel organizations of various types to strike down "capitalist roaders," some of the cadres in Ma's unit began to organize themselves. Pai recruited six or seven members of Ma's section for a rebel organization.[30] Initially the rebels confined their activity to general propaganda about the goals of the Cultural Revolution, with no attacks on specific individuals. However, by this time the leading Kwangtung Provincial Party Committee officials were already under considerable fire, and this added to Ma's own sense of foreboding.

The mood in Ma's unit changed markedly with the seizure of power from the Provincial Party Committee by a Red Guard and rebel alliance in January 1967. Ma was incredulous upon hearing that the Provincial Party Committee had capitulated without a major fight (although there had been resistance and behind-the-scenes maneuvering prior to this time). With provincial leadership gone and as leading cadres stopped giving orders and running affairs, all regular work in Ma's unit ceased. And the various rebel organizations turned from general propaganda to planning attacks on specific cadres within the organization. February and March were months of suspended animation and confusion, with nobody clearly in charge and much jockeying for position for the coming struggle with the unit's "power holders." During this period much of the day was spent in Mao study or reading Cultural Revolution documents with no clear organization, and the leading cadres in the unit did not try to organize counter-rebel organizations as they did in some other units. More students began to come in and out of Ma's unit espousing various points of view. These student Red Guards took no direct hand in organizing his unit's rebels, but they did introduce new ideas and tactics. In March army representatives started to come into Ma's unit on rotation, but their role was primarily one of keeping order, and they did not try to direct the developing struggle.

Starting in April Ma and other section heads as well as all higher Party and administrative cadres in his unit were assigned to spend their time examining their misconduct in isolation from other cadres. Rebel leaders directed others to write ta-tzu-pao attacking all of these power holders. The army representatives began treating former leading

---

30. The term Red Guards (*hung-wei-ping*) is often used to refer to all of those who rose up against the leadership during the Cultural Revolution, but particularly the students, while the term rebel (*tsao-fan-p'ai*) is generally used to refer to those participants who were not students. However, in some instances the terms are used interchangeably.

cadres with disdain, earnestly lecturing them to confess their mistakes. Ma and the others spent much of their time writing repeated self-examination essays dealing with the charges made against them in the *ta-tzu-pao*. They were also expected to write *ta-tzu-pao* attacking each other, although most of these were devoid of any real content. From time to time they were subjected to mass criticism meetings run by rebel organizations, or were escorted to the large public rallies then being held to struggle important provincial officials.

Long accustomed to trust and consideration, many of the leading cadres became bitter at the sudden shift to isolation and humiliation. Ma felt that in the competitive atmosphere surrounding the writing of *ta-tzu-pao* many false charges went unchecked. The main charge against all the leading cadres was that they were "power holders" and "capitalist roaders," the latter referring particularly to the role played by Ma's unit in reintroducing free markets and private plots in 1962. These measures were now attacked as leading China back down the road to capitalism. Ma greatly resented charges that he harbored a desire to return to capitalism. He claims that all the leading cadres looked upon the 1962 measures as temporary, justified only by the severe economic problems of the period and in spite of the potential harmful effects of these policies in encouraging capitalist sentiments. Ma was also specifically charged with continuing to harbor a strong grievance against the Party for its treatment of his fiancée (who at this point, three years after the Four Cleanups criticism, had still not been released from her rural exile). It was also claimed that Ma did not support the "three red flags" sufficiently fervently, and that in past campaigns he had failed to examine his defects deeply enough. While Ma admitted a basis to some of these charges, he regarded their sum as unfair and distorted and challenged others to come up with any real evidence that he longed for capitalism or hated the Party. But his replies found no support among other cadres, and he remained effectively isolated before his critics. By this time most of the members of his section had hopped on the bandwagon by joining rebel organizations and attacking the leading cadres. Ma knew that many of his section-mates did not take very seriously the charges against him (some, such as Ch'en, privately told Ma of their sympathy for his plight). But he also knew that none of them would risk publicly supporting him against his more zealous critics, such as Pai. Thus the care with which Ma had built up solidary relationships with his co-workers counted for nothing as he stood isolated before the increasing barrage of criticisms. The friendship and protection that Ma had derived in previous years from his close relations with his division head now worked increasingly against him, as this man came under more and more virulent attack.

Ma was a proud and confident man, accustomed to fair treatment and trust. In the Cultural Revolution he felt himself suddenly subjected to unfair abuse, completely at the mercy of events outside of his control. In mid-1967 Ma was not yet the target for special criticism or struggle meetings, but he continued to deal with the day to day charges made against him in *ta-tzu-pao*. Increasingly resentful at being treated like a class enemy after years of loyal service, he resolved to leave China rather than submit to full scale struggle himself. In the latter part of 1967 the rebels turned the focus of struggle meetings upon the highest cadres in the office and then began working their way down to the smaller fry. Toward the end of the year the head of Ma's division was struggled, and Ma saw the writing on the wall and began to prepare his escape. In the spring of 1968 he arrived in Hong Kong.

KUNG CH'ENG-SHIH: A CITY ENGINEER

I conducted four interviews with 42-year-old Kung Ch'eng-shih. Like Ma Kan-pu, he came from an overseas Chinese family, although his father was a teacher, not a landlord. He studied engineering in college, graduating in 1951. At that time and in later years he lacked interest and tried to avoid involvement in politics, and he never joined the Youth League or the Party. After graduation he worked as a draftsman and engineer for a number of government agencies of the city of Canton, rising to become a rank eight engineer in 1956, a rank he retained without change in subsequent years.[31] In 1961 he was transferred to work as a civil engineer in a construction company attached to the city administration, and his work involved periods in his Canton office and frequent trips to construction sites in and around the city. In 1965 he was assigned to remain full time at a major construction site, and the following year most of his original unit joined him in the field. We will describe primarily his post-1961 work situation.

Kung worked in a construction section (*shih-kung k'o*) of about forty-five cadres, run by a section head and two assistant heads. The section was divided into four work groups, and Kung was appointed head of the smallest of these, a civil engineering group (*t'u-chien tsu*)

---

31. Engineers belong to an 18-rank classification system along with technicians, with ranks 3 to 9 generally reserved for engineers. Kung earned about 130 yüan a month (U.S. $52 at the official exchange rate), or somewhat more than Ma.

of six members. There were eight Communist Party members in the section who formed a Party *hsiao-tsu*. There was also a somewhat larger Youth League *hsiao-tsu*, but Kung cannot recall the exact size. At least half the cadres belonged to neither organization. In Kung's own group there were no Party members and two Youth League members. As in Ma's unit, the majority of the cadres came from former middle and upper class backgrounds, and all six members of Kung's group fit this pattern. In contrast to Ma's unit, however, a fair number of the cadres were engineering "experts" without a record of political loyalty and enthusiasm. There were also many cadres, particularly at the higher levels, who came from provinces outside of Kwangtung, and three of the cadres in Kung's group were "outsiders." Kung notes that, as the leader of his work group with acknowledged skill and experience, he was usually given a good deal of authority to make day-to-day work assignments. In the process he was able to cultivate close ties and develop strong influence over his subordinates, who usually backed him in minor disputes with higher authorities. Kung was felt to have a negative effect on the political activism of his subordinates, particularly the two Youth League members in his group, and for this reason he was not placed in charge of any political study rituals. Rather, his group was merged with another for such meetings so that criticism and discordant opinions could be effectively developed.

For political study the section was divided into two study groups. Often only about fifteen cadres were available for *hsiao-tsu* meetings in each group, with the rest in the field on work assignments. The heads of study groups were nominated by the Party branch and then elected by members of the group, but there was no set term of office. Kung says the changes in study leadership produced marked shifts in group atmosphere. In one period his study group was led by Lin, the section head, who was an old revolutionary cadre with little education. Lin was embarrassed to use political theory texts and articles because of the higher educational level of many of those he was leading in study. Instead he spent much of the meeting time reminiscing about his experiences in the revolution and his views about China's problems. Later a female Party member who led the study group ran things "by the book" and insisted that the cadres stay on the topic and do the required reading, a situation which Kung found much more tedious. Later an old worker was elected who, more like Lin in his approach, often let group discussions drift off to topics unrelated to study themes.

In the lulls between campaigns, Wednesday afternoon and evening and sometimes Saturday afternoon were the political study periods. Some of these meetings were spent listening to reports from leading cadres in the construction company or outsiders. Most were spent in *hsiao-tsu,* reading and discussing assigned texts and press articles. Mutual criticism was not a regular feature of these discussions. Sometimes when concluding a study theme the cadres would be asked to evaluate their own attitudes and criticize their shortcomings, but much of this was stated in generalities. The study group heads consulted with and reported to Party branch authorities on the methods and progress in political study, generally on an informal individual basis. One person in a study group was always assigned to take notes on the discussion for reference in reporting to Party authorities, but this was rarely done diligently. Sometimes a *hsiao-tsu* head would embellish discussion notes to make it appear that a meeting had been livelier than it was. Cadres in the field were supposed to carry out a regular plan of individual study, but Kung says this was not rigorously enforced and he doubts that even Party members complied very well unless there was a campaign in progress.

Most of the cadres in Kung's unit were trade union members, but Kung himself never became one. He never refused to join; he simply used various excuses and mislaid the entrance application forms given him by the union chairman, and after a while people forgot about him. It is clear from Kung's comments that the union was not very important in his unit. There were union meetings, generally scheduled for Friday evenings, but in times of heavy work these were often skipped. There were no union *hsiao-tsu,* or political study within the union framework, and it was mainly concerned with welfare assistance and arranging cultural and athletic events. The fact that Kung was able to avoid joining the union (he says he just didn't want to bother with paying dues and attending more meetings) may indicate not only the low importance of the union, but the generally lax attitude taken by Party officials within his unit toward organizational matters.

Monday evenings were set aside for work conferences unless campaign schedules intervened. Usually work conferences were held in the section to discuss the past week's work and future plans. Occasionally the cadres split into their work groups to discuss such matters in more detail. Professional study sessions were generally held Saturday morning or afternoon in individual work groups. Sometimes Kung gave talks to his co-workers on technical topics, and sometimes the cadres studied technical journals individually.

Livelihood self-examination meetings were supposed to be held twice a month, although sometimes these were convened less regularly. Some-times these sessions involved the entire section, and at other times the cadres met in their study groups. The format was similar to that described by Ma—each cadre was expected to examine his contribu-tions and defects during the past period and to receive criticism from the group. Kung states that mutual criticism was rarely effectively developed except during campaigns, and what criticism there was often was not truly mutual but directed one way, from Party and Youth League members and activists toward more backward cadres.[32] Kung was not able to recall specific examples of serious problems which were dealt with in such sessions. Kung also mentions a process of annual summations and the selection of advanced workers very similar to that described by Ma Kan-pu.

Kung illustrates the relatively weak development of mutual criticism with his own situation. He was one of the most backward individuals in his unit politically, and he never even feigned much activism. As an "expert," he regarded himself, and was regarded by others, as "relying on technical skills to eat" (k'ao chi-shu ch'ih-fan). He was also characterized as not demanding political progress of himself (pu yao-ch'iu chin-pu) and as having the attitude of a hired hand (ku-yung ssu-hsiang), i.e., working mainly to earn a living with little concern for the goals of his unit or the state. Yet he was not the target of constant criticism for such attitudes. Most of the criticism was for minor matters, for what he terms "chicken feathers and garlic skin" (chi-mao suan-p'i). In his self-examinations Kung would confess that he had day-dreamed through a speech or had not read an article which had been assigned. In political study sessions he tended to participate minimally, speaking only after others had spoken and paroting what had already been said, a habit referred to as "reheating a cold meal" (ch'ao leng fan).

Despite his evident backwardness and lack of interest, Kung was usually able to avoid serious trouble. This was partly because he tended to keep his true feelings to himself and rarely voiced com-plaints. He also cultivated close relations with his work group and was generally able to avoid criticism from that source. He possessed techni-cal skills which could not easily be replaced. Also, political work was

---

32. Kung says there were few activists among the non-Party non-Youth League cadres, and that throughout this period there was little effort to recruit such cadres for Party and Youth League membership. This lack of political recruitment tended to reinforce the separate identities of the members and non-members of these organizations.

not run well or heavily emphasized in his unit, and therefore others felt no great pressure to change Kung's attitudes. Kung was easy going and jovial and used his sense of humor and way with words to soothe animosities and prevent conflicts. He also feels that it was a general national policy during this period, reflected in a speech by foreign minister Ch'en Yi in the fall of 1961, to treat apolitical experts with more consideration than had been the case in the past.[33] Finally, and perhaps most important, Kung was able to cultivate close relations with one of the top administrators (ching-li) in his construction company, an individual who, although an old revolutionary cadre, came from a village near Kung's own home area and shared other background characteristics with him.

Kung says his unit was divided by personal rivalries and cliques. Regional origins played a role in interpersonal disputes, with Kwangtung cadres (such as Kung and his patron the administrator) tending to support each other in conflicts with outsiders. He claims there was also a fair amount of suppressed tension between Party and Youth League members and non-members, as shown by a curious trend in the company's dormitories. About 80 per cent of the cadres, particularly those from other provinces, lived in dormitories provided by the construction company. Originally cadres had been assigned to apartments apparently at random, but they were allowed to exchange places with others. Over time, as people switched rooms to join their friends, the living space began to separate into two clearly defined areas, with Party members and some Youth League members concentrated in one area and non-members in the other. This separation caused some concern among Party authorities and led to suggestions that housing be reallocated to restore unit solidarity. However, the trouble involved in such a reshuffling prevented this action from ever being carried out.

Social relations were further complicated by nepotism within the unit—several leading cadres assigned their wives to jobs.[34] Kung claims that the arrogance and lack of ability of some of these women

---

33. *Chung-kuo ch'ing-nien pao*, September 2, 1961.

34. While nepotism was a common practice in traditional China, it has taken new forms since 1949. In recent years arranging a job for most relatives has been strongly frowned upon and has undoubtably decreased. However, the arranging by leading cadres of jobs for their wives (who traditionally would not have worked at all) in the same or a nearby unit seems to be fairly common. It has been noted that the ninth Central Committee of the Chinese Communist Party elected in April 1969 included the wives of Mao Tse-tung, Lin Piao, K'ang Sheng, Chou En-lai, and Li Fu-ch'un. Some of these women, of course, have earned some prominence in their own right.

led to resentment among other cadres. He notes that a cadre named Liao, who replaced Lin as head of his section in 1963, managed to get himself and his wife picked as advanced workers every year although this honor was generally reserved for deserving lower cadres. Cadres also tended to behave in a subservient way toward their superiors, by currying favor, a practice referred to literally but politely as "patting the horse's rump" (*p'ai ma p'i*). He gives the example of a leading cadre in his unit who ran into several of his subordinates who had just caught a large fish from a reservoir near a work site. He complimented them on the size of the fish, and when he returned home he found it sitting on his table. Subordinates rarely criticized superiors publicly, while superiors often used their positions to attack rivals and subordinates who displeased them. These attacks reinforced the insecurity of the ordinary cadres and encouraged them to cultivate the friendship of higher level cadres as protection against such attacks. Kung characterized personal relationships as "complex" (*fu-tsa*). The English translation misses the full meaning: it was hard to tell the true feelings and intentions of others, and the universalistic prescriptions set forth by China's leaders for comradely relations and solidarity within organizations could not be relied upon. Without the cultivated protection of some leading cadres the individual would be left defenseless against the capricious attacks of others. The contrast in this respect with Ma's account of his unit could not be more marked.

Kung also sought to escape from the complexity of interpersonal relationships by maintaining close friendships with several other ordinary cadres in his unit. He was on good terms with two of the cadres within his own section, but on the job he treated them the same as others and retained a certain amount of social distance. They would, however, arrange to meet after work in a teahouse to drink and relax. Occasionally Kung would even give them and himself false work assignments so that they could sneak off the job and meet in a teahouse during the day. His closest friend was a cadre from another section in his company, a man named Fan who was something of a social isolate because he had been declared a rightist and had spent a term in labor re-education after 1957 (see Chapter 9). Kung often gave Fan technical advice which helped him in his work and gradually they became close friends. Over time Kung learned that he could trust Fan not to reveal confidences, and he even dared discuss with him the possibilities of escaping to Hong Kong. They also listened to the Voice of America on a crystal set Kung had built. Thus in addition to the generally lax political atmosphere in his unit, Kung was able to find a few friends with whom he could share his true feelings of alienation, and these friends kept him from feeling totally isolated politically.

In 1961, soon after Kung joined this unit, a campaign was launched to deal with cadre errors called *"kung-ssu pu-fen, tuo-ch'ih tuo-chan"* (failure to separate public from private, appropriating extra food and other goods for personal use). Cadres who had abused their positions during the food shortage of this period were expected to confess these errors. Each individual was supposed to conduct a self-examination of such abuses, starting with the leading cadres in the company and working down through the rest of the staff. The administrator who was Kung's patron confessed to having sold some wire belonging to the unit and using the proceeds to purchase additional food for his staff. Since his error was motivated not by personal greed but by concern for others he was subjected to criticism but was not given a fine or other sanctions. Other leading cadres revealed a variety of minor acts of graft, and in some cases during their confessions they broke into tears before the assembled cadres. Kung feels that the tears represented skillful acting, designed to help these cadres "pass the gate," for after the campaign their humility quickly disappeared and they resumed their former ways.[35] Lower cadres such as Kung were not the main focus of this campaign and passed the gate with perfunctory self-examinations.

In 1962 Kung applied for permission to visit relatives in Hong Kong, and the following year this act got him into trouble. (At the time his superiors, if they had learned of his application, made no comment to him about it.) [36] Early in 1963 another campaign was launched which Kung feels may have been part of the Socialist Education campaign. However, the focus of the activity in Kung's unit was unclear, and cadres with a variety of errors were dealt with. A core leadership small group composed of the leading cadres in the construction company was set up to organize campaign activities. (Kung calls this the "campaign office.") Cadres with particularly serious errors were subjected to criticism in special "battle small groups" (*chan-tou hsiao-tsu*) set up by the campaign office, and then in large struggle meetings before the entire staff. Lin, the section head, was subjected to criticism

---

35. This pattern of being concerned with getting through a campaign rather than with reforming one's defects was termed *kuo-kuan ssu-hsiang*—passing-the-gate-thought.

36. Kung claims that in many instances leading cadres would learn of minor errors of their subordinates but would not raise them for discussion. They would store them up for use as ammunition in future campaigns. Thus it was impossible for a cadre to know what things were held against him at any time.

for suspicion of graft, but not enough evidence could be found, and he was eventually let off without sanctions. A cadre in the personnel department did not fare as well. He was charged with accepting bribes from others to alter their dossiers and with changing his own dossier to improve his record. After criticism and struggle he was demoted in rank and transferred to work elsewhere. A cadre in the general service section was accused of accepting bribes to alter the distribution of rations. He was let off after several struggle meetings with only a warning. Kung was criticized in his own section (not in the battle groups) for wanting to leave China. He defended himself by saying that there was nothing illegal about applying to go to Hong Kong, and that he merely wanted to spend a brief visit with relatives and then return. No action was taken against him.

At about the same time a major error within the unit was handled somewhat differently. The Party general branch secretary had been having an affair with his wife's sister, and when the sister became pregnant he bribed a doctor to perform a secret abortion.[37] The doctor apparently informed on him during this campaign, and the Party secretary fell into disgrace. However, the entire matter was handled within the Party, and the secretary was not subjected to struggle meetings before his subordinates.[38] Kung says he learned of the details of the case because the discipline and secrecy of the Party organization in his company were not very strict. The Party secretary was deprived of his post and sent to a cadre farm to engage in agricultural labor.[39] Kung heard that the farm chairman, who was lower in rank than the Party secretary, treated him like a royal visitor. He overlooked the fact that the Party secretary did not work in the fields when everyone else did. After a month the Party secretary was able to arrange a job

---

37. Abortions were legal during this period, so the secrecy must have been due to the circumstances involved.

38. Errors by Party members are often handled within the Party, in semi-secrecy from outsiders. The rationale is that publicly proclaiming such errors would harm the prestige of the Party itself. However, such secrecy leads to resentment from non-Party members who feel that members get separate and special treatment. Such feelings led to criticisms of the Party during the "100 Flowers campaign" in 1957 and to the demands for "open door rectification" of the Party (i.e., with non-Party members participating) during the Cultural Revolution.

39. Many bureaucratic offices in China at this level have maintained cadre farms, perhaps shared with other units. The labor would be provided by cadres going in rotation to put in manual labor stints, as well as by cadres who had committed errors and had been assigned to longer periods of reforming themselves through labor. These cadre farms seem to provide some precedent for the much more extensive network of "May 7th cadre schools" set up after 1968 (see fn 4).

in the Party organization of another unit and escape his rural assignment. Kung says this case reinforced in his mind the privileges of power and the hypocrisy of the "mass line."

Later in 1963 the section chief Lin was transferred to work at a construction site, perhaps as a result of the earlier unproven suspicion of graft. The new section head, Liao, who has already been mentioned, was less favorably disposed toward Kung. Lin had recognized his own low level of technical ability and had allowed Kung a certain degree of work autonomy. Liao, who had spent a year or two in technical training, tried to retract this autonomy and take personal charge over work assignments in Kung's group. Kung appealed to his friend the administrator, who supported him against Liao. This conflict led to constant criticism of Kung by Liao, as well as continued enmity between Liao and the administrator. Kung characterizes Liao as a "laughing faced tiger," meaning he was jovial with others but behind their backs he was always looking for ways to attack them.

In 1965 Kung was transferred to the main work site of the construction company. He mentions that the Four Cleanups campaign described by Ma was supposed eventually to be carried out in his unit, but that the Cultural Revolution intervened. Soon after Kung's transfer all cadres, technical personnel, and workers were assigned to study Mao Tse-tung's works systematically. Kung, who regretted the renewed emphasis on political study, was assigned to a study group with the Party secretary and other leading personnel. In early 1966 most of the other cadres from Kung's unit were transferred into the field to join him, but his original work group was dispersed, and he now led a group of three other cadres. The amount of time cadres had to spend both in manual labor and in political study was markedly increased, but Kung did not foresee the Cultural Revolution. As before, he tried to ignore political events as much as possible.

In the summer of 1966 the company's Party organization began to mobilize the workers and cadres to expose the errors of others in connection with the growing Cultural Revolution. After several large mobilization meetings explaining the general themes of the new campaign, all the cadres were organized to post ta-tzu-pao revealing errors and criticizing others. A new campaign office set up by the Party leadership organized selected cadres into a "battle small group" to lead the way in writing ta-tzu-pao. As more and more posters appeared Kung saw that his name was appearing with disturbing regularity. He realized that he had become one of the campaign targets, as his minor errors and disputes of the past ten years appeared on local walls for all to note. Kung also noticed that other cadres were beginning to avoid him during work. In the fall of 1966, after a prolonged period of writing and collecting *ta-tzu-pao*, Kung and five other cadres were subjected to a series of highly organized struggle meetings. At the first meeting Liao read off the charges against Kung, and then members of the battle group led other cadres in further criticism. Kung claims that each member of the battle group who spoke concentrated on a different charge and spoke for the same amount of time, suggesting careful advance planning. Kung thought he could fend off the charges as long as his close friends remained loyal to him and did not reveal confidences. His closest friend Fan was pressured by members of the campaign office to reveal evidence of Kung's errors, and Kung spent a nervous period wondering whether he would be betrayed. However, Fan and his other friends continued to focus on "chicken feathers and garlic skin" in wall posters and meetings, and Kung was reassured.

The list of charges was long, but principally Kung was criticized for his backward thoughts and for exerting a bad influence on those around him. He was also denounced as a bourgeois technical authority and for his bourgeois habits (such as frequenting teahouses). His application to go to Hong Kong and the instances in which he had made favorable comments about foreign technology were cited as evidence of his low regard for China. When an earlier work accident was brought up, an attempt was made to shift the blame from those earlier found at fault to Kung. It was also claimed that Kung read decadent novels. A Youth League member had once seen Kung reading a Japanese book and had asked to borrow it. When Kung refused he became suspicious, and later made the charge that it must have been a decadent novel (*huang-se shu*). Kung claimed (falsely) that it had not been a decadent novel but a political work, and that he had taken it out from a local library, which certainly wouldn't harbor decadent books. He argued against the other charges as well, while his critics dug for new charges. These meetings were tense, but there was none of the physical violence of the struggle meetings taking place in many other organizations at about this time. After each struggle meeting Kung wrote out a new self-examination dealing with the charges raised. The next meeting would start with Kung reading his essay, which would be attacked again for its insufficiency.

After several such meetings it was decided that Kung did not fall within the category of counter-revolutionaries, but that he had committed serious errors. He was assigned to sit in his office all day reading Mao's works and further examining his errors. After Kung had done

this for about a month, not very diligently, cadres in his unit got wind
of documents from Peking saying that good people had been wrongly
struggled throughout the country and should be rehabilitated. The
collected self-examinations and confessions were termed "black materials" and were to be returned to those who had written them. Kung's
Party unit grudgingly acceded to this demand and held a large meeting
in which the formal rehabilitation of Kung and the five others was
announced, and their self-examination materials were turned over to
them. For a brief time after this Kung and the others were treated
almost as heroes and he resumed his old habits, such as frequenting
teahouses, with no fear.

With the national atmosphere clearly shifting in favor of "rebels" of
various types, cadres in Kung's unit began to organize into groups to
criticize the unit's Party authorities. In the winter of 1966–67 these
authorities tried a new defensive tactic. They organized some loyal
cadres into groups designed to support the Party leadership and attack
the rebel groups. However, by this time the authority of the Party
leadership was sufficiently undermined so that "real" rebel organizations far outnumbered this "false" organization. Kung was urged to
join several rebel groups, but in spite of his grievances with the Party
over his recent ordeal, he felt it was safest to remain uninvolved. In
the spring of 1967 a coalition of rebel organizations declared it was
seizing power from the leading cadres in the company, and from that
point on the Party secretary, Kung's patron the administrator, and
all the other leaders down to the level of section head were deprived
of their authority and subjected to supervised study and struggle meetings. Soon after this power seizure the rebel coalition split into factions
arguing among themselves about how to deal with the "power holders"
who had been deposed. From early 1967 on there was little regular
work, and when possible many of the cadres, including Kung, simply
went home. In the summer of 1967 most work stopped completely as
the factions in Kung's unit began to fight each other and join the
factional battles raging around Canton. Kung spent most of this period
with his wife in Canton and did not keep up with these events.
Representatives from the army had arrived in his unit in late spring,
but they had not been able to restore order. Some cadres went off to
other parts of the country, some to investigate the past activities of
various "power holders," and others simply to participate in the
general "exchange of revolutionary experience." As time went on
Kung returned to his work place less and less often, and finally, in
January 1968, he escaped to Hong Kong.

GENERAL PATTERNS AND CONTRASTS

Comparing the accounts given by Ma and Kung of the organization of political study in the early 1960's, the basic study routine, with study groups, political study meetings, professional study meetings, and livelihood self-examination meetings, is common to both. In both cases the political study routine was less elaborate than the ideal described in Chapter 4, and there was more differentiation between political study meetings and meetings for airing mutual criticism (the livelihood self-examination meetings). During campaigns in both units the pace of meetings was intensified and political study and mutual criticism merged and predominated over other kinds of meetings (e.g., professional study). The campaigns seemed to fall into recognizable patterns, with a period of concentrated study and mobilization, the collection of information about problem cadres through group meetings and *ta-tzu-pao,* large criticism and struggle meetings, and then a thought construction stage—all directed by the leading cadres. Even the Cultural Revolution, so unprecedented in many ways, tended to fit much of this pattern, and in fact the experience in past campaigns conditioned the way ordinary cadres and leaders reacted to the Cultural Revolution. Cadres tried to discover who the targets were and to disassociate themselves from and criticize those targets. In the Cultural Revolution the significant difference was that the leading authorities in the unit came to be the targets rather than the directors of the campaign; in fact, there was no unified direction, but simply various factional groups reacting to encouragement in the mass media. Ordinary cadres, often with no strong emotional commitment, disassociated themselves from the Party leadership as they had from targets in past campaigns and grouped themselves behind various rebel organizations. Many of these were led by individuals who did feel a stronger sense that these leading cadres were evil and corrupt. This kind of adaptive response facilitated the rapid undermining of the once strong authority of the leading cadres.[40]

---

40. It should be noted that there are precedents in previous campaigns for leading cadres, when themselves under criticism, standing aside until cleared or sanctioned. If an individual leading cadre had erred, he might be dropped from the core leadership group of the campaign. If the entire leadership was suspect, higher levels might send a work team to direct the campaign, and the entire leadership would cede authority to the work team. However, the standing aside of the leadership and the assumption of power by a new leadership group formed from their subordinates is more of a novel development. This notion of the leadership standing aside when in error was formulated in Mao Tse-tung's 1943 "Resolution of the

Despite these and other similarities, the differences between the two case studies stand out sharply. The solidarity and strict political atmosphere of Ma's unit contrasts with the "complexity" and laxity described by Kung. This difference may be due in part to the different personalities and outlooks of my two informants. Ma clearly looks back fondly on the good old days, while Kung has a considerably more jaundiced view of the past. However, there are also consistent patterns in the accounts which help us to understand the differences in atmosphere, and which can alert us to some of the characteristics of organizations which may be important in creating a strict or lax political atmosphere.

What are these patterns? Ma's office was a provincial unit which was perceived by its members as important and influential within the power structure. The unit was quite selective, and generally only those meeting both technical and political criteria remained for long. Their work involved helping to formulate and implement basic economic policies. Kung's unit, in contrast, fell under a lower administrative level, that of the city of Canton. His company was involved in construction and not policy making, and technical skills were needed which in some cases might be more important than political qualifications. These differences seem to have contributed to the sense of self-confidence and importance characteristic of Ma's unit, and the contrasting "hired hand mentality" that characterized Kung and others in his unit. In Ma's office there was great stability of personnel among both leading and ordinary cadres. A large number of the cadres came from similar backgrounds, had shared common problems and triumphs, and had successfully passed through various political campaigns. A high percentage of these cadres belonged to the Party or the Youth League, and over the years their common identity as cadres became more important than their particular identities as economist, Northerner, or old revolutionary cadre. In Kung's unit, in contrast, there was more turnover in personnel at all levels and more heterogeneity, and thus more potential for cleavages. There were also fewer Party and Youth League members, and a lower record of success in "passing the gate" during campaigns.

Ma's unit certainly came closer than Kung's to carrying out political study and group criticism according to the norms prescribed by China's elite. These rituals were engaged in more seriously and conscientiously, with criticism fairly open and lacking in personal animosity, and they

Central Committee of the Chinese Communist Party on Methods of Leadership." See Boyd Compton, *op. cit.*, p. 178.

seem to have reinforced, rather than undermined, solidarity within the unit. In Kung's unit these activities were often poorly run and criticism tended to be superficial or laden with personal or group vindictiveness. Evasion and hypocrisy were not attacked on the spot; cadres accumulated minor errors which added to their insecurity about the future (i.e., fear that these errors would be blown up into a major charge during a future campaign). In Kung's unit political rituals seem to have aggravated rather than reduced existing conflicts and animosities.

In spite of these different atmospheres, neither Ma nor Kung feels that political rituals were very effective in changing the political attitudes and thoughts of fellow cadres. Ma feels that his co-workers had pride and self-confidence that they were good, loyal cadres and so felt little pressure to change their attitudes. Successes in rectification campaigns reinforced this confidence. In Kung's unit cadres knew they fell short of the elite's demands for proper thinking and behavior. The pressure to meet those expectations was not substantial, however, and they were able to find ways to adapt to the pressures of cadre life without changing their attitudes. It would be a mistake to take these assessments at face value, since they may be heavily laden with retrospective cynicism. Nonetheless they alert us to the possibility that for effective attitude change to take place it may be important to create within the individual a compelling sense that he needs to change, and perhaps that others around him are "progressing" and will leave him behind if he does not alter his views. Several of my other informants mention that in the early years after 1949 criticism rituals had taken place within a general atmosphere in which people felt the need to progress or be left behind, but that later these activities became viewed more as a part of organizational life to be adapted to in various ways. Campaigns over the years had as one aim the revival of insecurity and the pervasive need for individual change, but from the accounts of my informants it is questionable whether even the Cultural Revolution, designed to "touch men's souls," was successful in restoring the mood of the earlier years.

From our comparison of these two accounts, we would expect that other units characterized by a low level in the national hierarchy, many lines of cleavage and few bases of solidarity, and high personnel turnover will have a lax political atmosphere. On the other hand, where there is greater selectivity of personnel, fewer bases of cleavage, and higher organization rank we would expect a much stricter atmosphere. However, these two patterns are not the only ones which can occur. The organizations of some of my other cadre informants fit neither pattern clearly. Some of these accounts describe a fair amount of stability and solidarity among leading cadres, but a high turnover among ordinary cadres, with most other cleavages (regional origins, Party membership, etc.) reinforcing the major division between the leaders and the led. In this situation what seems to have developed, other things being equal, was a more rigid authority relationship than in either of the accounts presented here. Political study and mutual criticism were pushed more vigorously and engaged in more diligently than they were in Kung's unit. But these activities were more formal and regimented than in Ma's unit, with cadres seeing in the criticism of their peers the manipulation of their superiors. In such units there was less venting of grievances by subordinates and less forming of protective relationships with superiors than was the case in the units presented in this chapter. The result was a political atmosphere that was in some sense intermediate in strictness between the two cases presented, with fairly vigorous political rituals, but without the desired amount of interpersonal solidarity and effective social pressure. In sum, neither of my case studies is in any exact sense representative of the accounts of all my informants, much less of all organizations in China. However, the comparison does help illuminate features of cadre organizations which seem to influence the kind of political atmosphere which develops and thus, presumably, how effective a given organization will be in changing the attitudes of its participants.

Certain other ways in which the accounts of other informants differ from the two presented should be noted. The political study routine in all units was similar, but there were many variations in specifics (e.g., some claim there was only one political study meeting a week, while others mention as many as three). There were substantial disagreements about the role of unions. It is not clear which kinds of cadres belong to unions and which do not (there was no union in Ma's unit, but there was a union in Kung's unit). Some kinds of cadres (e.g., teachers) seem generally to belong to a union, while there are instances among my informants of cadres working in similar units, but with a union organization in one unit and not in another. Most of my informants agree with Kung that the union was not very important, focusing mainly on welfare and recreational activities. However, there are important exceptions. One informant mentions that in her unit there was a union organization which formed its members into *hsiao-tsu* to carry out regular political study and discussion activities and mutual criticism. I am unable to explain these differences, and more research on the role of the trade unions among cadres seems desirable.

There were several kinds of laxity in the political atmosphere mentioned by my cadre informants. Most say mutual criticism tended to be superficial and pro forma except during campaigns. And most did not have to report on, or account for, their activities outside of work hours and were able to maintain a private life and outside friends, some of whom by their negative attitudes undermined social pressure within the organization. Several informants mention that the Youth League often played an ineffective role in political life in their units. In many cadre units, as in those described in this chapter, there were few non-member youth to be led, while in others non-member youth were those who did not join the Youth League in school and were no longer motivated to join. The Youth League, in the absence of "masses" to lead, tended to function mainly as an ideological watchdog over its members. Several informants mention that many Youth League members in their units had already passed the maximum age limit (25) but continued to participate since dropping out would have indicated a desire to escape the rigors of Youth League discipline. But this proportion of over-age members served to emphasize the political control role of the Youth League as opposed to its vanguard role. My other informants confirm the view that the most vigorous political study and mutual criticism occurred during the periodic rectification campaigns, but they share the skepticism already noted that real attitude changes resulted from these campaigns.

The Chinese Communists have consistently emphasized political study and criticism rituals as part of cadre life, although there have been periodic shifts in the strength of this emphasis. In so doing they hope to avoid a mechanical obedience to authority such as was fostered under Stalin in the Soviet Union, and they also hope to break down the influence of kinship, local origin, and other ties which permeated the traditional Chinese bureaucracy. These activities are expected to create a unified and disciplined corps of cadres willing to respond with creative initiative to the demands of the elite. By their leadership the cadres set the tone for the rest of society. In practice the effectiveness of these rituals in manipulating the behavior of cadres seems impressive, but the elite has been consistently disappointed in its quest for attitude change and organizational unity. The intensive assaults on the defects of cadres during campaigns are blunted by the adaptive behavior of the cadres. And in some cases political rituals aggravate existing cleavages and interpersonal tensions, thus making not only unity but attitude change difficult to achieve.

VI

STUDENTS AND
POLITICAL RITUALS

The importance of education in traditional China is well known. The educational ladder and the examination system provided some opportunity for youths of humble origin to move up in society, and a high level of education was a guarantee of public esteem. Today the motivation to get ahead via education retains its importance in the minds of the Chinese masses, while the concerns of the ruling elite are somewhat different: they desire to turn out people with training and motivation suited to the present and future political and economic needs of China.

In traditional China the intensive study of Confucian classics was emphasized as a guide to personal conduct and to the correct behavior of officials. Much of the schooling was conducted by scholars who had not succeeded in gaining public office themselves and had to be content with tutoring the next generation, sometimes individually and sometimes in small schools run by families, clans, or villages. The weaknesses of China in the nineteenth century in relation to her foreign intruders led to a re-examination of traditional education and to the foundation of modern schools, with mathematics, science, and the liberal arts increasingly replacing Confucian literary works. In accelerating fashion after the defeat of China in the Sino-Japanese war in 1895, and particularly after the downfall of the Ch'ing dynasty in 1911, new educational ideas and practices were introduced from Japan and from the West. There was in these years a great deal of ferment and debate over how to improve education and what role education should play in solving China's problems. During the period of Nationalist rule (1927–1949) a wide variety of experiments in mass literacy training, polytechnical education, and other fields was begun.[1] Eventually a national educational system emerged based on Western, and primarily American, models. The core institutions in this system were the primary schools (six years full primary or four years of lower primary), lower middle schools (three years), upper middle schools (three years) and universities (four or more years). These schools, particularly above the primary level, tended to be concentrated in urban areas. The emphasis was on general liberal arts rather than on technical and practical skills, and lower level schools were primarily oriented to preparing students for higher level schools. Efforts to develop more practical and technical education took place mostly outside of these core institutions. While foreign educational ideas were very important in remolding Chinese schools, there was also a partial reaction against these ideas during the Nationalist period, and an attempt was made to reemphasize elements of China's heritage and traditional moral training in education.

In the eyes of the Chinese Communists the Nationalists had substituted foreign liberal arts training for the study of the Confucian classics, but the purpose of the game was the same: getting ahead in the system without concern for the welfare of the masses. In Nationalist schools passive listening to lectures had replaced individual tutoring, but the idea that acquiring a certain amount of knowledge from the sages would qualify one to join their ranks remained.

In the 1930's and 1940's in their isolated border areas the Communists had been developing their own educational policies and institutions, based on different considerations. In a situation of nearly constant warfare, schools had to serve very immediate and practical needs. Short term training in technical and leadership skills and spare time literacy and political education were needed to support the war and production efforts. The institutional forms varied: evening and winter schools for peasants, training classes and intensive cadre schools and universities (generally with terms of study from six months to two years), and a wide variety of other approaches.[2] Given the pressing

---

1. For some of these issues and developments see Chow Tse-tung, *The May Fourth Movement* (Cambridge, Mass.: Harvard University Press, 1960); and Sidney D. Gamble, *Ting Hsien* (New York: Institute of Pacific Relations, 1954), Chap. 9.

2. See Peter Jordan Seybolt, *Yenan Education and the Chinese Revolution 1937–1945*, unpublished Ph.D. dissertation, Harvard University, December 1969; also M. Lindsay, *Notes on Educational Problems in Communist China* (New York: Institute of Pacific Relations, 1950).

needs of this period, little attention could be paid to general liberal arts education or to long term training of scientists or other highly trained personnel. Over the course of time these necessities became virtues, and educational practices initiated at the time continue to shape policies in China today.

As mentioned in Chapter 3, students during the Yenan period, at least in higher level schools, were divided into *hsiao-tsu* and took part in a wide variety of economic and political activities in addition to academic study. The *hsiao-tsu* were necessitated in part by the shortage of teaching personnel and textbooks, which made sharing and mutual help important. But this group approach also fit with the Chinese Communist emphasis on involving the masses in disciplining and re-educating themselves.

When they came to power after 1949 the Communists undertook a systematic reform of the national educational system, relying in part upon their Yenan experiences and in part upon the advice and aid of the Soviet Union. In the Soviet Union, the progressive educational experiments of the 1920's had given way to a highly centralized school system emphasizing the rapid output of large numbers of skilled technical personnel to fill the needs of the five-year plans. Political controls over schools and curricula were important to Stalin, but the main task of Soviet schools was to impart as much knowledge as possible. In practice this meant a heavy reliance on lectures, grades, examinations, and individual competition, all carried out under the watchful eye of teachers with newly re-emphasized authority and disciplinary powers.[3] Students who could not successfully compete for places in higher educational institutions were shunted off into technical schools (*tekhnikums*) or trade schools, or directly into the job market. After 1949 the Chinese combined this Soviet model of education with their Yenan experiences as a source of inspiration for educational policy.

After the Chinese Communists established military control over a region they moved to reform the schools, first by eliminating Nationalist political organizations and indoctrination courses. Young Pioneer and New Democratic Youth League organizations were established in the schools (for ages 9–14 and 15–25 respectively) in place of their Nationalist counterparts. A variety of campaigns involved students and teachers in remaking their schools and the society outside the

---

3. The best summary of these shifts is Ruth Widmayer, "The Evolution of Soviet Educational Policy," in *Harvard Educational Review*, Vol. 24, 1954, pp. 159–175; see also George L. Kline, ed., *Soviet Education* (New York: Columbia University Press, 1957).

schools (recall here Ma Kan-pu's mention of campaigns to control inflation). In the thought reform campaign of 1951–52 students and faculty members were organized into *hsiao-tsu* and assigned to study and discuss Marxism-Leninism, the thought of Mao Tse-tung, and the doctrines of the "New Democracy," the official policy line of that period.[4] Students and faculty members were expected to criticize their own pasts in light of these new ideas, and to progress to new levels of political consciousness.[5]

An important theme of the thought reform campaign was the denunciation of the previous glorification of things Western, a theme given special emphasis because of the concurrence of the Korean War. Many other activities of this period, such as reading Soviet novels, going on fields trips to observe land reform, and conducting propaganda about the Korean conflict contributed to the effort to change student attitudes. Schools varied, however, in the strength of the new political organizations, and in some more was done to change student attitudes through the medium of lectures and exhortation than through organized group pressure. The most important or difficult targets of thought reform, potential cadres and recalcitrant intellectuals, were for the most part taken outside of the existing schools and subjected to more intensive training and re-education in special institutions, such as the newly created "revolutionary universities." [6] In the efforts at political re-education within schools the Communists relied primarily on their own earlier experiences, rather than on Soviet precedents.

Institutional and curricular reforms were also undertaken in these years. Existing schools were in some cases reorganized or amalgamated, and in expansion plans technical and scientific education was stressed in an effort to redress the Nationalist emphasis on general education and the liberal arts. Specialized secondary schools were set up on the model of the Soviet *tekhnikum*. But the basic school system left by the Nationalists was preserved: the six-year general primary schools (a

---

4. Mao enunciated the doctrine of the "New Democracy" in 1940 to distinguish the transitional stage in the Chinese revolution between capitalism and socialism, in which some political and economic power would continue to be held by bourgeois classes. See his essay "On New Democracy," in *Selected Works of Mao Tse-tung*, Vol. 2 (Peking: Foreign Languages Press, 1965), pp. 339–384.

5. Two very different personal accounts of the initial takeover period in universities are available: Maria Yen, *The Umbrella Garden* (New York: Macmillan, 1954); and William G. Sewell, *I Stayed in China* (London: George Allen & Unwin, 1966).

6. For a discussion of these revolutionary universities, see R. Lifton, "The Thought Reform of Chinese Intellectuals: A Psychiatric Evaluation," in *Journal of Social Issues*, Vol. 13, no. 3, 1957.

reduction to five years was planned but never carried out) and the six years of general lower and upper middle schools. Most of the reforms took place within this basic structure, designed to adapt it to the new economic and political realities. Courses and textbooks were subjected to a general reform and eliminated where they did not seem relevant to China's needs. New texts were needed, and in these years many teachers used improvised teaching materials or translated Soviet texts. The predominant teaching method of previous years, the lecture, was criticized as leading to excessive student passivity. Efforts were made to develop class discussions and to build laboratory work, class trips, science clubs, and similar practices into school life. The authority of traditional teachers was attacked, and students were urged to be more questioning and critical of their teachers. During the thought reform campaign the lessening of the teacher's status was accelerated by having some faculty members confess their errors publicly before fellow teachers and students. In some cases the innovative spirit in school life went further, with students in their small groups discussing which questions should be included in examinations and grading each other afterward.[7] In this period collectivism reached great heights at some institutions, with the same small group studying together, eating together, and sleeping in the same dormitory room.

During the years 1948–1952 academic study was disrupted by the final stages of the Civil War, the campaigns in and around the schools, and the great amount of time spent reforming and reorganizing schools. As the elite moved from consolidation of its power to the long-term development effort, the conflict between these disruptions and academic study became a matter of some concern. Participation in social reforms was an exhilarating experience for many students, but at the same time the inability to make optimal use of educational opportunities could be frustrating. Reforms had made the educational system more relevant to China's needs, but now it was necessary to fully utilize the schools to transmit the knowledge and skills needed for long term development.

In response to such concerns, and in connection with the launching of the first five-year plan, educational policy underwent a number of changes in the period 1953–1956, most of which tended to bring Chinese schools closer to Soviet models. Political activities and campaigns intruded less into schools, and great stress was placed on im-

---

7. Pai Chih-chung, *Chung-kung chiao-yü p'i-p'an* (A critique of Chinese Communist education) (Hong Kong, 1955), pp. 150–152.

proving school discipline and on reemphasizing academics. *Hsiao-tsu* were now as concerned with encouraging academic study as with fostering thought reform. The innovations in student involvement in grading and examination construction fell from sight, the lecture became the main teaching method again, and students competed for high grades and a place on the honor roll. A strict student code of conduct, based on the Soviet code, was adopted in 1955.[8] The political course followed Soviet practice by assuming the form of other courses, with formal lectures, texts to be learned, and examinations to be passed. As educational emphasis shifted toward training for technical expertise, the remaining burdens of political study were perceived as onerous by some, and the position of student political leaders was undermined, or so it would seem from the events of 1957.

In the spring of 1957, during the period which is termed the "hundred flowers campaign" in the West, students and teachers voiced their criticisms of the existing educational system, and many of these criticisms were directed at the political controls and political study burdens placed upon students and teachers.[9] The criticisms unleashed, particularly in the universities, revealed to China's elite the superficiality of much of the thought reform of faculty members and students in earlier years, and also raised serious concern over the consequences of excessive emphasis on academic subjects. In the anti-rightist campaign of late 1957 the "hundred flowers" critics were dealt with. Many "rightists," both students and teachers, were expelled and assigned to labor re-education. Subsequently the number of hours devoted to political study was increased, and new required readings were assigned.[10] The formalism of political study in the previous period was attacked, and students were urged not to passively learn new political concepts, but to thoroughly examine and improve their own attitudes.[11] Sub-

---

8. The code is translated in Theodore H. E. Chen, ed., *The Chinese Communist Regime* (New York: Praeger, 1967), pp. 319–320. For the comparable Soviet code see an appendix to B. P. Yesipov and N. K. Goncharov, *I Want to Be Like Stalin*, translated by George S. Counts and Nucia P. Lodge (New York: John Day, 1957). Many other Soviet organizational policies were adopted in Chinese schools at this time, such as the regular classroom meetings; see *Kuang-ming Jih-pao*, February 6, 1956.

9. See Dennis Doolin, *The Politics of Student Opposition* (Stanford: The Hoover Institution, 1964); also R. MacFarquhar, *The Hundred Flowers Campaign and the Chinese Intellectuals* (New York: Praeger, 1960).

10. See H. Arthur Steiner, "The Curriculum of Chinese Socialist Education: An Official Bibliography of 'Maoism'", in *Pacific Affairs*, Vol. 31, no. 3, 1958.

11. See New China News Agency dispatches of September 11 and 13, 1957, in *Survey of the China Mainland Press*, no. 1630.

102 SMALL GROUPS AND POLITICAL RITUALS IN CHINA

sequently group discussion techniques were once again emphasized as were student criticism of teachers, group participation in grading, and similar practices. In 1957 it was ruled that political criteria should take precedence over academic qualifications in selection for higher education. (Prior to this time academic qualifications were primary and political criteria secondary.) At the same time there was a great emphasis on breaking down the isolation of schools, on getting students involved in manual labor and in outside political activities. Schools set up agricultural plots and industrial workshops, and students were sent off to engage in other kinds of labor. (Previously, students had participated in labor from time to time, but not on a regular basis.)

At this time there was increasing dissatisfaction with the core educational institutions, the general primary and middle schools and universities retained from the Nationalist days. These schools were now turning out more and more scientists and engineers, rather than lawyers or Confucian scholars, but in the process status striving and individualism continued to be fostered. After 1957 efforts were made to develop schools with lower level technical training, and to adjust popular aspirations to the idea of going to school in order to become no more than a literate and skilled manual worker. The desire to expand educational opportunities of this type without overburdening the state budget led to a new development of people-run (*min-pan*) and half-work half-study schools, which would be partially or completely self-supporting.[12] This period also saw an expansion of spare time educational facilities, such as the "red and expert" schools and colleges, which were designed to impart skills without divorcing students from labor.

Thus after 1957 the amount of time spent by students in labor increased greatly, an effort was made to revitalize political indoctrination, and educational facilities were expanded and decentralized. In all of these changes the harm of relying too much on Soviet precedents

---

12. People-run schools had played an important role in education in the Yenan period. See Peter Jordan Seybolt, *op. cit.* There is much confusion over the types of schools which sprang up after 1958. Some people-run schools were ordinary primary and middle schools financed by local units of various types (communes, Overseas Chinese Association, etc.). Some were financed in part by local economic enterprises but were expected to be partly self-supporting through school economic activities. In half-work half-study schools the labor performed by students was expected to help finance the school, thus lessening the burden on the state, local organizations, and the students' families. The most prominent type of new school was the agricultural middle school, which combined the people-run and half-work half-study features. See R. D. Barendsen, "The Agricultural Middle School in Communist China," in R. MacFarquhar, ed., *China Under Mao* (Cambridge, Mass.: MIT Press, 1966).

was proclaimed, although by a curious coincidence somewhat similar reforms were being introduced in the Soviet Union at this time under Khrushchev.[13] As Soviet experience was increasingly rejected, it was often the model of education during the Yenan period which provided the alternative.

The collapse of the Great Leap Forward campaign led to a severe reaction against these educational reforms, typified by the statement of Liu Shao-ch'i that the main business of students was academic study.[14] The economic problems of the years after 1959 led to a general educational retrenchment, and many of the schools set up during the previous few years were curtailed or closed down.[15] The pendulum once again swung back toward an emphasis on improving the quality of schooling and avoiding the disruption of education by other activities. "Expert" for a brief period became a favorable term rather than a pejorative. As Kung Ch'eng-shih mentioned in the previous chapter, in 1961 the foreign minister Ch'en Yi symbolized this trend in a speech advocating treating experts well and eliminating much of the political study burden from technical schools.

Thus in the years 1961–1963 schools were once again partially isolated from the disruptions of political and economic campaigns. Labor stints for students continued, but on an institutionalized and limited basis (for instance, for one afternoon a week, and for two weeks at the end of the year). But there was not a full swing back to the policies of the years 1953–1956, and certain key issues remained under debate. Perhaps the most crucial issue involved the criteria to be used in promoting students to higher level schools, and here the balance placed on academic and political qualifications apparently fluctuated from year to year. This issue was a critical one because of the changing demographic situation of the schools after 1961. The expansion of schools in the 1950's had produced an ever-larger cohort of students coming up from

13. For a description of these reforms see Jeremy Azrael, "The Soviet Union" in James S. Coleman, ed., *Education and Political Development* (Princeton: Princeton University Press, 1965); and N. DeWitt, *Education and Professional Employment in the USSR* (Washington: National Science Foundation, 1961).

14. Quoted in *Kuang-ming Jih-pao,* January 16, 1959. There is a question of emphasis involved here. In Mao Tse-tung's important May 7th Directive (1966) he also states that the main task of students is to study, but then he proceeds to outline their obligations to engage in industrial work, farming, military affairs, and "criticism of the bourgeoisie." The Directive is quoted in full in Peking Review, no. 32, 1966, pp. 6–7.

15. See Don Munro, "Egalitarian Ideal and Educational Fact in Communist China" in John H. Lindbeck, ed., *China: The Management of a Revolutionary Society* (Seattle: University of Washington Press, 1971).

lower levels, but the retrenchment of the economy and the educational system after the Great Leap Forward meant that access to higher schools and to jobs was relatively much more restricted.[16] The graduate at each level was faced with two primary alternatives: gaining acceptance into a higher school or being sent to the countryside to engage in agricultural labor. This predicament was markedly different from the situation of expanding opportunities in earlier years.

Since 1964 the pendulum has swung again back toward an emphasis on schools as inculcators of proper political and labor attitudes and not just as purveyors of knowledge. The half-work half-study schools, curtailed in the early 1960's, have been revived and proclaimed as the ideal for all schools.[17] In the Cultural Revolution the "bourgeois" educational line of the previous period was roundly attacked, and in recent reforms most of the educational ideas of 1957–1960 have been revived. Emphasis is being increasingly placed on politicizing school life and on gearing down the educational system and student aspirations. The period of schooling is being shortened, and students are told to expect to spend a limited amount of time in school and then to apply their skills in positions involving manual labor. At this writing

---

16. Available statistics are spotty. Some idea of the results of educational expansion can be seen in the following figures:

FULL TIME ENROLLMENTS (THOUSANDS)

	Primary	General middle	Specialized middle	Higher Education
1949/50	24,391	1,039	229	117
1953/54	51,664	2,933	668	212
1957/58	64,279	6,281	778	441
1958/59	86,400	8,520	1470	660
1959/60	90,000	n.a.	n.a.	810
1960/61	n.a.	n.a.	n.a.	955
1961/62	n.a.	n.a.	n.a.	819
1962/63	n.a.	n.a.	n.a.	820
1964/65	126,000	23,100	n.a.	700

n.a. = not available

SOURCES: Figures from 1949/50 to 1958/59 and for 1959/60 for primary schools from Leo A. Orleans, *Professional Manpower and Education in Communist China* (Washington: National Science Foundation, 1961), pp. 32, 35, 42, and 61. The other figures are from Barry M. Richman, *Industrial Society in Communist China* (New York: Random House, 1969), pp. 138, 139, 147 and 164. The 1964/65 figures should be regarded as tentative, since they came from an interview of Charles Lynch with a Chinese official, rather than from published statistics.

17. Donald Munro, "Maxims and Realities in China's Educational Policy: The Half-Work, Half-Study Model,' in *Asian Survey*, Vol. 7, no. 4, 1967.

the universities, the former pinnacle of the educational system, are still in the process of being reformed and re-established, with many of the details of their future operation and role still uncertain. These recent debates and reforms are too complex to go into here, but the core issues are largely the same as those involved in the dialectical policy shifts of the past two decades.

TAI HSIAO-AI: A STUDENT

Here we adopt a somewhat different approach from the previous chapter by presenting several schools as they are described by the same informant, a young man we shall call Tai Hsiao-ai.[18] Tai was 22 at the time I talked to him in the summer of 1969, and altogether we held seven discussions. In the process we covered his experiences from primary school up through upper middle school to the time he left China near the end of 1967.

Tai Hsiao-ai was born and spent his early years in a rural area on the outskirts of a *hsien* capital city in Kwangtung province. His father had fled to Taiwan when the Communists came to power, but since his mother had received a divorce soon after Tai was born this relationship was not held against either her or her son. In fact the family's class status was a very favorable one—worker, based on Tai's mother's job in a factory.

THE PRIMARY SCHOOL

In 1955 Tai entered primary school in his home village. Student organization in this school was not highly developed. From first grade, students formed *hsiao-tsu*, one per classroom row, but until at least the last year or two of primary school these groups were largely a formality. Few activities were organized on the basis of *hsiao-tsu*, although students did line up in their groups to go places, much as American schoolchildren line up by rows. A political course was introduced in the upper primary grades (Tai does not recall which year), but it was run much like any other course. *Hsiao-tsu* did not conduct political

---

18. Altogether I interviewed 23 individuals about their experiences as students, 16 of these solely about their student days, and 7 in connection with interviews about other stages of their careers. Some of the students were interviewed about more than one school, so that altogether I received descriptions of three primary schools, fourteen middle schools, and nine universities.

discussions or mutual criticism. They were supposed to help maintain discipline, with the *hsiao-tsu* head reporting any misbehavior of members to the teacher. But even this role was carried out poorly. The girls tended to be more orderly in class than the boys, but it was always the boys who were chosen as *hsiao-tsu* heads, apparently due to the traditional male bias of the children. The more rambunctious boys were often ineffective in supporting the discipline of the teacher. Classroom discipline was a frequent problem since there were some students who, again influenced by traditional peasant views, thought they were wasting their time in school. For these unruly students the threat of criticism or even of being held back a year had little chastening effect.

In the upper primary grades students began to join the Young Pioneer organization (Tai joined in his third year), but this did not markedly affect the political atmosphere. There were some indoctrinational aspects of Pioneer activities, such as learning revolutionary songs and listening to stories of modern heroes, but much of the activity concerned hobbies and recreation and had little political content. In the Pioneer organization as in the general classroom it was the teacher (who served as Pioneer adviser—*fu-tao-yüan*) who planned and organized all activities, with student officers playing little role. Tai feels school authorities recognized that primary school students were still too young to be able to run political discussions or criticize each other properly, particularly in view of the constant problems created by the unruly students. Most matters were left in the hands of the teachers, and school life was not highly politicized. It is important to note that during this period the anti-rightist campaign took place (1957) and was followed in 1958 by the onset of the Great Leap Forward. Neither of these campaigns had a major impact on the lives of the students in Tai's school—they were only dimly aware of their significance.

Students at this stage were not highly involved in school life. Since there were few organized after-school activities, most students went home and played with nearby friends after school, unsupervised except by their families. In their play they might be thrown together with older children no longer in school who had little respect for the activities and norms of the school. Tai mentions that he proudly wore his Pioneer neckerchief while in school, but on the way home he would hide it in his pocket in order to avoid the taunts of some of the older children.

Although life in Tai's primary school was not highly politicized, the process of differentiating students and picking those most suited for further schooling began in the earliest grades. At this stage the most basic qualification for special attention and encouragement from the teacher was being well behaved in class, although both intelligence and class background were also important. Tai tended to be rather quiet and shy compared to many of his fellow students, and he also tried to please his teachers by studying hard. These traits, combined with his worker classification, meant that he always received good conduct marks and comments on his report cards.[19]

In 1960 Tai moved to Fukien province where he finished primary school and started lower middle school. Early in 1963 he moved back to his original home and transferred to a middle school on the outskirts of the *hsien* capital near his home. There Tai finished his lower middle school education.

THE LOWER MIDDLE SCHOOL

Students were again split into *hsiao-tsu* according to classroom rows. The *pan chu-jen* (the home room teacher, literally the class master) arranged the seating so that shorter students and those with poor eyesight sat in front, and so that each *hsiao-tsu* had a rough mixture of different types of students: male and female, good and poor students, politically activist and backward students. Each year the fifty or so students in the classroom elected seven class officers: a class head (*pan-chang*), assistant head (*fu-pan-chang*), study officer (*hsüeh-hsi wei-yüan*), labor officer (*lao-tung wei-yüan*), physical education officer (*t'i-yü wei-yüan*), livelihood officer (*sheng-huo wei-yüan*), and a culture and recreation officer (*wen-yü wei-yüan*).

The study officer was responsible for aiding the academic (not political) study of the students. He was supposed to check whether students were having problems in their studies and report such problems to the appropriate teacher. He also edited the wall newspaper put up by the students each week, which publicized class activities and related them to general current events. The labor officer guarded the tools the class used on labor stints and helped organize this activity. Two hours a week were spent in labor around the school, and this was called the labor course. In addition the students went on organized

---

19. For a description of a primary school in another area of China, Northern Shensi, see Jan Myrdal, *Report from a Chinese Village* (New York: Signet Books, 1966), Chapter 30. It should be noted that schools on Taiwan bear marked organizational similarities to Mainland (and Soviet) schools reflecting in part the common Leninist ancestry. See Richard W. Wilson, *Learning to be Chinese* (Cambridge, Mass.: MIT Press, 1970), pp. 69–77.

rural labor stints for about two weeks each year during vacations. The physical education officer organized sports teams within the class and arranged competitions with teams from other classes. The livelihood officer was responsible for economic and minor housekeeping matters in the class, such as collecting the money and distributing the tickets when the class went to see a local movie. The culture and recreation officer helped organize drama and singing teams and a variety of cultural activities within the classroom. The class head and his assistant supervised these activities. Collectively these seven were referred to as class cadres (*pan kan-pu*), although this did not imply any sort of government position or pay. In the third year of lower middle school a new type of officer was added, the course representative (*k'o tai-piao*). There was one representative for each of the major courses studied, appointed by the teachers rather than elected by the students. The course representatives assisted the study officer by checking with students on problems in particular courses, and then referring these to the teacher concerned. Tai Hsiao-ai remarks that, counting class cadres, course representatives, *hsiao-tsu* heads, and Communist Youth League officers (to be discussed shortly), nearly half of the students in the class held some kind of office and a few students held two offices.

In theory the classroom cadres were under the supervision of the school student association (*hsüeh-sheng-hui*). All students in the school elected the officers of the student association, and their posts corresponded to those within the class: chairman, vice chairman, study officer, and so on. In fact this relationship was more one of coordination than supervision, and the student association arranged activities which transcended individual classrooms, such as all-school basketball competitions or participation in an outside political demonstration. In matters within the classroom the students and class cadres were under the direct supervision of the *pan chu-jen,* whose rough American equivalent is the home room teacher, but whose responsibilities extend more heavily into matters of character training and political tutelage.[20]

Tai is unclear about the administrative structure of the school, both because the time he spent in this school was relatively brief (about eighteen months) and because students generally had little contact with

---

20. The organization of the classroom is not far different from the Soviet model, except perhaps somewhat more highly organized. See the discussion in Urie Bronfenbrenner, *Two Worlds of Childhood, US/USSR* (New York: Russell Sage Foundation, 1969). The teacher's role is also similar. See F. Vigdorova, *Diary of a Russian Schoolteacher,* Rose Prokieva, trans. (New York: Grove Press, 1960).

the administrators. The two top administrative officials were the principal and the academic dean, while the Communist Party branch held ultimate authority within the school. The *pan chu-jen,* as the key staff member in each classroom, reported to the school administration on teaching matters and to the Party branch on political matters, but Tai is not sure about the mechanics of this practice. (Many of the top administrators also held posts within the Party branch.) Tai does know that the teachers were organized into their own study *hsiao-tsu.*[21]

While in Fukien Tai Hsiao-ai had remained active in the Young Pioneers, and when he returned to his home region and entered the new lower middle school the Youth League, the next stage after the Pioneers, was just beginning to organize students to enter its ranks.[22] At the time there were already three Youth League members in Tai's class. These three were all somewhat older than the other students, having worked for a period after primary school. Initially many students were hesitant to enter the Youth League because it made much greater demands of time and discipline on its members than did the Pioneers. Tai had not given the matter much thought, but he soon became interested in joining. He says that he "usually liked to be activist"; that is, he was anxious to please his teachers and to be respected by other students, and he tried to be among the first to volunteer for any new venture. Tai had been elected class study officer and this, combined with his class background and record of proper behavior, made him a good prospect for League membership.

In the spring of 1963 the three Youth League members began holding League courses (*t'uan-k'o*) two or three times a month. Students who wanted to enter the League were invited to listen to talks on the rights and responsibilities of League members, the history of the League, admissions procedures, and current political topics in general. Sometimes higher League officers in the school gave talks, and sometimes those present read and discussed articles in *China Youth Daily,* (*Chung-kuo Ch'ing-nien pao*) the official newspaper of the Youth League. This activity was more truly voluntary than many supposedly voluntary activities in China, and Tai noted that more and more stu-

---

21. According to informants who were teachers, their political study was carried out in course groups (*k'o-tsu*), which were sometimes called teaching research groups (*chiao-yen-tsu*). Here all of the teachers teaching one type of course would gather both for political study and for discussions of how to improve instruction.

22. The Pioneers are very much a mass organization, enrolling the majority of the school children eligible. The Youth League is more selective, while the Party itself is even more selective.

dents attended the course as graduation time approached and students became more concerned about bettering their prospects for admission to upper middle schools.[23] At the start of the third and final year of lower middle school the League course was supplemented by the individual "cultivation" (*p'ei-yang*) of specially selected students. Youth League members talked individually to these prospective members at least once a week, asking them about their conduct and thoughts and why they wanted to join the Youth League. Tai was one of those selected, and he had weekly talks in rotation with the three League members in his class. Near the end of the term these talks took place two or three times a week. Qualities such as diligence, good class background, and political enthusiasm all played a role in making a student eligible for membership, but it helped if he could distinguish himself by some especially meritorious act. Tai previously had been well behaved and studious, but he had never been particularly concerned with trying to influence others to be more activist or diligent. His general shyness tended to make him feel intimidated before the more unruly members of his class. But now he had a special incentive to change this pattern. Tai took advantage of a regular row *hsiao-tsu* meeting to criticize harshly another group member who was always fooling around in class. The fellow was somewhat stunned by the attack, since this kind of criticism was rare, and Tai had never been a vigilant defender of classroom order. But he could make no reply. In one of Tai's regular talks with his cultivators, he mentioned this incident and was praised for speaking out. Tai mentions that he customarily included minor self-criticism of his own conduct in these talks, for instance admitting day-dreaming during class, since such admissions were expected.

Near the end of the term Tai's cultivators were satisfied with his performance, and he was directed to write a final essay telling why he wanted to join the Youth League. By this time motivations for joining had been discussed so frequently that Tai knew very well which kinds of motivation were seen as proper and which were frowned upon. In his essay he stressed his desire to serve his country rather than his desire to earn prestige and improve his chances of getting into higher schools. Tai and one other student then attended the next League *hsiao-tsu* meeting, where they read their essays to the three existing members, who voted their approval. This vote was then confirmed by the League branch for the entire school year, and Tai became a League

---

23. In the final months about two-thirds of the students in Tai's class were attending. This pattern of gradually increasing attendance is confirmed by other middle school informants.

member. He began to attend the weekly League life meetings (*t'uan sheng-huo*). His League *hsiao-tsu* eventually came to have nine members, who were led by a *hsiao-tsu* head. The League branch had a secretary (*chih-pu shu-chi*), a propaganda officer (*hsüan-ch'uan wei-yüan*), and an organizational officer (*tsu-chih wei-yüan*).

Now that we have sketched the basic organizational structure of this lower middle school, we can turn to the kinds of political meetings and activities which were conducted within it. A one-period class meeting was held once a week, generally on Wednesday afternoons, and the usual format was for the *pan chu-jen* to discuss the activities of the past week and to praise and criticize various students for their study and labor. Then he would announce the activities for the coming week and tell how they would be organized and carried out. If an issue required class discussion and opinion the students would break down into their *hsiao-tsu*, and then would reconvene as a class with heads reporting on the opinions in their groups. But usually the entire period was spent listening to the *pan chu-jen*.

A formal political course was held two times a week, and in addition *hsiao-tsu* were supposed to spend about the same amount of time discussing point by point the material covered in the text and lectures of this course. Tai describes these sessions as closer to rote learning than to debate or thought reform. The study outline was reviewed to make sure that everyone understood all the terms and concepts, and then students quizzed one another on the material covered. There was no emphasis on students' examining and criticizing their own improper attitudes. In addition, at irregular intervals *hsiao-tsu* held meetings to discuss general student behavior during the preceding period, but in such sessions there was little mutual criticism, as the startled reaction of the student criticized by Tai attests. *Hsiao-tsu* could also meet for academic purposes, for students to work on homework assignments or laboratory exercises together. It was the *pan chu-jen* who decided what kinds of meetings to hold and when.

Hsiao-tsu also served as the forum for discussion of major speeches given by school officials at all-school assemblies. They also were the units for organizing student labor around the school or on rural labor stints, and for discussing afterward who had labored well. Semester summaries (*nien-chung tsung-chieh*) were also discussed within *hsiao-tsu*. These summaries followed more or less the pattern of the cadre summations mentioned in the previous chapter. Each student wrote a summary of his academic study, his labor, and his political thought; these were then read to the group, subjected to criticism, and turned over to the *pan chu-jen*. In fact, Tai says, the summaries tended to be rather brief (one or two pages) and written in a pro forma fashion. Few real revelations were included, and the criticism from other students tended to be perfunctory. The *pan chu-jen* supposedly relied on the summaries in deciding on the conduct marks and comments to be placed on each student's report card. Tai feels however, that the summaries were so stereotyped, and the teacher knew the students so well anyway, that they served little real purpose.

The *hsiao-tsu* were thus the basis of a wide variety of activities, and yet there was no particular loyalty toward one's own group. Students tended to view *hsiao-tsu* as arrangements for the administrative and disciplinary convenience of the teachers rather than as solidary social units. *Hsiao-tsu* were organized by the *pan chu-jen* with no regard (and in many cases with purposeful disregard) for friendship ties among students. Tai had three of four fairly close friends in his class with whom he used to play basketball after school. But these friends were split up throughout the various *hsiao-tsu*. Tai's best friends were not in his class, in fact not in the same school at all. They were friends from his neighborhood, youth he had grown up with. He spent many of his after-school and vacation hours with these friends, rather than with fellow students. He says that his situation was by no means atypical. For students who lived a fair distance from school, as many did, the logistics of getting together with classmates was difficult, and the food rationing system made it embarrassing to invite fellow students home for meals. During the summer vacation the isolation from school life was almost complete, since no efforts were made to organize student life at this time. As a result of these factors the *hsiao-tsu* and the school itself often did not correspond to the social groups which were of importance to students, and this fact tended to weaken their influence.

Another problem in the school political atmosphere was the weak role of student officers, including the *hsiao-tsu* head. The teacher monopolized so much of the direction of student activities that student officers tended to show little enthusiasm or initiative. Tai as study officer rarely went out of his way to check on study problems unless prodded by teachers. The *hsiao-tsu* head in theory had an important role to play in directing social pressure and in improving student political attitudes. But in practice this job tended to be regarded as of minor importance, with the more outstanding students competing for higher offices in the class, the student association, or the Youth League. As a result the *hsiao-tsu* head was looked upon as "nothing special," and the office often fell to students who were not very interested in holding it. The *hsiao-tsu* heads did run meetings, but took little interest in investigating the inner thoughts of group members or in correcting student behavior. Tai feels that, due to their low prestige, *hsiao-tsu* heads would not have been very effective in influencing fellow students even if they had been highly motivated.

Mutual criticism therefore tended to be poorly developed among students, with criticism from teachers much more important in maintaining order. Criticism rituals were more regularly carried out within the Youth League, but even there they tended to be formalized and superficial. Most of the things confessed during "League life" meetings were matters of common knowledge, and various kinds of deviance known to other League members were often not mentioned. The status of the Youth League was somewhat ambiguous. It was supposed to be a vanguard, setting an example for other students, but the concentration of control over student affairs in the hands of teachers and administrators tended to deprive the Youth League of this role. Some of the more unruly students would even laugh at League members and try to give them a hard time. Tai conveys the ambiguous status of League members by stating, "they had high prestige but were not too well liked." In other words officially they were a vanguard, but at least some of the students felt there was also "nothing special" about League members and resented their currying favor with teachers and being too critical of other students. Tai feels that there was some justification for these feelings since the League members, while generally better behaved than other students, were not above mischief.

Tai mentions several examples of student misbehavior which went unreported. Some of these were minor, such as fooling around or secretly reading a novel in class. Cheating was also widespread among the students, League members included, but was never the subject of group criticism. Once while in the countryside doing labor Tai and a group of friends stole and ate some fruit, and again the matter was never brought up for confession or criticism. For the most part students were unconcerned about reporting the misbehavior of others.

There were two major cases of misconduct, but students were not involved in dealing with them at all. During an examination two students changed seats so that they would be in a position to cheat, but the teacher noticed them, criticized them, and reported the matter to the *pan chu-jen*. Tai is not sure how the matter was handled after that, but the next the students heard of the affair was when they saw the penalties posted outside the academic office—each offender received a large demerit (*ta-kuo*).[24] No student discussions were held, and the two students were not subjected to any sort of special criticism meeting.

In another incident some belongings of a teacher were stolen. One student was suspected, and for several days running he was called out of class for talks with the principal. Then an all-school assembly was held in which the details of the theft were publicly revealed and the principal announced the penalty: the thief was expelled from the Pioneers and from school. He was ordered to remove his Pioneer neckerchief in front of the assembled students and then to leave. Again no student discussion sessions were held, and the thief was not subjected to criticism from other students. The assembly was not a struggle meeting with students rising to denounce the offender, but simply a meeting to announce the penalty and to warn others. In both cases the school authorities and teachers took charge of disciplinary action, and student involvement was nil. Tai feels, however, that there were good reasons for the teachers and administrators to monopolize school leadership. His fellow students were often not highly involved in school, and they tended to be immature and often poorly behaved. Tai feels that if the teachers had tried to rely more upon student leadership the result would not have been very good, since the ability and motivation for leadership on the part of most students was so small. But the result was admittedly a political atmosphere which fell far short of the ideals prescribed by China's elite.

The period of Tai's lower middle schooling was one of relative calm in terms of political pressures and campaigns. By the time of graduation in mid-1964 the national mood had changed with the start of the Socialist Education campaign, but the impact on Tai's school was not marked. Students did start to study information about the People's Liberation Army and its heroes, particularly Lei Feng, but this activity was fitted into the regular study and meeting system. New revolutionary songs and stories were learned, but as yet there was no institutionalized study of the thoughts of Chairman Mao.

In the spring of 1964 preparations were made for the application of Tai and his classmates to upper middle schools. Ideological work was conducted called "two kinds of preparation for one red heart" (*yi-k'o hung-hsin ti liang-chung chun-pei*). Students studied articles about the critical national importance of agriculture and listened to their teachers explaining the value of the life of the peasant. As a climax of this

---

24. Tai recalls that the available administrative sanctions were small demerits, large demerits, probation (remaining in school), and expulsion.

activity the students signed pledges that they would go to the country-side to engage in farming if they were not accepted into upper middle school. Tai knew that his chances of continuing school were good, due to his good grades, his League membership, and his class background. When it came time to fill out his preference form (chih-yüan-shu) he listed a provincial specialized upper middle school as his first choice.[25] Tai then took the standard placement examination along with his classmates, and a few weeks later he received word that this technical school had accepted him. Of his graduating class almost half were admitted to upper middle schools, most to local general schools. Of the roughly thirty students who were not accepted, Tai says, only seven or eight lived up to their pledges to settle in the countryside. The remainder stayed at home, lived off their families, and tried to find some kind of urban employment, if only odd jobs. This estimate seems to confirm Tai's feeling about the poor political atmosphere in his school, since, once out from under official supervision, many students failed to live up to the demands made upon them.

THE TECHNICAL MIDDLE SCHOOL

On the bus going to his new middle school on the outskirts of Canton, Tai Hsiao-ai met other first year students from his home area and formed initial friendships, particularly with two other boys. The three boys hoped to room together, but they soon learned they were to be split up and dispersed among students from other parts of Kwangtung province. In fact, Tai's two new friends were assigned to other class-rooms. They also learned that their new hsiao-tsu would be identical with their dormitory rooms, rather than being based on classroom seating. The class of forty-nine was divided into seven rooms and thus seven hsiao-tsu, four in the boys' dormitory and three in the girls'.

The new students were given a welcoming speech by the principal, who also served as Party secretary of the school. This man, a Northerner with a past career in the army, spoke with pride of the special nature of the school, its good equipment, and the high expectations he held for the students. In this speech and in subsequent orientation

---

25. These specialized middle schools (chung-chuan hsüeh-hsiao) were generally terminal rather than leading on to college. However, they had the advantage of training students in fairly specific skills and making job placement pretty certain upon graduation, reducing much of the insecurity felt by general middle school students. Tai was worried about getting through school quickly in order to help the family's finances, so he opted for this technical school.

activities it was made clear to the students that activities besides academic study, particularly political activities and labor, were regarded
as very important. The students were made to feel that the quality of
the job they would receive upon graduation would depend to a significant extent upon how they fared in these aspects of school life. Tai
also noticed an atmosphere of enthusiasm among his fellow students.
Most seemed anxious to meet the high expectations of the principal
and if possible to become student leaders, rather than just to get by.
The number of League members in the entering class was not much
higher than in Tai's lower middle school graduating class (thirteen as
opposed to nine), but the general level of activism seemed much higher.
There were none of the unruly students who disrupted discipline in
Tai's primary and lower middle schools, and there were also few of
the "white-expert" types who concentrated on academics and avoided
politics. Tai attributes these differences to the selection process of his
new school—in selecting students from all over the province political
activism must have been given more weight than was the case in ordinary middle schools.

The basic organizational structure of the new school was not far different from Tai's lower middle school. Below the principal and assistant principal were five committees of administrators and teachers
responsible for teaching and research (evaluating teaching methods),
educational affairs (setting schedules, keeping teachers' personnel dossiers), student affairs (overseeing student activities), labor (arranging
both rural labor and work practice in the technical specialty), and
school affairs (finances, plant maintenance, etc.). Policy direction was
in the hands of the school Party branch, and of forty-five teachers
about fifteen were Party members. The principal, as mentioned, also
served as Party branch secretary, while the assistant principal doubled
as Party branch assistant secretary. Tai is not positive about this, but
he thinks that the proportion of teachers who were Party members was
higher than in his lower middle school. (This figure of one-third Party
members is higher than that mentioned by any of my other informants
from middle schools.)

The school's 750 students were divided into five classrooms in each
of the three grades. Each class had a *pan chu-jen* assigned to it. The
class cadre positions were the same as those in lower middle school:
class head, assistant head, study officer, physical education officer,
labor officer, livelihood officer, and culture and recreation officer. The
hsiao-tsu arrangement by dormitory rooms has already been mentioned, and each of these groups had a head. At first there were no

course representatives, but after teachers familiarized themselves with the new students these positions were filled as well. Two minor class offices were added. In each *hsiao-tsu* one student was selected to act as correspondent (*t'ung-hsüan-yüan*), whose function it was to keep an eye out for any good deeds or accomplishments of group members and write them up for the weekly wall newspaper. Also four members of the class were designated as newspaper readers (*tu-pao-yüan*). Each morning before school the students were assembled and in rotation on different days these officers read key articles from the press to all present. There was also a student association for the entire school, with officers corresponding to those in each classroom. Upon entry Tai Hsiao-ai was elected to the posts of assistant class head and also student association study officer, although this kind of doubling up was rare. He mentions that it was the general practice to include one first year student on the official slate of nominees for student association offices. Initially students were nominated for these posts by their teachers, who had access to student files and recommendations from lower middle schools. Later on the student association officers organized the nomination and election of their successors, and there was much continuity of leadership from year to year.

In addition there was a Youth League branch. At first a branch was organized for the entire first year class, but after a couple of months the Youth League was reorganized with a branch in each classroom, and a general branch for the entire school. Later, as new members were cultivated and accepted (there were twenty-three League members, or ten new ones, by 1966), two League small groups were formed in Tai's branch. Weekly League life meetings were generally held in these *hsiao-tsu,* with classroom branch meetings called to deal with major issues and problems.

The basic organizations and offices in this school are not far different from Tai's lower middle school,[26] and in fact seem to be fairly standard for middle schools in China during the early 1960's. But there were shifts in the relative importance of different organizations. The most important was the diminished role of the *pan chu-jen* in the

---

26. In addition to the organizations mentioned there was a student militia. A select minority of students, primarily those from favorable class backgrounds, were chosen for the school's basic militia (*chi-kan min-ping*), which had regular training and exercises. The rest of the students were considered the ordinary militia (*p'u-t'ung min-ping*), and had only one or two brief militia exercises per year. This division parallels that in rural communes—see Chapter 7. The militia organization existed in Tai's lower middle school, but was largely a formality, with little activity or training.

technical school. The *pan chu-jen* exercised less direct leadership over student affairs than in Tai's lower middle school and often receded into a background advisory role, leaving the task of immediate leadership to student officers. The *pan chu-jen* continued to exercise general supervision over the activities of these officers, and he was a member of the informal leadership group (*ling-tao hsiao-tsu*) including the class head, assistant head, and League branch secretary, which met frequently to plan class activities. But he left many kinds of problems, discipline included, to student cadres. The weekly classroom affairs meetings were now run by the student cadres, and sometimes the *pan chu-jen* was not even present. In general, student officers were quite diligent. Tai mentions that the class officers informally recruited other students as their "backbone elements," that is, people they could count on to help them in their jobs of writing articles for the wall newspaper and arranging cultural events, and so forth.

The student association was somewhat more important in the technical school than in Tai's lower middle school. Student association officers kept tabs on how student activities were being directed in each class and periodically called meetings of all class officers and of, say, all class study officers, to check on how well they were doing their jobs. The student association was in turn under the supervision of the student section of the school administration.

The role of the Youth League was ambiguous in the technical school, but for somewhat different reasons than in Tai's lower middle school. The Youth League did not perform much of a vanguard function, in spite of the fact that five out of seven of the major class officers were League members. In fact there was a fair amount of friction between these class officers and the League officers, because the responsibilities of class officers were much broader than had been the case in lower middle school. In addition to the duties implied by their titles, classroom officers served as political and indoctrinational leaders as well, directing political discussions and talking to students about individual thought problems. But this was theoretically the role of the Youth League officers, and the two groups fought to establish control over this important activity.

From the first days in the technical school Tai's life was filled with political activities of various sorts. Study of the writings of Mao Tsetung was made a daily ritual. Students read Mao's works individually and listened to the newspaper readers for an hour before breakfast each morning. Monday, Wednesday, and Friday evenings were specified as *hsiao-tsu* study and discussion periods. At least once a week this session was devoted to a "livelihood self-examination" meeting as in cadre units. Tuesday and Thursday evenings were left for academic homework, but even this was generally a *hsiao-tsu* activity. Three hours a week were devoted to the political course, and some of this time was spent in group discussion. If topics were left undiscussed, additional group meetings could be scheduled in the afternoon or evening. The nature of the political course also changed. The lectures were concerned more and more with the thoughts of Chairman Mao and discussions of class struggle, rather than with basic tenets of Marxism-Leninism. The entire school schedule was more flexible than had been the case in Tai's lower middle school. The various kinds of political discussions were not sharply distinguished from one another, and the times allotted to them were often switched or academic classes pre-empted (although the reverse situation, of classes interfering with political study, never occurred).

Students were involved in competition for the titles, "five-good student" (good in politics, thought, study, labor, and relations with classmates) and "four-good classroom," competitions modeled after similar activities in the People's Liberation Army. At the beginning of each semester school authorities announced the criteria for selection. Throughout the semester, in livelihood self-examination meetings and classroom affairs meetings, individual behavior and defects were constantly expressed and evaluated in terms of these criteria. Then at the end of the semester *hsiao tsu* convened to nominate "five good" students. Each individual reported on his own conduct during the past semester according to the established criteria, and group members added their comments. This evaluation procedure replaced the semester summaries found in Tai's lower middle school. The group as a whole decided whether a student had been five-good, or perhaps only four, three, or fewer good. There was no limit on how many in the group could be nominated. After the *hsiao-tsu* meetings there followed a meeting of class cadres and *hsiao-tsu* heads in which the latter reported on those chosen by their groups. Then the cadres discussed the nominees and added or subtracted a few names, either to compensate for the varying quality of *hsiao-tsu* or to include the names of class cadres who, because of the tensions arising out of their leadership roles, were often not nominated by their own groups. The final list of nominees was submitted to the entire class for comments or criticisms. Then it was voted on and sent to the school Party branch, which approved and announced the five-good students for the entire school. Tai was picked for this honor each of the three times the selection was held prior to the Cultural Revolution.

The emphasis placed on this competition had an important influence upon school life throughout the term, and students were very anxious to be chosen for the "five-good" title in spite of the fact that the immediate rewards were purely honorary. (Of course the possible benefits in terms of future job placement may have added to student motivation.) The competition gave rise to serious tensions. Even though the criteria for each good were stated in advance, they tended to be vague and abstract; there was room for personal feelings and conflicts to enter the selection process. In some cases as a result of such conflicts a student picked as a labor activist after a rural work stint was not even judged as good in labor at the end of the term. Tai says many of the students found the frequent evaluations and competitions fairly painful, and during the Cultural Revolution they decided to have no more of such competitions, specifically because of the way these had disrupted classroom unity.

The four-good classroom competition was less important. A class meeting was held to discuss the good points and shortcomings of their class with respect to the four established criteria. Then the class officers wrote a summary report of these comments. The reports were read to the student association and League general branch officers, meeting in joint session, who made the selection of four-good classrooms. Tai's class was never picked for this honor. It should be noted that there was no competition for good *hsiao-tsu,* but only for individuals and classrooms, and the individual competition was given much greater emphasis. In this competition grades played very little role, although study was one of the criteria to be considered. Although many class officers had low grades due to the great time burden of meetings and other activities, they were still generally chosen for such honors, and their poor grades did not greatly concern them.

Political attitudes were subject to other types of systematic evaluation. Students were expected to submit weekly written evidence of the progress of their thinking. This evidence could take two forms. All students were encouraged to keep diaries, but diaries of a very non-secret sort. Students recorded in their diaries various events and activities, their impressions of them, and how their political attitudes had been influenced by them. These diaries would be handed over to the *pan chu-jen* once a week for inspection. The diaries were modeled after those of Lei Feng and Wang Chieh, the two most prominent army heroes and models of this period.[27] Alternatively, a student could

---

27. See *Lao-tung jen-min ti hao erh-tzu Lei Feng* (Good son of the laboring people Lei Feng) (Peking, 1963); *The Diary of Wang Chieh* (Peking, 1967).

turn in a study comprehension report (*hsüeh-hsi hsin-te*). The content was not very different. The student discussed a political study article he had read during the past week, his thoughts about its meaning and importance, and how he was trying to apply its ideas in his daily activities. Tai mentions that a basic article such as Mao Tse-tung's "Serve the People" might be studied several times during the year, and each time students tried to think of something new and different to put in their comprehension reports. Tai feels that the diaries and study reports were not too effective in influencing student attitudes, since they were written with their audience (the *pan chu-jen*) clearly in mind. Many students wrote up these materials fairly carelessly, and they were not given heavy emphasis by the *pan chu-jen*.

In 1965 new kinds of political activities were initiated. One was the "red pair" activity (*yi-tui-hung*). The idea was that an activist student should be teamed up with a relatively backward student, and the two of them should have frequent heart-to-heart talks on political topics in order to bring the backward member up to the other's level. If both members of the pair could be selected as five-good students at the end of the term, they could be called a red pair. But there were inherent conflicts between the five-good and red pair activities. The more activist member of each pair was trying to distinguish himself from other students in order to be judged five-good, and he was often disinclined to share the spotlight with his partner. The more backward members in turn often resented the patronizing airs of some of their tutors. In any case after a "high tide" of red pair formation one semester, this activity fell off and ceased to be important.

Later in 1965 two other activities were added. First there were the meetings held to tell the uses of Mao Tse-tung's thought (Mao Tse-tung *ssu-hsiang chiang-yung-hui*). All students read various writings by Chairman Mao and then wrote essays on ways in which they had put Mao's ideas into practice. In response to this and other activities (particularly the study of heroes) the school was swept by waves of good deeds. Students got up early to clean their dormitory rooms or to mend a classmate's clothing, and then wrote about how Mao's thought had inspired them to perform these deeds. Tai mentions some humorous aspects of this activity. Students racked their brains for novel good deeds to perform, and an innovation by one student led to many imitations. Also many students performed acts unselfconsciously which they later gave Mao credit for. For instance Tai and a classmate once found a lost child wandering around the school grounds and helped her find her way home. He felt this act was motivated by simple human kindness, but later they both included it in their reports on the use of Mao's thoughts and received a good deal of praise. Tai also notes that a fair amount of ambivalence existed toward some kinds of good deeds. One member of Tai's *hsiao-tsu* went to get wash water for his roommates and received not praise but criticism from the others, who said they could easily get the water themselves. In the highly competitive atmosphere of this school it was often better to perform a good deed that was impersonal than to help another person since the recipient might interpret the deed as an effort to put him in a bad light.

After the reports on applying Mao's thoughts were written, students read them out in class meetings. Then the best essays were chosen, and the authors represented the class by reading these essays before an all-school assembly. There all 750 students listened to the best examples of how to apply Mao's thoughts and then returned to their classrooms to discuss what they had learned.

A similar activity of this period was the writing of family histories (*chia-shih*). Each student wrote about some features of his family's past, with the emphasis on the exploitation and suffering experienced prior to 1949. The purpose was to strengthen class (in the socio-economic sense) feelings and to keep students from forgetting the need for continual struggle against class enemies. Again classroom meetings were held at which students read aloud their compositions. And again the best essays were selected for presentation in all-school assemblies. Tai states that many of these essays were vivid and tragic, and that in the assemblies many of the girls broke into tears upon hearing them. Most of the students, including Tai, took this activity quite seriously and were moved by what they heard. On reflecting upon these sessions later in Hong Kong, Tai was suspicious that many of the details in these family histories were false, culled from novels and newspapers of the period. But at the time such doubts had not arisen. The Mao's-thought-use and family history meetings were held about once a month, the former somewhat more frequently than the latter.

Besides these organized political activities, there was also much individual ideological work to be done upon students. Tai and his fellow student officers were constantly on the lookout for students who were dissatisfied, who were having problems, or who were not participating fully in school life. The officers consulted and picked one of their number to have an individual talk with such a student. There was a general form used in such talks, called a "heart-to-heart talk" (*t'an-hsin*). First the cadre inquired about whether the student was feeling well and how his family was. After this initial show of concern he went on to mention the specific problem or failing and explore its origins. This method of approaching problems was felt to be more effective than simply criticizing a student, either individually or in a group meeting. It is interesting to note that generally male cadres were designated to talk to female students and female cadres to male students. This was not due to any romantic interests, for in this school the official strictures against young romance were pretty rigidly observed, i.e., there wasn't any. Rather this approach seems related to the competitive atmosphere which had developed. Apparently the competition for scarce political honors did not extend too much across the sex line, perhaps because the *hsiao-tsu* in which evaluations took place were separated by sex. If a male tried to do "thought work" on another male (or female on another female) it would be resented more than in the mixed sex situation.

There were, finally, many miscellaneous activities designed to affect student political attitudes. Each class organized propaganda teams which prepared skits, songs, and speeches on political themes. Representatives of these teams were formed into an all-school propaganda team which went outside of the school to conduct propaganda. In periods away from school on work assignments political activities were continued. Twice a year the students went to a rural commune to engage in agricultural labor. In the countryside, meetings for the study of Mao's thought were held every evening, and students lived with local peasants and interviewed them about their past sufferings. Also, the commune organized older peasants to "speak bitterness" to their guests about life under the Nationalists. And students tried to do good deeds for local peasants. All these activities, not just the work performed, were considered in picking labor activists at the conclusion of each rural work stint. In the summer of 1965 many of the students went to work in a nearby factory rather than going home. During this period the regular evening study sessions were kept up, and students sat in on the political meetings of the workers. Tai was so impressed by the strict political atmosphere of his technical school that he wrote a letter to one of his lower middle school teachers, advising him of ways to improve the lax political atmosphere of his school.

The highly politicized nature of the technical school certainly led to changes in the behavior of students. Tai says that during this period he was able to get over some of his timidity and throw himself into running student activities and doing ideological work among his fellow students. The impact of these activities on student attitudes, however, is less certain. The Chinese press in this and later periods has been filled with tales of ideological transformations: the evil and selfish individual who, upon reading some of Mao's writings, sees the light and resolves to follow Mao's teachings. But in Tai's school an unexpressed but strong suspicion greeted any similar claims to ideological progress. While the students felt they had few serious ideological problems, they recognized that there were no selfless individuals in the mold of the heroes Lei Feng and Wang Chieh among them, nor were any likely to arise. Student cadres and activists were in the paradoxical situation of encouraging their more backward mates to progress ideologically, but at the same time being unhappy and skeptical when these students claimed such progress, since this would undermine their own special prestige. Tai gives an example of one student who was very activist and who qualified for Youth League membership under any criteria, but was voted down when he applied for admission, apparently simply because his admission would have made the entrenched Youth League officers seem less activist by comparison. Tai does not see his former classmates as totally individualistic and scheming, however. Rather, they had a general mixture of selfish and altruistic motives, a mixture Tai does not think changed too much over time. Students of various motivations and degrees of activism generally phrased much of their discourse in ideological terms. Nobody felt hypocritical about using lofty words about the class struggle or serving the people to characterize and justify his ordinary daily activities. This language had become the accepted form of discourse. Whatever the alteration in the students' underlying attitudes, the fact that they at least analyzed situations and actions in ideological terms must be considered an important kind of thought reform.

There were few examples of student misbehavior and mischief in the technical school. Tai feels that there was virtually no cheating. The disciplinary tone was set very early, when one student cheated on a test by looking at his textbook. After the examination he reported on himself and declared he did not want the grade. He was praised by the teachers for his confession, and the other students were somewhat amazed, never having heard of such an incident before. After this there was no cheating that Tai was aware of. There were no other major instances of student misbehavior that Tai can recall, and for the most part individual talks and *hsiao-tsu* criticism sessions succeeded in solving or squelching problems before they got out of control. The impression Tai gives is of students highly motivated to conform to the strict discipline of the school, although many kinds of checks and reports on individual behavior reinforced this self-control.[28]

The major problem in the political atmosphere was that interpersonal conflicts went unresolved. The tensions of competition were aggravated by the regional and linguistic differences among students. The students came from all over Kwangtung province and tended to herd together into five groups on the basis of their regional origins: the Canton city region, the Hakka areas of northern Kwangtung, the Swatow area in Northeastern Kwangtung, the T'aishan area in the south, and Hainan Island. Initially the students from different areas had to speak Mandarin to communicate, since their local dialects were partly or completely unintelligible to each other. In the initial period of homesickness, students tended to congregate with people from their home area, with whom they could communicate easily. When school got started, however, all the student organizations cut across these regional lines, and students were urged to overcome their attitudes of localism (ti-fang chu-yi).

This proved to be a difficult task. Regional loyalties and conflicts continued to create problems right up to the Cultural Revolution. Tai's closest friends, as mentioned, were from the same region, but in different classrooms. Tai was proud of the relatively high number of student leaders who came from his region, and he tended to feel superior to students from some of the other areas, particularly those from Canton, who tended to be more bourgeois (for example, they were flashier dressers) and less involved in student affairs than other students. Tai had a sort of paternal feeling for other students from his area, and he made special efforts to help them adjust and keep out of trouble. With close friends from home Tai would often downplay the ideological jargon and tell of his dislike for certain other students or give them tips on how to get on the right side of the principal and other authorities.

Localism was vividly illustrated by the situation in Tai's own hsiao-tsu. The seven members of the group tended to form two factions. The leading faction consisted of Tai and two others from his home area, one of whom was the hsiao-tsu head while the other served as class labor officer. They tended to support each other in arguments with the other four members, who were informally led by Wang Hei-jen, the

---

28. Here we should note that Tai may be exaggerating the good behavior of fellow students. Since he was a class officer assigned to deal with deviants, students so inclined could be expected to conceal their misbehavior from him if possible.

League organizational officer (later switched to propaganda officer). These four came from two of the other regions of Kwangtung province. Tai Hsiao-ai and Wang Hei-jen detested each other, and Tai says for his part this feeling stemmed from an early selection of activists in which Wang Hei-jen had spread false rumors about Tai in order to keep him from being selected. From then on the two were constantly in conflict. Various efforts were made to reconcile them. In livelihood self-examination meetings each confessed that he had been harboring a dislike for the other, and then they pledged to try to work together and forget past feelings. They conducted similar self-criticisms in class cadre and Youth League meetings. For a short time after such a meeting the two might get on tolerably well, but then some new incident would reignite the hostilities, and the cycle would start all over again. The conflict between Tai and Wang was only one of many such conflicts among students, although perhaps one of the more acrimonious. Individual talks and group meetings could not remove the basic causes of such conflicts, which were rooted in regional differences and personal rivalry.

Tai notes that over time the importance of regional differences tended to decline somewhat as students developed friends from other regions, and all learned Cantonese, which came to be the language of informal discourse. In the case of Tai's own *hsiao-tsu* the decline in regional solidarity did not result in wider unity, but in an even more Hobbesian world. First one of the four members of Wang Hei-jen's faction "defected" because his faction-mates had been picking on him. Soon after Wang's faction fell apart the same thing happened to Tai's clique. The *hsiao-tsu* head coveted the job of the labor officer, and so he criticized the latter for being a poor laborer. Tai Hsiao-ai supported the labor officer and succeeded in getting him re-elected, but as a result he alienated the *hsiao-tsu* head. The result by early 1966 was general bickering and resentment within the group.

In June of 1966, as Tai Hsiao-ai completed his second year in the school, the Cultural Revolution broke into full bloom, and during the next year and a half until he left China the tight organizational structure we have described fell apart and new forms emerged. We do not have room here to discuss the drama of the Cultural Revolution in this school in detail,[29] but certain events of the period are of interest for the light they throw on the strength of the relationships and

---

29. Tai's account of the Cultural Revolution has been published in book form. See Gordon Bennett and Ronald Montaperto, *Red Guard* (New York: Doubleday, 1971).

attitudes which were built up among the students in the previous two years.

In the initial stage of the Cultural Revolution in this school the existing organizational structure changed little. The principal directed the students to attack ten of the teachers, who had been singled out by the Party branch as "demons and monsters" (*niu-kuei she-shen*) who had a bourgeois influence upon students. After a few weeks of this activity the students became disenchanted with the extent to which the principal was pulling the strings, particularly when they heard that in other schools in the area students were organizing their own Cultural Revolution activities. The students succeeded, as they did in many other schools, in getting a work team sent by the Provincial Party Committee to take over the direction of the campaign from the school Party branch and the principal. The work team rehabilitated the ten teachers and then organized the students to begin attacking the "powerholders," i.e., the principal and other leading cadres. The work team dissolved the old *hsiao-tsu* and formed new organizations. Many of the former classroom cadres were organized into a core small group (*ho-hsin hsiao-tsu*) which was responsible for leading class activities, under the supervision of the work team. Several activists from the class were then organized into a shock small group (*t'u-chi hsiao-tsu*) which was supposed to set an example for other students by participating actively in writing wall posters and similar activities. The remaining students were formed into five combat groups (*chan-tou-tsu*), with male and female students now mixed together.

During this period the students divided their attentions between studying Mao's works and collecting and posting criticisms of the former school leadership. Classes had long since been suspended (it was July now anyway), and students gave all their energies to these activities. The Youth League and the *pan chu-jen* ceased to play an important role in the school, and, as dormitory *hsiao-tsu* ceased being units for evaluation and criticism, roommate tensions eased somewhat.

By August the work team had left, under attack in this school as elsewhere for directing student activities too strictly and stifling mass initiative, just as the principal had done at an earlier stage. In the ensuing period the combat groups fell apart, and students gradually formed new kinds of groupings from which Red Guard organizations eventually emerged. With direct supervision and control gone, it is interesting to examine what the bases for these new groupings were. In October of 1966 Tai Hsiao-ai and some other students formed one such Red Guard group. At first they had only fifteen members, although they later grew in size. All but two of the original members came from Tai's home region, and included the other two students from this area in his original *hsiao-tsu*. But only four of these original members came from Tai's classroom, the others belonging to other classes and even classes in different grades.[30] This group was not based simply upon regional loyalties and friendships, however; in fact, Tai's former best friends had a falling out with him, and they ended up in other groups. These friends did not get along well with one of the leading students in the new faction, but there was also an ideological issue involved. This concerned the hereditary nature of political purity. Before the Cultural Revolution students from the "five kinds of red" backgrounds (*hung-wu-lei*—poor peasant, lower middle peasant, worker, revolutionary cadre, or revolutionary soldier) made up about 30 per cent of the student body and monopolized the leadership posts. When the first Red Guard organization was formed these same students tried to control things by restricting its membership to students with the same class backgrounds. Tai, in spite of his own qualification on these grounds, felt that this limitation was wrong, that behavior and not class background should be the measure of redness or political loyalty. Opposition to the five kinds of red restriction was one factor uniting the 15 students who joined with Tai Hsiao-ai to form a new Red Guard group. In opposing the five kinds of red limitation Tai was breaking with his former best friends, who supported this restriction. Thus the bases for group formation were complex. Tai explains that those who formed factions tended to share similar views and to get along well together. Getting along meant in many, but not all, cases being with people from one's home area. Similar ideas often, but not always, meant the same class background and the same former position in the student leadership hierarchy. In later months, however, these principles broke down as people switched back and forth between competing factions.

In late 1966 and in 1967 the focus of activities shifted increasingly away from attacking the school's "power holders" to outside activities. Increasing amounts of time were spent away from the school in various activities: raiding private houses to destroy the four olds, traveling to Peking to exchange revolutionary experiences, visiting nearby factories, and joining factional allies for battle in the city of Canton.[31]

---

30. In a published account about a school in Shanghai the pattern was somewhat different, with entire classrooms joining the same Red Guard factions together, which may indicate greater classroom solidarity to begin with than existed in Tai's school. See Neale Hunter, *Far Eastern Economic Review*, June 22, 1967.

31. See the detailed account in Gordon Bennett and Ronald Montaperto, *Red Guard, op. cit.*

The faction increasingly replaced the school as the meaningful social unit, and large and opposing factional alliances emerged in the city of Canton which recruited their support from competing Red Guard groups in different schools, factories, and other organizations. All systematic Mao study and other organized political indoctrination now ceased as students threw themselves into unsupervised Red Guard activities: collecting information about opposing factions, preparing for battles, etc. When organizational control was removed Tai's fellow students did not drop the ideological jargon and start openly advocating personal or regional interests. Rather the rhetoric of Maoism, which had formerly been used to combat factionalism, now was put forth by all sides in justification of the ever more bitter conflicts between groups. Each faction felt that it was ideologically correct, while its opponents were motivated by hypocritical and selfish motives. Without a strong Party to interpret and implement this ideology, the Maoist faith which had been built up in the previous period served as an intensifier of conflict rather than as a source of unity.

During 1967 Tai experienced a growing sense of disillusionment with Red Guard activities, partly because the Red Flag faction which Tai's Red Guard group attached itself to experienced a number of severe defeats in battles with the rival East Wind faction. The East Winders received considerable support from the Army, apparently with the tacit consent of Mao Tse-tung himself. Tai began to feel that he and other Red Guards were being cynically used by Mao for his own purposes, and that loyalty to Mao was not being appropriately rewarded. These feelings were reinforced by advice he received from friends of his family on a visit home, and his depression deepened. When an opportunity arose late in 1967 he escaped to Hong Kong.

GENERAL PATTERNS AND CONTRASTS

Here we will review apparent reasons for the differences between the political atmospheres of the two middle schools attended by Tai Hsiao-ai in our effort to gain further insight into the organizational variables which affect the political atmosphere.

First, there was an important difference in the external environment. Tai entered lower middle school during a period of relative calm in terms of national political campaigns, while during his years in technical school political campaigns and pressures escalated nationwide. This external factor is not by itself sufficient to explain the differences, since some of my other informants mention a relatively lax political atmosphere in their middle schools even in the years 1964–

1966. In other words, some schools seem to be more responsive to changes in national policy and emphasis than others. Perhaps the greater responsiveness of Tai's technical school was due to the fact that this was a provincial level school rather than a county or city run school.

The technical school also possessed stronger internal political leadership than Tai's lower middle school, represented by the powerful ex-military principal and the strong Party representation among teachers. As a technical school transmitting occupational skills rather than preparing students for college there was automatically less emphasis on pure academics than in most general middle schools, and consequently more room for politics. This school was very selective and chose students who were already relatively activist in politics. The students felt a sense of honor to be studying in such a special school, a feeling less characteristic of students in general middle schools. It was also a boarding school, which meant that students, particularly those from areas outside Canton, were isolated from outside reference groups and had their energies and attentions focused inward on school affairs. Partly for this reason the school and the classrooms and *hsiao-tsu* within it were regarded by students more as important social units and less as mere administrative conveniences than was the case in Tai's lower middle school. The students, in addition to being selected in part for their high levels of political activism, were simply older and more mature than lower middle school students, and thus could be expected to be more capable of organizing and leading their own activities. Student leaders were given important roles to play, and as a result students saw discipline and political pressures coming from their classmates rather than simply from school authorities.

The result of all these and perhaps other differences was that the political atmosphere in Tai's technical school was much stricter than in his lower middle school. Cheating on exams, mutual protection of friends, lack of concern for political activities, and unwillingness to criticize others were all virtually absent from Tai's technical middle school. But as a byproduct of the provincial level of this school and the heavy emphasis placed on gaining political honors there was a competitive atmosphere which somewhat undercut the effectiveness of the political atmosphere. Students saw criticism not as a sincere and constructive effort to help them progress ideologically, but as an effort to put them in a bad light so that their critics could monopolize the political honors. Those who were singled out for praise did tend to guard their special status jealously and view competitors suspiciously.

It should be emphasized again that this competitive atmosphere was not the result of some sort of "bourgeois academic" emphasis on grades but of a very different, even contrary, emphasis on developing political purity.

How do these two middle schools compare with the schools described by my other informants? In general the organizational structure of middle schools of various types does not seem to vary too much. The political atmosphere described for other middle schools, both upper and lower, tends to fit the lax pattern of Tai's lower middle school. Some informants mention that no five-good competitions were initiated in their schools, while others mention daily study of Mao's writings starting only in 1966, two years after Tai had begun this activity. As one might expect, there tended to be a stronger emphasis on academics in these other schools than in Tai's technical school. In most other accounts ideological work was conducted by teachers with some help from Youth League officers, while classroom officers confined their activities to non-political matters. Thus the Youth League often has more of a vanguard role than Tai describes. Several of my other informants mention more bitter conflict between students of good and bad class status and between activists and backward elements than Tai describes for either of his middle schools. And my other informants generally feel that their *hsiao-tsu* were poorly led and organized and lacked a sense of solidarity.

Students were also in most other accounts not so involved in school life and activities as in Tai's technical school, but preserved private lives and outside friends as in Tai's lower middle school. Many other middle schools have boarding facilities, but often only for a minority of students who live too far away to commute easily. Even schools which do have boarding facilities do not always make these the locus of political activities. It is interesting to note that since the Cultural Revolution much attention has been given in the press to the fact that students in the past had free time after school which they often used in non-constructive ways, i.e., in ways which undercut the political pressures developed within the schools. Recently extensive efforts have been made to develop organized after-school activities for youth which will carry over the political pressures developed during school hours.[32]

Several of my other informants mention poor quality political leadership from the *pan chu-jen* and other teachers. The expansion of edu-

<hr>

32. See, for example, *Kuang-ming Jih-pao*, April 3, 1968; *Jen-min Jih-pao*, April 15, 1971.

cation since 1949 in China has led to serious problems in training sufficient teachers to meet the demand,[33] and even many of the teachers trained since 1949 seem ill equipped for their role as political tutors. This may be due in part to changing mobility patterns. The status of teachers is not as high as in traditional China, but teaching is still looked upon as an honorable profession by many, particularly by youth from the former middle and upper classes. Students of worker and poor peasant backgrounds who do well in school may be channeled upward to careers in political leadership or science, while students from the former bourgeois classes who are screened out from such positions may find teaching an attractive alternative. In any case my informants (including the teachers I interviewed) state that a large percentage of even young middle school teachers come from such "bourgeois" backgrounds. These teachers are in a strange position when it comes to leading activities designed to increase the proletarian consciousness of their students. Perhaps for this reason, during the Cultural Revolution one of the reforms of the educational system proposed was the abolition of the post of *pan chu-jen*. The *pan chu-jen* was charged with having a harmful ideological influence on his students.[34]

Viewed together these other student accounts tend to highlight the distinctiveness of Tai's technical school. The strict political atmosphere in this school was apparently due to the joint operation of several factors (selectivity of students, strong Party representation among the teachers, de-emphasis on academics, boarding school), which seem rarely to be found together in other Chinese middle schools.

There are certain general features of Chinese middle schools and the political rituals within them which set them off from other kinds of organizations. Political rituals seem to be somewhat more formal and highly structured among students than among cadres, although perhaps not as highly formalized as in the ideal political rituals described in Chapter 4. For students part of this activity is connected with a formal political course, an element lacking in other organizations. In almost all the political activities of students there is a strong emphasis on instruction and on learning new concepts rather than on rectifying old attitudes. Students are not generally considered to have evil pasts of which they must rid themselves. Rather their minds are

---

33. T.H.E. Chen, *Teacher Training in Communist China* (Washington, D.C.: U.S. Office of Education, 1960).

34. This and other reforms are contained in Central Committee draft recommendations translated in *China Topics*, May 23, 1967.

seen as a *tabula rasa,* to be filled with correct thoughts. This makes student political rituals somewhat different from cadre political rituals. Mutual criticism tends to be muted, and students are not subjected to constant rectifications or struggle meetings. We can see this contrast by looking back at the new political activities of the 1960's described by Tai Hsiao-ai on the one hand and by Ma Kan-pu on the other. For instance, in Ma's unit family histories were written primarily to get cadres to confess unrevealed skeletons in family closets and to assume a sense of guilt for past family misdeeds. The family histories written in Tai's school were designed simply to bring out any incidents which might heighten class sentiments among the students. Middle schools up until the Cultural Revolution also tended to be isolated from many of the political campaigns of these years, or to experience them in milder forms than did cadres and other segments of the population. In many cases campaigns were studied rather than participated in, and even when students did participate they were not subjected to the systematic rectifications that cadres experienced. Partly as a byproduct of this emphasis on instruction rather than on thought reform and rectification, there tended to be little relative mobility within the student power structure. Most of my informants noted that students with the proper qualifications (such as Tai) tended to be noticed at an early age and placed in positions of leadership. In a new school it was generally students who had held such positions in previous schools who were nominated to hold them again. In later elections there might be a fair amount of switching around of jobs among student leaders, but little vertical mobility. With no rectification campaigns to "purge" student leaders, the opportunity for other students to move up was limited.

Some of the preceding generalizations need to be qualified when we look at universities. In organizational details, universities are not far different from middle schools. Students are organized into departments, and within departments into subjects and specialties. Students in the smallest subdivision (e.g., first year students of English within a foreign languages department) are considered a class and are further subdivided into *hsiao-tsu.* The student association, the Youth League, and even particular class offices tend to correspond to those of middle schools. Evidence for the position of *pan chu-jen* at the university level is conflicting, with some of my informants mentioning such a position and others denying its existence. I am unable to explain this disagreement.

Universities tend more often than middle schools to have students living in dormitories, as in Tai's technical school, and thus relatively isolated from outside influences. Students are again somewhat older and more mature, more capable of assuming leadership positions. At this level a greater percentage of students are generally Youth League members, and some may start to join the Communist Party. The Youth League and other student organizations tend to play an important vanguard and leadership role in universities, directly under Party supervision (without extensive mediation by teachers, as in middle schools). A critical feature differentiating universities from middle schools is the breakdown of the isolation from political events and campaigns. The universities' importance in training future elites and their visibility makes them more sensitive to changes in national political moods than institutions at lower levels. University students participate directly in political campaigns and undergo rectification campaigns much like cadres. The general effect of all of these differences is to give universities a somewhat stricter political atmosphere than most middle schools. However, this may not always be so. In periods in which academics are stressed and grades are emphasized more than politics in selecting students for these institutions, the greater responsiveness of universities may lead to a sudden loosening of the internal political atmosphere. Also, the conflict between "bourgeois academics" and political authorities seems to be sharper in universities than in middle schools.

In the 1960's political rituals were developed fairly extensively within China's student population. But a variety of features of school organization and student life tended to make the political atmosphere in schools, particularly in the lower grades, less strict than that existing in many cadre organizations. School authorities were able to control and influence the behavior of the students during school hours. However, there was growing concern that not only were schools not properly inculcating the correct political attitudes among the "revolutionary successor" generation, but also that schools were often themselves the source of many harmful attitudes. In the Cultural Revolution the educational system ground to a halt, and in its wake extensive reforms are being implemented. It remains to be seen whether these changes, designed in large part to create a stricter political atmosphere within schools, can successfully overcome the kinds of organizational problems discussed in this chapter.

VII

PEASANTS AND
POLITICAL RITUALS

The Chinese Communists have succeeded in breaking down the isolation and inertia of the peasant village as no earlier Chinese government had. The ruling elites of traditional dynasties valued this inertia, since it enabled them to pursue minimal goals in rural areas (primarily tax collection and the prevention of disorders) with a remarkably small bureaucracy.[1] Although periodic efforts were made through a variety of devices, such as the *pao-chia* system (described in Chapter 3) to extend imperial control to the villages, for the most part local power remained in the hands of village and clan elders who emerged naturally from the rural social structure.

The Kuomintang decried the inertia of peasant villages and made some efforts to effect rural social change and bring the peasantry into national life. The governmental bureaucracy was extended below the county level to the township (*hsiang*), the *pao-chia* system was revived, and under a variety of auspices efforts were made to extend rural education, develop peasant cooperatives, and introduce other changes.[2] However, on a nationwide scale the Nationalists were unable to mo-

---

1. See Kung-chuan Hsiao, *Rural China: Imperial Control in the Nineteenth Century* (Seattle: University of Washington Press, 1967).

2. See Sidney D. Gamble, *Ting Hsien* (New York: Institute of Pacific Relations, 1954); James C. Thomson, Jr., *While China Faced West* (Cambridge, Mass.: Harvard University Press, 1969), Chaps. 3–6; and Lucien Bianco, *Origins of the Chinese Revolution, 1915–1949* (Stanford, Stanford University Press, 1971), Chap. 5.

bilize the peasantry for social change with much success, and, particularly in later years, were increasingly unwilling to as well. Of course, the strife and upheavals of the first half of the twentieth century did a great deal to force an awareness of national events upon rural villagers. But the completion of the process, the penetration of the government into the daily affairs of peasant villages, occurred only under the Communists.

The Chinese Communists developed their ideas and skills in rural organization over three decades of desperate struggle for popular support, and in the Yenan years they perfected most of the techniques they would use in organizing villages after 1949. In rural affairs the Soviet model was less important than in other policy realms, such as education and industry. In fact, the Soviet model of forced collectivization, accompanied by dreadful social costs and problems that continue to this day, served more as a negative example. The Chinese Communist elite knew how to go about penetrating and gaining support within villages, while their Soviet predecessors clearly did not.[3] The Soviets could absorb the drop in production that resulted from collectivization in order to gain greater central control over agricultural deliveries to the cities, but Chinese authorities could not so easily afford such a drop, since Chinese villages were generally closer to subsistence minimums. The requirements of fighting a guerrilla war against Japan and the Kuomintang and later of pursuing ambitious development plans made it necessary to avoid alienting the peasantry by arbitrary measures of external coercion. During the Yenan period numerous measures were adopted to develop close ties between the villages and the ruling Communist elite. The final culmination of these efforts was the land reform, carried out in areas of North China in 1946–1948 and in the rest of the country during 1950–1952. As Ezra Vogel has pointed out, land reform involved much more than simply redistributing land from the rich to the poor. It led to the consolidation of Communist control over village life throughout China.[4]

The tactics of land reform varied in different periods and areas, with a primary difference between many northern villages, where land reform was preceded by years of earlier Communist organizational ef-

3. See Thomas P. Bernstein, "Leadership and Mass Mobilization in the Soviet and Chinese Collectivization Campaigns of 1929–30 and 1955–56: A Comparison," in *China Quarterly*, no. 31, July–September 1967.

4. Ezra F. Vogel, *Canton under Communism* (Cambridge, Mass.: Harvard University Press, 1969), Chap. 3.

forts, and villages in the south that had recently been under Kuomintang control.[5] But a brief review of the "ideal stages" of the land reform process can give us some notion of the careful planning that
went into revolutionizing the rural social structure.[6] The land reform
effort was initiated by specially trained teams of organizers, the land
reform work teams, which were dispersed into the villages. The work
team members were supposed to seek out elements in the village who
had grievances against the status quo (poor peasants, women and
youth with grievances against the family system, and minority clans
and nationalities who resented their inferior positions). Through intimate talks with these selected peasants, work team members were
supposed to get them to connect their grievances to the existing class
structure within the village. This process was known as "speaking bitterness and digging out the roots" (su-k'u wa-ken). Once some of the
peasants had been brought around to making these connections, they
were urged to recruit some of their friends to join in the discussions.
In this manner the work team cultivated a widening network of supporters from among the village disgruntled and oppressed. These individuals would form the basis for new organizations which would solid-
ify the separate identity of the formerly exploited (e.g., a peasant
association with landlords and rich peasants excluded, a women's association, a militia drawing heavily on activist youth). Through this
process the old orientations of villagers versus outsiders or fellow clan
members (rich and poor) versus members of rival clans were supposed
to give way to a new primary social cleavage, that between the former
village elite and the rest of the village population. The complex ties
of kinship, mutual aid, and joint social life which cut across class
lines had to be severed by promoting class struggle.

Once a core of support for the work team and its class analysis had
been developed, the new organizations took action against individual

---

5. For a variety of discussions of the land reform campaign and the problems it
confronted, consult David and Isabel Crook, *Revolution in a Chinese Village: Ten
Mile Inn* (London: Routledge and Kegan Paul, 1959); C. K. Yang, *A Chinese Village in Early Communist Transition* (Cambridge, Mass.: MIT Press, 1959); Ezra
Vogel, *op. cit.*; Franz Schurmann, *Ideology and Organization in Communist China*,
2nd ed. (Berkeley and Los Angeles: University of California Press, 1968), Chap. 7;
William Hinton, *Fanshen* (New York: Vintage Books, 1966); and G. William Skinner, "Aftermath of Communist Liberation in the Chengtu Plain," in *Pacific Affairs*,
Vol. 24, no. 1, 1951.

6. These stages are abstracted from a review of press articles about land reform
primarily in the south, such as *Nan-fang Jih-pao*, January 4, 1952, March 22, 1952,
July 4, 1952, July 9, 1952, July 31, 1952, September 3, 1952; *Ch'ang-chiang Jih-pao*,
March 10, 1952.

members of the former elite for past injustices, thus demonstrating
the vulnerability of the rich to concerted mass action of the poor. The
climactic form of mass action came in the struggle meetings which
preceded the actual redistribution of land. Redistribution of land
without struggle was viewed as unsatisfactory. If the members of the
former elite were not thoroughly humiliated, they could use their
old ties and influence to regain authority. In 1927, in his "Report on
an investigation of the peasant movement in Hunan," Mao Tse-tung
had outlined this tactic:

This sort of thing is very common. A tall paper-hat is stuck on the head of
one of the local tyrants or evil gentry, bearing the words "Local tyrant so-
and-so" or "So-and-so of the evil gentry." He is led by a rope and escorted
with big crowds in front and behind. Sometimes brass gongs are beaten and
flags waved to attract people's attention. This form of punishment more than
any other makes the local tyrants and evil gentry tremble. Anyone who has
once been crowned with a tall paper-hat loses face altogether and can never
again hold up his head.[7]

In addition, if the new "activists" did not lead the way in struggling
the former elite, they would not be "steeled in struggle" and would
not provide reliable and dynamic leadership in the future. And without struggle the bulk of the peasants who were "middle-of-the-roaders"
could not be pushed into taking sides and joining the revolution.
Therefore members of the former elite were paraded in front of the
other villagers and subjected to struggle in all its colorful forms:
spoken bitterness, demands for redress of specific grievances, threats,
demands for confessions and signs of humility. If their earlier work
had been done well, the work team members could sit on the sidelines
and leave the running of these struggle meetings to the newly recruited activists.[8]

In practice land reform often was far different from this ideal form.
In some villages the peasants stuck together in fear and distrust of
the outside organizers, and violence and threats were used to drive
a wedge into the village. The zeal of both the outside organizers and
their new rural recruits produced a reign of revolutionary terror in
many areas, in which members of the former elite and their supporters in other classes were not only humiliated, but also beaten, tor-
tured, and executed. Some activists used the struggle process to settle

7. Mao Tse-tung, *Selected Works of Mao Tse-tung*, Vol. I (Peking: Foreign Languages Press, 1967), p. 37.
8. It should be noted that in many northern villages the stages were somewhat
different, since local leadership responsive to higher Communist authorities had
already been built up during the pre-land reform period.

old scores with personal enemies, and sometimes took advantage of their new power to enrich themselves and to seduce local women. On the other hand, in some villages land reform was characterized as simply "walking across the stage," that is, redistributing land without much class struggle. In such villages the mass of the population might sullenly go along as the work team pushed through village reforms. In other cases landlords and traditional elites managed to worm their way into positions of leadership in the new organizations. The great variety of village conditions throughout China and their varied responses to the land reform campaign make generalization extremely difficult. Nonetheless it seems clear that, in spite of these "deviations," the result of the land reform campaign was a fundamental change in the rural social structure, with newly recruited elites displacing former elites and taking charge of a wide variety of new organizations which had been established in the countryside, all under the supervision of rural Party authorities.

The land reform campaign was followed by a re-examination stage, designed to correct a variety of abuses, and then a consolidation stage. Consolidation was aimed at maintaining the momentum and spirit built up during land reform in order to carry through other rural changes. Peasants were enrolled in spare time literacy and political study classes, activists were given special leadership training, and those who had distinguished themselves during land reform were recruited into the Party and the Youth League. Health campaigns and newspaper study groups were initiated, and production mutual aid groups were established. But running counter to these efforts was the strong desire on the part of many peasants and activists to sit back and enjoy the fruits of land reform or simply to concentrate on the ever pressing demands of farming.[9]

In the years since the land reform campaign, peasant involvement in political activities has been subject not only to the dialectical shifts in policy originating from Peking, but also to the seasonal fluctuations of rural work. At no time have all peasants been involved in regular political study and mutual criticism as these take place in *hsiao-tsu* in other settings, and the smallest work units (mutual aid teams, later work groups and production teams) have not carried out these political rituals as have urban work groups.[10] Rural cadres and activ-

---

9. See Thomas P. Bernstein, "Problems of Village Leadership after Land Reform," in *China Quarterly*, no. 36, October–December 1968.

10. There are occasional reports of well run rural newspaper reading and study groups in these early years. See, for instance, *Nan-fang Jih-pao*, June 2, 1952; *Jen-min Jih-pao*, January 20, 1955.

ists have been involved in some kinds of political study on a regular basis, and during the high tides of campaigns and during some agricultural slack seasons increasing numbers of ordinary peasants have been involved in such activities as well. However, in the lulls between campaigns and during agricultural busy seasons, attentions have shifted back to the enduring problem of getting enough to eat, and even cadres' and activists' political life has often been neglected. Subsequent campaigns (collectivization, communization, rural socialist education) have attempted to reinvolve the mass of the peasants in village and national political life using many techniques similar to those of land reform: outside work teams, cultivating new activists, speaking bitterness, and struggling the remaining members of the former elite. But after each "high tide" this involvement has fallen off, as peasants returned to farming and family concerns. Whenever this happens the potential for the re-emergence of traditional autonomous groups based on kinship and clan loyalty is strengthened, and this re-emergence was apparently particularly forceful during the economic crisis of 1960–1962.[11]

Since 1963 there has been a more sustained effort to reorient peasants toward broader commune and national concerns and programs. In this period, particularly in the wake of the Cultural Revolution, there have been a variety of efforts to develop among the ordinary peasants group political rituals very similar to those of urban dwellers. In some cases this has even taken the form of family study groups, in which a child leads members of the group, particularly his parents, in criticizing their selfishness and political backwardness, in the hopes of earning the honorary title "all red family" (ch'uan-chia-hung).[12]

---

11. See, for example, C. S. Chen, ed., *Rural People's Communes in Lien-chiang*, trans. by Charles P. Ridley (Stanford: Hoover Institution Press, 1969); and John W. Lewis, *Leadership in Communist China* (Ithaca: Cornell University Press, 1963), pp. 235–238.

12. *New China News Agency* (Peking), April 8, 1969; *Jen-min Jih-pao*, June 11, 1968; Wen Hui Pao (Shanghai), August 29, 1969, trans. in *Survey of the China Mainland Press*, no. 4263; *Jen-min Jih-pao*, December 7, 1968; *Kuang-ming Jih-pao*, December 9, 1968; *Kuang-ming Jih-pao*, December 17, 1968; *New China News Agency* (Canton), January 9, 1969; *Wen Hui Pao* (Hong Kong), January 9, 1969; *Kuang-ming Jih-pao*, January 13, 1969; *New China News Agency* (Nanking), January 23, 1969; *Wen Hui Pao* (Hong Kong), February 9, 1969; *New China News Agency* (Tsinan), February 10, 1969; *Kuang-ming Jih-pao*, February 26, 1969; *Jen-min Jih-pao*, February 6, February 14, May 13, and May 14, 1969.

CHANG NUNG-MIN: A SUBURBAN PEASANT YOUTH

Chang Nung-min was 23 in 1969, when I interviewed him in five sessions for a total of fifteen hours.[13] At the time of land reform his
family was classified as a rich peasant household. They had farmed
some of their land themselves, but they still rented out enough and
exploited others enough to be included among the "four bad elements," [14] although they were treated more leniently than those classified as landlords. Chang's parents felt their children had no future in
the countryside because of the stigma of bad class status,[15] and they
strongly encouraged their children to study hard and get ahead
through education. Chang tried to follow this advice, even studying
for a time with a private tutor to prepare for the upper middle school
examinations. He successfully completed upper middle school in 1963,
but then he could not get into either a university or an urban job,

---

13. Altogether I interviewed 23 former peasants or fishermen. Unfortunately all
of them come from Kwangtung province. My efforts to find peasants from other
provinces proved unsuccessful. There are features of rural life in Kwangtung that
set it off from some other provinces: a separate identity reinforced by linguistic
differences, large numbers of returned overseas Chinese and continuing ties with
those still overseas, predominantly rice agriculture with fertile land and fairly
abundant rainfall, high population density, relatively large villages and strong clan
organizations, less aversion to women doing field work than in some other areas,
later liberation from the Kuomintang and, at least in the early years, weaker rural
Party organizations, and so on. (The interested reader should consult Ezra Vogel,
op. cit., Chap. 1.) However, in spite of these regional peculiarities a description of
a Kwangtung commune is not completely irrelevant for understanding communes
elsewhere. Kwangtung is itself very diverse internally, with different linguistic
groups, mountainous and valley regions, national minorities, and so on. My informants come from a variety of diverse areas within Kwangtung, and yet present
many common features. This internal consistency leads me to believe that Kwangtung communes may not be so very different from communes elsewhere.

14. The "four bad elements" (*ssu-lei fen-tzu*) were those classified as landlords,
rich peasants, counterrevolutionary elements, and bad elements (thieves, bandits,
etc.) at the time of land reform. In 1957 this was enlarged to "five bad elements"
to include the rightists, although there were few rightists in rural areas. These elements were subject to special supervision and controls, and often had to submit
regular reports on their conduct to the local security defense committee and ask
special permission for a variety of activities. See, for example the 1952 "Provisional
measures for the control of counter-revolutionaries" translated in T.H.E. Chen,
The Chinese Communist Regime (New York: Praeger, 1967), pp. 296–298.

15. Children of bad elements are not subjected to the same controls and restrictions as their parents, but are nonetheless discriminated against in a variety of
ways. From time to time there have been debates about whether such children
should be treated in this way, or like any other rural youths. See R. Baum and
F. Teiwes, *Ssu-ch'ing: The Socialist Education Movement of 1962–1966* (Berkeley
and Los Angeles: University of California Press, 1968), pp. 93–94, 117.

and he was forced to return to his native village to engage in agriculture.

Chang's commune was located on the outskirts of Canton. It had a
population of 30,000 and was subdivided into twelve production brigades. Chang lived in a large village of 3,000 people which constituted one brigade. His brigade was divided into sixteen production
teams, each based upon neighborhoods within the village with roughly
200 inhabitants. Within Chang's team only 90 to 100 people were regularly engaged in agricultural production; the rest were mostly children and old retired peasants. About 80 per cent of his village was
also surnamed Chang, with the remainder split among a half dozen
or so other surnames. The Chang clan did not, however, form one
cohesive social unit. For as long as people could remember there had
been rivalry and disputes among branches of the Chang clan almost
as intense as those between the Changs and outsiders. This commune
was a relatively affluent one, due in part to its proximity to Canton.
While the major crop in terms of area was rice, a large amount of
land was given over to vegetable cultivation, and vegetable sales provided the commune with a constant flow of cash income.

In 1963 Chang's production team (sheng-ch'an-tui) had six officers:
team head (tui-chang), assistant team head (fu-tui-chang), bookkeeper
(k'uai-chi), cashier (ch'u-na), work recorder (chi-kung-yüan), and custodian (pao-kuan-yüan). Chang says that nominations for these offices
came from higher authorities in the brigade and were followed by
general team elections. In his team there was little turnover in leadership from year to year. As the titles suggest, the primary duties of
team officers concerned economic management. The bookkeeper handled the financial records, the cashier handled all disbursements, the
work recorder noted the tasks performed by each person each day and
the work point value of those tasks, and the custodian was responsible
for the storage and care of farm implements and other valuables. The
team head and his assistant assigned members to various work tasks,
planned overall team economic activity, and supervised their subordinate officers. Although the officers were referred to as team cadres, they
were not paid by the state. Rather, they earned work points for their
own labor and also work point bonuses to compensate them for the
time spent in administrative work. The value of these points then
depended upon the team's harvests, in a manner to be described
shortly.[16]

---

16. Rural cadre positions vary somewhat from place to place, as do their specified duties. See Jan Myrdal, *Report from a Chinese Village* (New York: Signet

Team meetings were not held on a set schedule, but were convened by the team head whenever needed. Most meetings were concerned with discussions of agricultural work and plans and they were quite informal. The team officers were not apolitical, and from time to time they did call meetings for other purposes: to transmit a higher directive on strengthening the rural militia, to alert team members to major national events, or to exhort all present to show their political and patriotic enthusiasm through their efforts in the fields. However, these officers had no major responsibility for political training or propaganda within the team, and their primary concern was always production. Within the team there were three Party members and four Youth League members when Chang returned in 1963, but there was neither a Party nor a Youth League *hsiao-tsu*. These organizations had their branches at the brigade level.

Many kinds of non-production activities were centered at the brigade level. The overall direction of both production and non-production activities originated from the brigade Party branch, which was assisted by the Youth League branch, and it was these units which had primary responsibility for political work among the peasants. The brigade had a militia battalion headed by a man who served concurrently as head of the local security defense committee (*chih-an pao-wei wei-yüan-hui*).[17] The team had a basic militia platoon of twenty-five members, but most militia activity was run from the brigade battalion, rather than independently by each team. At the brigade level there was also a Women's Association, but Chang (who obviously is not in the best position to testify) feels that this organization was not very important. Its officers sometimes conducted birth control propaganda, tried to mediate marital disputes, and encouraged women to work more in the fields. At the brigade level there were also economic officers basically paralleling those of the team (brigade head, assistant head, bookkeeper, etc.).

Thus in 1963, when Chang returned to his native village, there was a difference between the centers of economic and political life in his commune. Political activities and other kinds of non-production concerns were centered at the brigade level, directed by the brigade Party branch

---

Books, 1965); and A. D. Barnett with Ezra Vogel, *Cadres, Bureaucracy, and Political Power in Communist China* (New York: Columbia Univ. Press, 1967), p. 419. The work point bonuses for cadres were subsequently criticized.

17. On the role of security defense committees, see Jerome A. Cohen, *The Criminal Process in the People's Republic in China, 1949–1963: An Introduction* (Cambridge, Mass.: Harvard University Press, 1968), pp. 113–119.

and its various auxiliary organizations. Team cadres and activists in these organizations were drawn out of their homes for a wide variety of brigade-centered activities. In some cases (e.g., the basic militia) a sizeable number of team members were involved. But for many if not most team members involvement in such activities in 1963 was marginal. For the ordinary peasant the team functioned primarily as an economic unit. It supervised his labors during the day, but in the evenings, unless there was a special event or a meeting, he returned to his family and spent his spare time with relatives and friends, tending his private plot, and so on. For such a peasant there was no regular newspaper reading or study *hsiao-tsu*, nor was there regular mutual criticism or summations and self-examinations. In this period the free time of most youths also went largely unsupervised. There was one attempt to run a Youth League course to cultivate new members, but not all youths were encouraged to attend; instead, only four or five specially selected individuals from Chang's team attended, and even they skipped the League course meetings when field work demanded too much energy. Some general exposure to political topics came to team members from agencies outside of the commune, such as the propaganda, drama, or movie teams which visited the area every month or so.

As a result of the marginal involvement of many of the peasants in community life and political affairs, when rural cadres tried to act against various minor kinds of deviance they could not always count upon the support of public opinion. Although Chang had been in school during the economic crisis years of 1960–1962, he knew that a variety of kinds of misbehavior had occurred during this period which the cadres had not been able to check. A number of peasants in his team had ignored the demands and pleas of cadres and had abandoned farming to go into private trading activities. Various kinds of graft and mishandling of public (i.e., team) property occurred. Traditional patterns of behavior surfaced throughout the village, even in some of the families of cadres: wedding banquets, religious worship, celebrations of traditional holidays, etc. There was also a great deal of outspoken and uninhibited complaining from peasants about their difficult economic plight, which they blamed on government policies and cadre enforcement of those policies.

The Socialist Education campaign was launched in late 1962 in an effort to check such "spontaneous capitalist (and feudal) tendencies," and by mid-1963 when Chang returned home most of the "spontaneous elements" had returned to farming and many kinds of forbidden behavior had been curtailed, as peasants and cadres responded to the writing on the wall. But the task of criticizing those who spent money on wedding feasts or ran off to engage in trade fell mainly to the basic level cadres and activists. Most of the local peasants were anxious to labor well and to improve the general prosperity of the area, but they were reluctant to criticize fellow peasants who erred and were content to leave this distasteful job to the cadres. Such peasants were not for the most part hostile to the cadres, to whom they were bound by ties of kinship and friendship, but they were not anxious to aggravate their relationships with other team members by criticizing offenders. So while many of the major kinds of deviance of the "three difficult years" were eliminated, the result in Chang's village was not unified pressure from below for everyone to conform to the elite's demands. In fact, complaints and gripes about official policies and about cadre behavior continued to be relatively freely voiced with no *hsiao-tsu* rituals to control their expression.

The partial involvement of the peasants in public affairs can also be seen in the way work points were assigned at the time Chang returned. The prevailing system was a complicated one. All members of the labor force had been evaluated in team meetings and assigned a personal work point rating according to their strength and skill. (The procedure was that of self-report and mutual-evaluation, mentioned in Chapter 4.) If a peasant was assigned to a task for which piece rates were not suitable (e.g., tending cattle, repair work), then he received either a time rate for that job or his individual work point rating (e.g., 9 points per day). For other jobs piece rate work point values were assigned to the job itself, for example weeding a field at 15 points per mou (a mou is roughly ⅙ acre). An individual doing such a job would receive the total work points assigned to it whenever he finished, and a group would split up the total work point value assigned to the job, either equally or in proportion to their individual work point ratings.[18] Team cadres were supposed to check whether work was up to quality standards or not, and to order it redone or dock a portion of the assigned work points if it was not. The peasant's actual income was derived by dividing his share of the total work points of the team into the produce and income the team retained after satisfying the demands of the state, providing funds for investment, and replenishing seed stores. In Chang's village the profitable vegetable trade with Canton made it

18. See the more comprehensive discussions in A. Nathan, "China's Work-Point System: A Study in Agricultural 'Splittism'," in *Current Scene*, Vol. 2, no. 31, April 15, 1964; and Chen Mae Fun, "Paying the Peasants," in *Far Eastern Economic Review*, November 3, 1966.

possible to make partial advance distributions of income about once a month, with a final accounting and adjustment at the end of the year. Most communes, in contrast, seem to have had only one or two distributions a year, after the major harvests.

Public opinion and mass involvement did enter the work point system at some points. Initially team members had discussed in open meetings the point values to assign to specific jobs as well as to individuals. (Actually the basic discussion of these issues took place during the period of agricultural producers cooperatives, 1956–57, when a similar system was in use. This system was abandoned with the advent of people's communes in 1958 but revived after 1960.) Also, team members freely complained to team cadres about their work assignments and work point ratings. But there were no regular meetings in Chang's team to announce and review monthly work point totals, as existed in some other communes. The day-to-day decisions on work points were made by team cadres, and the burdens of this task were quite heavy. A large amount of time had to be spent inspecting work done and computing work point totals. Other peasants were not involved in any systematic way in checking the quality of work or criticizing those who labored poorly. Most peasants were content to let the cadres bear the main burden for quality control and criticizing other peasants.[19]

Chang, as the son of a rich peasant, should have been the focus of special political re-education efforts to see that he did not inherit a "rich peasant mentality" from his parents or transmit such a mentality to other youths. In fact almost the opposite was the case. Chang was excluded from some activities, such as the League course, which were designed to influence the political attitudes of rural youths. When he did attend political meetings, he was allowed to participate minimally, to the extent of sitting in the back and dozing off. Chang was admittedly one of the relatively backward youths in his team when it came to politics, but he experienced neither general pressure from cadres to improve nor criticism from other young peasants. Young people in his team were in fact a highly fragmented lot, split not only by traditional clan and kinship rivalries, but also by differences in class origins, education, and political activism. Chang did not associate much with activist youths from other classes, but neither did he experience much conflict with them. He went his own way and they went theirs. He had

---

19. This general problem is discussed in R. Birrell, "The Centralized Control of the Communes in the Post-'Great Leap' Period," in A. D. Barnett, *Chinese Communist Politics in Action* (Seattle: University of Washington Press, 1969).

several close friends his own age within his village, mostly youth of other "bad" class families, and with the closest of these friends he could discuss freely his feelings about anything. With these friends the topic of conversation was rarely politics, but most commonly sports, romance, or general village gossip, although Chang did tell them that ever since his return home he had been thinking of escaping to Hong Kong. There was no pressure on these friends to reveal such confidences. In general Chang felt that he could get by and keep out of trouble if he worked satisfactorily in the fields, even if he remained politically backward. He felt that his backwardness was in fact what was expected of the son of a rich peasant, and that if he tried to express enthusiasm about politics such sentiments would not be believed.

During the period from 1963 until Chang left China in late 1967, a confusing variety of changes took place in his village, and political non-involvement became more and more difficult. The Four Cleanups campaign of 1963–64 ushered in a wide variety of changes. Chang states that his commune was a "test point" (shih-tien) for this campaign in Kwangtung province,[20] and was thus one of the first areas affected. In late 1963 an outside work team came down to Chang's commune, sent by the provincial directorate of the campaign. About forty members of the team were assigned to Chang's brigade, and two or three members were dispersed into each production team. During the early period they carried out the "four togethers" (living with, eating with, working with, and consulting with the peasants) and asked selected peasants about their problems and the local situation. They focused their attentions on the poor and lower-middle class peasants, and, as in the earlier land reform campaign, they tried to find a few who were willing to speak out about their grievances. They tried to point out to such peasants the ways rural life had improved since 1949 and to convince them that all of these gains would be undone if the poorer peasants didn't speak out against capitalist and feudal tendencies which had re-emerged during the previous period. Through the use of time honored techniques for reviving class emotions, such as telling family histories and thinking of bitterness and recalling the sweet (yi-k'u ssu-t'ien—referring to contrasting the post-1949 gains with prior suffering), the work team members cultivated a core of poor and lower middle peas-

---

20. A "test point" refers to a location where the tactics of a campaign are initially tried out. The term "strong point" (chung-tien) refers to an area where the tactics which were worked out in a test point are first applied generally. From strong points the campaign tactics are then spread gradually to other villages until everyone is involved.

ants, many of whom had not served as cadres or been considered activists in the past. These individuals formed the basis for the new Poor and Lower Middle Peasant Association.[21] After this organization had been formed, the campaign evolved into a round of almost daily meetings. Some were meetings of team poor and lower middle peasants or of all such peasants in the brigade. Some were mass meetings of all team or brigade members. Some were enlarged cadre meetings at the brigade or commune level, with representatives attending from among the poor and lower middle peasants at lower levels. Chang, as the son of a rich peasant, was excluded from many of these meetings and only attended the general mass meetings.

After initial mobilization meetings the focus of the campaign shifted to criticizing the "four bad elements" within the commune. It was felt that the harmful influence of these elements had led to the capitalist and feudal tendencies which had occurred. However, Chang says in his village the supervision of the four bad elements had remained fairly strict during the period 1960–1963, and it was usually only poor and middle peasants who dared go off into trade or other unorthodox activities. The heads of four bad element households were subjected to public criticism in a variety of meetings, but no major errors were found, and so the focus shifted to the "spontaneous elements" themselves. Here, too, the treatment was generally lenient, with fines or the confiscation of the gains from private economic undertakings supplementing public criticism.

After the ice had been broken and the targets of the campaign clarified in the criticism of four bad elements and spontaneous elements, the work team directed the focus of attack against bad cadres. While Chang and his family had attended many of the meetings held to criticize the earlier targets, they were generally excluded from meetings

21. The peasant association which was formed during the land reform became moribund after the development of mutual aid teams and then cooperatives in the early 1950's. The primary aims behind the establishment of a new poor and lower middle peasant association after 1963 seem to have been to reaffirm the separate class identity of these peasants and to prevent the erosion of their class consciousness and a strict class line in the villages, as well as to have a local mass organization which could supervise and control the abuses of rural cadres. See the discussion in Baum and Teiwes, *op. cit.* Franz Schurmann suggests that Mao Tse-tung tried to establish these associations as a counter to the control of the Party machine in the villages, but was thwarted in this effort by Liu Shao-ch'i, who kept these associations from generally emerging until about 1966. My informants lead me to believe rather that these associations were set up in many areas in 1963, and that, whatever Mao's aims might have been, the rural Party organizations were able to control them much as they did other mass organizations. See Franz Schurmann, *op. cit.,* supplement.

called to deal with cadre errors. They only learned afterward of the details. The commune Party secretary and commune accountant, it seems, had connived together in embezzling about 20,000 yüan (U.S. $8,000 at the official rate) of public funds for their personal use, and they had ordered odd job workers on the commune to take commune-owned logs and build them private houses. These two cadres were struggled in a meeting called by the work team at the commune headquarters, with each team sending representatives. Both were expelled from the Party, had their houses confiscated, and then were sentenced to periods of labor reform by the local people's court (see Chapter 9). The errors of cadres at lower levels were generally less serious, as were the penalties received. In Chang's team it was discovered that the head had awarded himself extra work points, and that before 1949 he had stolen some cows from a local merchant. He was publicly criticized in team meetings, and a fine was levied against him, to be taken out of his future work points, but he was permitted to retain his office. Both he and the assistant team head were criticized for arrogance and for favoritism in work assignments, particularly for assigning relatives to the best jobs. Over the course of several weeks the cadres at all levels in the commune had to "pass the gate" by examining their errors in the previous period, all under the direction of the work team. Chang feels that the tone of the campaign was relatively mild, with an emphasis on propaganda and persuasion rather than on struggle and sanctions, and this emphasis seems to fit the relatively optimistic tone of official campaign documents prior to the fall of 1964.[22]

Coinciding with this campaign was an effort to inject more politics into production team life. In the spring of 1964 members of the work team and the new Poor and Lower Middle Peasant Association tried to establish a systematic political study routine. Monday, Wednesday, and Friday evenings were designated as political study periods, and all members of a production team were expected to meet in the team assembly hall or on the team threshing grounds to read newspaper articles, study Mao's writings, and discuss production tasks. Typically, a literate poor peasant would read some passage from a newspaper or pamphlet, give some explanation of its meaning in his own words, and then ask those present to split into informal groups for discussion. Initially the emphasis was on getting across political ideas rather than on examining prevailing attitudes. This effort at regular intensive study ran into various problems. Those leading the meetings (mostly the new Poor and

---

22. See R. Baum and F. Teiwes, *op. cit.*

Lower Middle Peasant Association activists) had had no special training in conducting these sessions, and they had difficulty both in explaining concepts and in making the discussions interesting. Attendance varied, and people often showed up late, dozed off, or chatted
during the meetings. With the departure of the work team and the
onset of the agricultural busy season in mid-1964 this study activity
was abandoned.

Early in 1964 special youth study activities had also been established.
At this time China's leaders were especially concerned about training
"revolutionary successors," and in the rural areas this meant in part
trying to organize spare time activities for working youth to keep them
from falling under the influence of old ways of thinking.[23] In Chang's
team youths were expected to participate with other team members in
the Monday-Wednesday-Friday study meetings, but in addition special
youth activities were organized on Tuesday and Thursday evenings.
The work team and the brigade Youth League branch guided the establishment of what was simply called a youth group (ch'ing-nien-tsu),
composed of all working youth in the team. The work team nominated
three members of the youth group for the position of head, and the
members elected one from these. The Tuesday and Thursday sessions
differed from the all-team meetings. Sometimes there would be study
and discussion of Mao's works, but often the activity was simply recreation—ping-pong, chess, chatting, and reading. Most sessions were a
mixture of politics and recreation, with, for example, the singing of
revolutionary songs followed by sports period. These meetings were not
run very strictly, and there was no organized mutual criticism. Youth
of all backgrounds, including Chang, found this activity very enjoyable,
and attendance remained high even after the work team departed. The
Youth group provided new recreational activities for rural youth as
well as a previously unavailable outlet for their oganizing abilities. In
early 1965 three girls who had been active in the Four Cleanups campaign and in organizing youth group activities were inducted into the
Youth League, thus enlarging the core of activist youth within Chang's
team.

Chang feels that some of the underlying problems in his commune,
such as the tension between clans and between cadres and ordinary
peasants, were not resolved during the Four Cleanups campaign. As a
final stage in this campaign there was a review of class statuses, and a

---

23. The direction of these efforts varied from place to place, with rural clubs,
cultural offices, and special study classes among the forms tried in various villages.
See *Jen-min Jih-pao*, July 8, 1964; *Chung-kuo Ch'ing-nien Pao*, July 4, 1964, January 16, 1964.

change in the official class designations of a few of the peasants.[24] Chang says that most of those reclassified in his team and brigade were cadres who got their status lowered from upper middle to lower middle peasant, or from lower middle to poor peasant. Some of the other peasants openly complained that this was simply a new instance of using public power for private gain, but the changes stood. In 1965 an experimental scientific plot was set up within the team to test new seeds and agricultural techniques. This, too, was the subject of much controversy, since, whatever the scientific merits of the plot, the work was less strenuous than ordinary field labor but still earned high work points. Those assigned to work on the experimental plot were mostly young activist youth, and many of the older peasants complained.

Many of these cleavages and tensions came to the surface during the attempt to reform the work point system. In 1965 Chang's commune began to study the new work point system introduced in the national model *Tachai* brigade in Shansi province.[25] Basically, the *Tachai* system was designed to simplify the calculation and awarding of work points, to stress political and labor attitudes more in relation to sheer quantity of work in awarding points, and to involve all team members in the task of quality control. The team was the basic unit for calculating work points, as before. The piece rates, time rates, and individual ratings were all discarded. Each day the team head called the roll at the beginning and at the end of work and noted the number of days' attendance by each laborer over the course of a month. The team head did not make a detailed quality check of areas and amounts worked, as had previously been the case. Once a month a team meeting was called to evaluate the work points each member would receive for each day he had worked. The criteria to be used in the assessment were abstract: political thought, technical skill, labor intensity, and labor attitude. Each team member in turn was expected to evalute himself over the past month in relation to these criteria, and then to estimate how many points he deserved per day. His estimate was then open to revision and criticism from other members of the team who were supposed, based

---

24. This re-evaluation of class statuses was supposed to be carried out as one of the final stages of the Four Cleanups Campaign, but it never seems to have occurred in most villages which did not fall in the campaign "test point" category.

25. The introduction of the *Tachai* system here was much earlier than in most areas, again reflecting the "test point" nature of Chang's village. A participant claimed in a Hong Kong journal article that introduction of the new work point system was supposed to be a final stage in the Four Cleanups Campaign. See Tai Tan, "Lun chung-kung nung-ts'un ssu-ch'ing yün-tung (hsia)," (On the Chinese Communist Four Cleanups Campaign [Conclusion]), in *Chung-kuo P'ing-lun*, no. 356, March 25, 1969, p. 14.

on their observations of his labor and attitudes during the past month, to suggest either a higher or a lower total. (Peasants were not, however, expected to wait to criticize poor work until these meetings. The hope was that in the daily work in the fields team members would now take an interest in prodding each other to work better. Thus more of the burden of quality control would be shifted from the cadres to the entire membership.) After all comments had been heard, an informal vote was taken on the work point rank of the peasant for the month, and that figure was simply multiplied by the number of days he had shown up for work. As before, the final value of the work points was not known until the year-end accounting, and it was calculated in much the same manner as before.

In implementing the *Tachai* system problems were encountered which still had not been resolved by the time Chang left China. The initial evaluation meetings were stormy affairs, and it sometimes took over a week of nightly meetings to agree on the ranking of all 100 members of the team labor force. The vagueness of the criteria made disputes inevitable, and personal and kinship animosities were vented in the discussions. The new system had the effect of upgrading young activists and downgrading those with undesirable class origins, and this shift was resented by older peasants and by the bad class elements within the team, the latter including Chang and his family. However, for many team members there was little change in the points they had been awarded under the older, more complicated system. Moreover, after the first few months the ratings tended to stabilize, and individuals could count on getting about the same rating they had had in previous months. As a result in subsequent evalution meetings only about half the labor force showed up. Those who stayed away were mostly poor and lower middle peasants. They had no fear that they would lose points for missing these meetings, since the primary standard for judging political thought came to be the peasant's class status rather than his political participation or enthusiasm during the previous month. The team head assigned points to those who did not attend the meetings, and he generally gave them the same as they had received in previous months. Thus the *Tachai* system lost much of its intended incentive effects, since the ratings did not accurately reflect changes in labor efforts or political involvement.

Another problem was that the hoped for common involvement in checking on and encouraging the labor efforts of others did not materialize. In the fields and in team meetings peasants were willing to criticize the efforts of members of rival clan branches and personal enemies, but they were still reluctant to interfere with or criticize their close friends and relatives. There was now more pressure from newly recruited activists on poor workers, but not general social pressure. As a result quality control was less well done than previously, and Chang feels that the new system allowed some peasants to loaf more. He claims the overall effect on production was negative. We should be cautious in accepting this judgment, since Chang was one of those who resented the new system because his own income fell. Previously he had been able to earn fairly high work point totals by working hard, but now due to his class status he was generally given a somewhat lower rating. Chang does note that some of the predicted benefits of the reform did materialize—work point bookkeeping did become simpler, and team cadres did have more time free to devote to other matters.[26]

In the winter of 1965–66 further changes were made in the political study routine in Chang's commune. At this time rural Mao-study activities were being encouraged in various areas throughout China, particularly in Kwangtung province.[27] In late 1965 three or four youths from Chang's team were picked to go to commune headquarters for ten days of training in the techniques of studying Mao's works, and after this several other groups were sent for similar training. Upon their return these youths became advisers (fu-tao-yüan) in the study of Mao's thought. They were expected to lead the way and to get other members of the production team to take up systematic political study. In early 1966 a new leadership post was created within the team, that of political instructor (cheng-chih chih-tao-yüan). Chang claims that a female Party member in his team was picked for this post directly by the commune Party committee first secretary. She reported to the brigade Party branch secretary and was considered equal in authority to the team head, but the manner of her selection gave her somewhat more power. Her appointment seems to have been an effort to bring the direction of political activities down to the team level and strengthen its leadership.[28]

---

26. See further discussion in Martin Whyte, "The Tachai Brigade and Incentives for the Peasant," in *Current Scene,* Vol. 7, no. 16, August 15, 1969.

27. Both the People's Liberation Army and the work teams of the socialist education campaign were involved in promoting rural study classes. For details see *Jen-min Jih-pao,* Feb. 24, 1966; Political department of the Kwangtung provincial military district of the Chinese People's Liberation Army, eds., *Mao Tse-tung ssu-hsiang chao-yao heng-p'i* (Mao Tse-tung's thought brightens Heng-p'i [commune]) (Canton, 1966).

28. None of my other informants mentions the creation of such a position in

At this time the Monday-Wednesday-Friday team political study meetings were revived. Now the political instructor led the sessions, and the advisers acted as her assistants. The focus of study was more strictly upon Mao's writings than had been the case in 1964. A common format was for the meetings to begin with some revolutionary songs. Then the instructor or an adviser would write a single Mao-saying on the blackboard, and explain its meaning and significance. Efforts were made to keep the topic simple and illustrations vivid and concrete, to avoid burdening those present with abstract theory. New emphasis was placed on putting Mao's thought into practice, which meant trying to get people to examine their behavior for ways in which they could conform more closely to Mao's ideas.

Attendance was poor. Chang thinks this was partly due to the political instructor, who was relatively young, fairly hot-tempered, and always ready to vent her anger at the lack of cooperation she received from team members. Some older peasants resented her arrogance and engaged in a test of wills with her, showing up late for study or thinking up excuses to avoid attending completely. Those such as Chang who came from bad class backgrounds had to be fairly diligent in their attendance in order to stay out of trouble, but poor peasants could afford to be non-cooperative. Even many of those who did attend (Chang mentions himself in particular) did not like to voice their views. As a result the advisers and other young activists tended to monopolize the discussions and self-examinations, while others remained passive observers. General mutual criticism of individual shortcomings did not develop. Thus the peasants in Chang's team were brought into regular contact with the study of Mao's thoughts, but were not fully involved in it.

The Mao study advisers did not confine their activities to these meetings. They spent some of their time going around to individual homes in the evenings to lead family Mao-study and some time leading songs and study in the fields during rest breaks. They also continued to receive follow-up training in Mao-study techniques through weekly meetings with the brigade level adviser.

Political activities, then, were increasingly injected into Chang's village in the years 1964–1966. These developments did provide greater exposure to political ideas and an outlet for the previously underuti-

---

his team. However, in the press there have been accounts of other efforts to bring political leadership down to the team level. One brigade in Kiangsu province established political team heads (*cheng-chih tui-chang*) in each team for this purpose. See *Jen-min Jih-pao*, October 11, 1967.

lized enthusiasm and organizing abilities of the youths. However, the political atmosphere was still relatively lax, and general political involvement and social pressure behind elite goals did not develop. Peasants were still not holding regular *hsiao-tsu* study and criticism meetings like cadres and students. Chang himself felt he had to attend most of the political activities which were open to him, but he was still not the target of special pressures because of his backwardness. He was criticized from time to time for not speaking in study sessions, but he knew that nobody expected him to become an activist, and the criticism was not very concerted. With the greater politicization of village life as well as his decreased income, Chang increasingly felt that there was no future for him at home; no hope of finding a wife, gaining a secure income, and staying out of trouble. He began to think more seriously about escaping to Hong Kong and even made several trips to scout out possible escape routes.

In the fall of 1966 the Cultural Revolution intruded into village life and produced further changes. The proximity of Chang's village to Canton meant that the turbulent events in that city had more impact than was the case in remote rural areas. The initial events were not far different from previous campaigns, with the commune Party authorities directing a new wave of criticism at the four bad elements in the village. This was accompanied by an activity referred to as "destroying the four olds" (old culture, old ideas, old habits, and old customs) and "establishing the four new"; teams of local students and militia members searched the homes of some local residents, particularly the four bad elements, and confiscated any "old" articles, such as jewelry, old books, religious objects, etc. Pictures of Mao Tse-tung and Mao sayings were then posted in houses in place of confiscated "old" pictures and shrines. The focus of criticism then shifted to "demons and monsters," individuals charged with current political errors. In a neighboring team a girl whose father had been executed during land reform was accused of ripping a picture of Mao in two and wishing a similar fate for Mao himself. A man who had seduced a girl and then tried to escape to Hong Kong was also named a "demon and monster," and the two of them were subjected to long and bitter struggle meetings by local youths. No one in Chang's team came under such attack, so his team sent representatives to view the struggle in the neighboring team. While some struggle meetings did take place, the activist youths spent most of their energies in propaganda activities, studying the press and posting *ta-tzu-pao*.

By late 1966 the commune Party officials had organized activist youths into a unified Red Guard organization to carry out these activities. However, prodded by students from the local middle school and occasional visitors from Red Guard organizations in Canton, these working youths began to direct their criticism away from the four bad elements and dragons and monsters and toward the commune Party authorities themselves. As in many other organizations, this shift in targets led to the outbreak of factional disputes, as some peasants were more willing than others to criticize the former "power holders." Chang says the more radical faction in his commune was led by dissatisfied demobilized servicemen and youths, while the other faction tended to be dominated by low level cadres and experienced peasants. Various Red Guard groups within these factions competed in holding meetings to struggle the various power holders, with the public invited. Chang attended most of these meetings, and he thinks that many others besides himself felt a great deal of secret enjoyment from seeing the former high authorities publicly humiliated. Most of the "crimes" with which these cadres were charged were related to the general complaints of stifling mass initiative and leading the commune back down the road to capitalism.

After repeated struggle meetings the commune head and the commune Party committee first secretary were removed from their posts and assigned to study Mao's works and write self-examinations. Other commune and brigade cadres were attacked in wall posters and in meetings, but no others were struggled; team cadres generally escaped criticism. The Red Guard organizations did not attempt to seize power as they did in many urban organizations, and after the downfall of the top two officials, the remaining cadres tried to keep things running.

There was some disruption of agricultural production and marketing in Chang's commune, particularly after some of the rural Red Guards started going off to join factional allies in battle in Canton in mid-1967, taking commune vehicles with them. Chang estimates that about thirty of the members of his team, mostly youths, actively participated in Red Guard activities at some time. The others attended some meetings, but for the most part stood on the sidelines and continued working in the fields. Chang himself was largely a bystander to these events. Although his home was ransacked during the "four olds" destruction, subsequent events did not involve him in any significant way.

Chang took advantage of the confused situation in late 1967 to make good his earlier plans to escape to Hong Kong. He left before it was clear how the Cultural Revolution conflicts within his commune would be resolved. When he departed there had been little change in personnel and more verbal hostility than real violence. He feels that much of the population believed that these events were a temporary phenomenon launched by Mao's supporters in Peking which would sooner or later run their course, and things would return to normal. There was, however, a significant number of youths in his commune who did get involved in political activities for the first time during the Cultural Revolution. Chang felt that it would be difficult to make use of this activism, since activists had joined factional groups which were bitterly opposed to each other. Future commune leaders, Chang thought, would face the problem of how to subdue this hostility while maintaining the enthusiasm. In any case Chang felt at the time he left that the Cultural Revolution had still not produced the kind of general political involvement and unified social pressure for Maoist goals which the leadership so clearly desired.

LIU HSIA-CHUNG: A LOWER MIDDLE PEASANT

Liu Hsia-chung is a 26-year-old former lower middle peasant from a commune in southern Kwangtung who was interviewed five times. Liu attended a rural primary school, graduating in 1958, and then took up full-time farming. Liu's village of over 500 inhabitants was divided into three production teams; Liu's team had 180 members, about 100 of whom were in the labor force. His brigade, made up from several surrounding villages, contained over 3,000 people and was divided into fourteen production teams.

Before 1949 there had been a history of intense clan conflict in Liu's village, particularly between his own kinsmen and the Su clan. The Lius had owned much more land and had dominated positions of influence in the village and had earned the animosity of the more numerous Su clan. During land reform the Communist work teams found their most eager activists among the Sus, and the Liu clan not only had several of its leading members struggled and executed but also was completely excluded from the new positions of rural leadership. The Lius nursed their wounds and contemplated ways to regain their influence. With this aim in mind they began grooming Liu Hsia-chung for a cadre position. Since his family had been one of the poorer ones in the clan they received the favorable lower middle peasant class ranking, and this, combined with Liu's education, made him a good prospect for a leadership post. Liu himself was not altogether enthusiastic, since he preferred to avoid major responsibilities, but he did not actively oppose the plans his relatives made for him.

In 1960 Liu was elected to serve as both team head and accountant, and the following year he was admitted to Youth League membership. However, later in the year Liu became fed up with serving as a cadre. During the agricultural crisis he had to try to enforce team regulations and he served as a lightning rod for peasant complaints. He therefore demanded to be replaced as team head, saying he was not experienced enough to bear the burdens. He was criticized for being selfish, particularly in Youth League meetings, but he remained adamant, and finally the brigade authorities accepted his decision.

In the following months Liu stopped working regularly in the fields and began going off with other local peasants to engage in private trade in the hopes of earning more money. When food was very short Liu even stole some poultry from his team to sell to earn enough to keep his family from running out of food. By 1963 the local agricultural situation had improved, and Liu's relatives urged him to return to regular work in the fields and to try to win back the good graces of higher authorities. He finally agreed to toe the line, and, in view of the chronic shortage of basic level cadres at this time, he was elected assistant team head. Later in the same year he was picked to serve on the brigade security defense committee, whose primary responsibility was the supervision and control of local "four bad elements."

The organization and daily routine in Liu's commune throughout the early 1960's were not much different from those described by Chang. The work point system was similar to the complex piece work arrangement described by Chang, and political pressures on ordinary peasants were few. Liu says there were no regular political study groups or mutual criticism rituals for ordinary peasants in his commune in these years. Brigade and team cadres held informal meetings almost nightly, and both brigade and team membership meetings were held at least once a month, mostly to discuss production activities. Team members also gathered together informally after work to receive their work assignments for the following day. Occasionally special team or brigade meetings were called to discuss major political events or campaigns. Party and League members were supposed to hold organizational life meetings every Saturday, but Liu says his League *hsiao-tsu* often failed to do so. (His team had a six-member League *hsiao-tsu*, but no Party *hsiao-tsu*. At the brigade level there was a Party branch and a Youth League branch.) Most of the free time of ordinary team members was their own, without organized political activities. There was no special activity for rural working youth at this time either. In the evenings Liu and his friends would gather to play pick-up basketball games, to walk into the nearby town for a movie or a snack, or

simply to wander the local streets in twos and threes. Liu testifies, as
does Chang, that unorthodox comments and criticisms of the government and its policies were voiced fairly openly during these years,
particularly during the most severe food shortages, and that those who
made such comments suffered few penalties. In general, then, he paints
a picture of a fairly lax political atmosphere.

As in Chang's commune, the political pressures began to increase
after 1963, although their timing was somewhat different. In the fall
of 1964, about a year later than in Chang's account, the Four Cleanups
campaign was initiated in Liu's village. The special district Party committee trained a campaign work team and dispatched it to Liu's
commune, and seven members were assigned to his team. There was
no initial period of dealing with the "four bad" and "spontaneous
elements," and the work team set right out to find and deal with the
errors of local cadres. The brigade and team cadres were assembled
at the brigade headquarters for three days of constant study and self-
examination. They were told that they had committed many errors
and abused their positions as cadres and should make thorough confessions before the masses. At the same time some of the work team
members went among the poor and lower middle peasants searching
out individuals who had grievances and could provide information
about cadre errors.

For the next several months there was a round of almost nightly
criticism or struggle meetings, mostly held in the brigade headquarters.
The errors of commune cadres were dealt with separately in special
meetings with representatives from the various brigades. Many abuses
and policy violations were uncovered. The brigade Party secretary had
embezzled a large sum of money. The brigade head had "lost his class
standpoint" by helping a related family classed as landlords to get
permission to leave for Hong Kong. Two team heads were themselves
from landlord families, chosen when none of the poor or middle
peasants would agree to serve. More than half of the team and brigade
cadres were found to have serious errors and were subjected to struggle
meetings. These cadres spent several weeks writing and revising self-
examinations and submitting to mass criticism. During the winter
months entire days were sometimes devoted to struggling a single
cadre.

Liu says the work team was clever at manipulating popular cleavages
and emotions. Those cadres with minor errors were shown leniency if
they would lead the way in struggling other cadres whose errors were
more serious. Clan rivalries were played upon to build up emotions

for the struggle meetings. Tactics such as these led to a much more tense emotional tone than occurred in Chang's village in the Four Cleanups campaign. Liu claims that three cadres he knew of were driven to suicide by the constant hounding and public humiliation.

Liu himself got into trouble at this time. His earlier speculation and trading were brought up, as well as his theft of team property. Liu was also charged with embezzling extra work points for himself, but he says this charge was false, a product of the fertile imagination of his enemies within the Su clan. The work team and the new core group of poor and lower middle peasant activists recruited by them decided, after struggling Liu several times, to remove him from his team and brigade offices and to fine him 250 yüan (U.S. $100 at the official rate). Liu was also severely criticized within his Youth League organization, but he retained his League membership.

Liu says that the Four Cleanups events badly shook much of the local population. The suicides and the severe penalties meted out to so many local cadres caused fear and resentment and aggravated the old problem of finding people willing to accept leadership positions. Liu at this time vowed to himself that he would never again let his relatives push him into accepting a cadre post.

In the spring of 1965 the work team left, after having installed new activists in many brigade and team posts and after having established a local Poor and Lower Middle Peasant Association to guard against future abuses by cadres. A few months later the work team returned briefly to announce that errors had been committed in the campaign, and that the work team would accept criticisms of its earlier activities. They admitted that their tactics had been excessively severe and thus had had a negative effect on local morale.[29] Because most of those attending the meeting were confused or fearful of future retaliation, few criticisms were offered and the demotions and fines were all allowed to stand. The resentments and tensions produced by the campaign remained.

Later in 1965 Liu again left regular field work to try to earn more income by private trade and speculation. Although he remained nominally a member of the Youth League and the Poor and Lower Middle Peasant Association, he increasingly withdrew from their activities and ignored the criticisms he received from cadres and activists. His relatives tried again to persuade him to resume regular work

---

29. This shift is connected with another change in official policies, toward the more lenient "23 points" which are associated with Mao's influence. See R. Baum and F. Teiwes, *op. cit.*

on the commune. In both 1966 and 1967 he was proposed for team cadre positions, but he refused to serve. His own family and close friends sympathized with him and stood up for him when he was criticized by others. Liu continued to work for the team when he chose to, and to spend the rest of his time in private economic activity.

In early 1967 the *Tachai* work point evaluation system was introduced in Liu's commune. The system and its problems were similar to those described by Chang Nung-min. At first the team members, accustomed to the old system, were anxious to know how the *Tachai* evaluations would affect their incomes. Each of the early evaluations took several evenings of bitter wrangling, and all of the cleavages between clans and other groups came to the surface in these meetings. The new criteria emphasizing political attitudes as well as work performance struck some peasants as unfair, since lazy peasants who were good talkers might earn more than hard workers. In fact there was so much criticism of others voiced in the evaluation meetings that the top ranks were almost vacant. Team members generally had their self-evaluations knocked down a rank or two by the judgment of their peers. The result was that almost everyone received a smaller monthly work point total than before the *Tachai* system was introduced. The final value of these points would not, of course, be known until the annual accounting, and might in fact be greater than income before *Tachai*. But since the accounting would not take place for several months, fears of income reductions could not be allayed, and criticism of the new system mounted. After a few months the hue and cry was so great that the team cadres quietly switched back to the old system.

In 1966, when the Cultural Revolution erupted in China's cities, Liu's commune remained fairly isolated from its impact. In the summer of 1967 his commune's Party committee did organize a group of working youths to go to the various teams to conduct Cultural Revolution propaganda. These youths posted *ta-tzu-pao* and banners and blackboard newspapers praising the good points of the Cultural Revolution. However, they did not organize Red Guards or any rebellious activities, and they were forbidden by the commune Party authorities from going outside to exchange revolutionary experiences with students, workers, or anyone else. So in fact the Cultural Revolution was virtually non-existent in Liu's commune in 1967, and most peasants still went about their daily routine.

In early 1968 changes did take place. First a preparatory revolutionary committee was established in the commune, composed of essentially the same people who had dominated the commune management and Party committees in the past. Then in June a new work team arrived to direct the final stages of the Cultural Revolution. The new work team followed tactics similar to those of the Four Cleanups campaign, recruiting young enthusiastic poor peasants to form a core group to lead the way in subsequent activities. The work team set out to reinvigorate the Poor and Lower Middle Peasant Association, which had not been very active or important in the years 1965–1967, and to reinstall the *Tachai* work point evaluation system. They also tried to establish a regular political study routine in each team. During 1965–1967, when in Chang's commune regular political study was being attempted, there were no similar attempts in Liu's commune. But now the work team began holding weekly team political study meetings on Sunday nights, using the youths who had been sent into the teams during the Cultural Revolution to conduct this activity. Only about thirty members of the team regularly attended these meetings, however, and occasionally the young study leaders could only muster eight or ten participants. Liu says there was no attempt to run family study classes or to study in the fields during rest breaks in his commune.

In the fall of 1968 the work team moved on to direct the "cleaning out of class ranks," aimed primarily at bad elements who had taken advantage of the Cultural Revolution to cause trouble. Local peasants, perhaps recalling the Four Cleanups turmoil, did not at first respond enthusiastically when asked to denounce bad elements in their midst. The work team then tried a new tactic: they set up "mass accusation boxes" at strategic locations so that local peasants could anonymously deposit charges against their neighbors. In this manner nine targets for "cleaning out" were eventually selected in Liu's team, and Liu was one of them. His capitalistic activities in 1961 and after 1965 were brought up again, and he was accused of setting a bad example for other poor and lower middle peasants. He was also criticized for individualism and selfishness for refusing to serve as a cadre. Liu suspected that the Sus had been especially zealous in using the mass accusation boxes to get him into trouble. He says he was confined for almost a month writing repeated self-examinations, and that he was subjected to three large struggle meetings. Finally he was expelled from the Youth League and warned to toe the proper class line in the future, but he received no other penalties. However, his constant run-ins with commune authorities, the Sus, and outside work teams had taken their toll, and Liu resolved to escape to Hong Kong at the first opportunity.

At the end of 1968 the work team moved on to direct the rectification of the local Party and Youth League. Party members were convened for lengthy discussion meetings to listen to suggestions and criticisms offered by non-Party poor peasant activists recruited by the work team. This activity was just getting under way in January 1969, when Liu, his wife, and two friends were able to steal a small boat and escape to Hong Kong.

GENERAL PATTERNS AND CONTRASTS

Certain basic differences can be seen in the features of the rural production teams described in the two case studies. Liu's team experienced the campaigns and policy shifts of this period later than, and in somewhat different form from, Chang's team. Regular political study activities for ordinary peasants came later to Liu's team and were even more poorly attended than in Chang's team. The Cultural Revolution, at least in its earlier stages, had much less impact on Liu's team. There were considerably greater problems in getting people to serve as cadres in Liu's commune than in Chang's. Although in neither commune was the political atmosphere very strict compared with the case studies in earlier chapters, Liu's commune had an even more lax atmosphere than Chang's.

We can point to several factors which may explain the different atmospheres in the two communes. Chang's commune was suburban, with a high standard of living and regular cash incomes, while Liu's commune was more isolated and apparently less prosperous (I have no reliable income statistics for the two communes). The nearness to Canton explains much of the greater impact of the Cultural Revolution on Chang's commune, while the higher standard of living probably contributed to better popular morale and less severe problems in finding peasants willing to serve as cadres. Chang's commune was also a test point for many of the campaigns of this period. As a result, campaigns and pressures to inject politics into rural life arrived in his commune earlier, and, particularly in the case of the Four Cleanups campaign, they took a very different form than they did in areas where they were applied later. Because of the pendulum shifts in the policies regulating the Four Cleanups, this campaign was fairly mild in Chang's commune, but quite severe in Liu's. And this difference seems to have contributed in Liu's commune to greater resistance to subsequent political activities, and greater reluctance by peasants to serve as cadres. There may be other factors affecting the political atmosphere in the two communes whose importance is more difficult to judge— the clan rivalries in Liu's commune seem more intense than those in

Chang's. If we want to understand the different political atmospheres in other communes it seems that we must consider such factors as the location of the commune, the prosperity and income trends, when and in what form that commune had been involved in various campaigns, the impact those particular campaigns had had upon ordinary residents and rural cadres, and the pre-existing social cleavages in the area.[30]

Certain general features of commune life in the early 1960's are reflected in these two case studies as well as in the accounts of other informants. There is general agreement that ordinary peasants had no regular political study *hsiao-tsu* during the period 1960–1963, and that the political life of even those who did have regular study activities did not approach the rigor of most urban organizations. Most political and other non-production activities were centered at the brigade level, while the lives of ordinary peasants were focused on production activities within the team.[31] Peasants had free time to spend in unorganized, often traditional ways, in informal socialization with family and friends, and in work on the private plot. General involvement in supporting the demands of rural cadres was absent, mutual criticism was not developed in any systematic way, and a considerable amount of open complaining was tolerated.

After 1964 various new activities were introduced, designed to politicize rural activities and to direct peasants' attention away from per-

---

30. There are other distinctive features of these communes. For instance, Chang's commune had a fairly high representation of women in positions of leadership and in the Party and Youth League. Women have not been well represented in rural leadership posts in China generally, although during the Cultural Revolution there was some effort to promote women in some communes. See Heilunkiang Radio, March 7, 1968. One estimate for Kwangtung Province in 1965 lists 25 per cent of production team offices as held by women and probably only 10 per cent of brigade offices and 5 per cent of commune offices. Janet Salaff, *Youth, Family and Political Control in Communist China,* unpublished Ph.D. dissertation, University of California at Berkeley, 1971.

31. All of my informants mentioned Party branches at the brigade, rather than the team level, and only a few mentioned Party *hsiao-tsu* within the team. It was reported in *Nan-fang Jih-pao* (January 14, 1960) that 20 per cent of the production teams in the province had no Party members, while 70 per cent had no Party branches (or 30 per cent had them). Since then two trends have worked in opposite directions. On the one hand, rural Party membership has presumably increased, although no statistics are available for the period since 1960. On the other hand, the large communes of 1960 were split up, as were their subordinate units, so that the number of teams in the province more than doubled from 198,000 in late 1960 to 440,000 in April 1963 (Ezra Vogel, *op. cit.,* p. 379). Since rural Party membership has certainly not doubled, I would expect that substantially less than 30 per cent of the production teams in the province had Party branches in the period we are dealing with, but that such teams did exist.

sonal and family affairs and toward the concerns and needs of the commune and nation. My informants feel, however, that the political atmospheres in their villages remained relatively lax, that there were serious obstacles to the thorough politicization of rural life. Study meetings were called at the team level, rather than in *hsiao-tsu*, and they tended to be poorly attended and to be dominated by a few young activists lecturing to a passive audience. Forums for mutual criticism tended to open the Pandora's box of traditional enmities and rivalries. Complaints about official policies could still be heard. Some sectors of the rural population saw the political demands made upon them as but another short term obsession of China's leadership which would eventually be forgotten.

There is a long history of close ties between the Chinese Communist Party and the peasantry, ties which eventually led to victory in 1949. Yet the efforts to introduce political rituals and organizational discipline into rural villages seem to be fraught with difficulties. The special obstacles which villages present to these efforts are not all obvious from the case studies presented; they become apparent only when we compare the rural setting with the other organizations considered in previous chapters. The low cultural level of many peasants (Chang mentions that almost half of the members of his team, mostly those over thirty, were illiterate), the tradition of isolation from national political life, the physical separation of peasants at work and in their homes and the consequent difficulties of organizing and supervising their activities, and the grinding burden of agricultural toil all contribute to the relatively sporadic nature of peasant involvement in political rituals. Capable and highly motivated rural cadres are also in scarce supply, and are themselves less easy to supervise than urban cadres. Where capable rural cadres are scarce they may be recruited for posts at higher levels, continually endangering the strength of basic level leadership. In any village there is already a complex set of social relationships lying under and complicating any attempt to establish political study groups and mutual criticism, whereas in many other organizations (schools, the army) such prior relationships are largely absent. Finally peasants, whatever the official value placed upon them in Maoist ideology, rank rather low in social prestige compared to those holding other occupations. This gives peasants a certain immunity from criticism and sanctions, since they have few privileges that can be taken away. This also means that elites will have difficulty rewarding rural activists, since the opportunities for mobility are relatively limited and the burdens of becoming a rural cadre make this form of mobility unattractive to many. All of these are relatively special conditions of rural life which, when compared with the situations of cadres and students, make regular political rituals and a strict political atmosphere difficult to establish and maintain.[32]

In spite of such obstacles, intensive efforts to politicize rural life continue. The mass media in the past few years have contained accounts of the organization of peasants into touring Mao Tse-tung's thought propaganda teams, rural Mao Tse-tung's thought study classes, and family Mao Tse-tung's thought study groups. Efforts are being made to develop mutual criticism among the peasants in sessions to "smash selfishness and establish the collective" (*p'o ssu li kung*). Individuals are expected to criticize themselves as well as family members and neighbors for selfish and individualistic behavior, such as refusal to serve as a cadre or reluctance to contribute household night soil to the collective lands.[33] Only time will tell whether these and similar efforts are simply a new "high tide" in rural politics to be followed by another lull, or whether the elite can find ways to deal with the problems discussed here and for the first time establish a system of regular political rituals for all peasants.

---

32. It may be questioned whether all of the Chinese leadership really wants to impose *hsiao-tsu* political rituals on the peasantry. Franz Schurmann, in the supplement to his *Ideology and Organization in Communist China* (2nd. ed.,), seems to argue that this might have been a goal of Liu Shao-ch'i, but that Mao Tse-tung opposes the regimentation that such an imposition would imply and favors the less organized, more spontaneous methods of mass meetings, speaking bitterness, and other such tactics to mobilize the peasantry. Whatever the truth to this contention, in the wake of the Cultural Revolution there has clearly been a vigorous effort to promote systematic group political study among the peasants. See the sources cited in footnotes 12 and 28.

33. For a particularly colorful example, see *Peking Review*, no. 47, November 20, 1970.

VIII

WORKERS AND
POLITICAL RITUALS

Mao Tse-tung confounded orthodox Marxists by basing his revolution on the peasantry rather than on the urban proletariat, but after their assumption of power the Chinese Communist leaders turned to the working class as the potential spearhead of the drive for economic development. The tumult of the previous half century had left the workers poorly organized and demoralized, ill equipped in many ways to play a spearhead role. Even in modern factories under Nationalist rule workers' organizations and involvement in national life were weak. Unions had little authority, either within the factory or nationally, and they continued to be regarded with some suspicion by the Kuomintang elite because of the dominance of the Communists in labor organizations prior to 1927.[1]

In addition the low level of economic development posed obstacles to effectively organizing the workers, both before and after 1949. One estimate for 1952 lists only 3.54 million workers in factories, mines, and utilities, compared to 13.5 million workers in handicraft workshops and 199.89 million workers in agriculture.[2] The preponderance of

---

1. J. Chesneaux, *The Chinese Labor Movement 1919–1927* (Stanford: Stanford University Press, 1968); I. Epstein, *Notes on Labor Problems in Nationalist China* (New York: Institute of Pacific Relations, 1949); Lucien Bianco, *Origins of the Chinese Revolution, 1915–1949* (Stanford: Stanford Univ. Press, 1971), pp. 82–87.
2. T. C. Liu and K. C. Yeh, *The Economy of the Chinese Mainland: National Income and Economic Development, 1933–1959* (Princeton: Princeton University Press, 1965), p. 69.

small scale traditional handicraft workshops presented special problems for labor organizers. Even large scale mechanized factories, however, experienced many of the problems which commonly occur when industry is introduced into an agrarian environment: an unstable labor force, semi-feudal hiring practices, and worker unfamiliarity and discontent with the impersonal nature of factory authority.[3]

Prior to 1949 the Chinese Communists had had little experience in running large scale industry. The precarious existence of the guerrilla and civil war situations and the depressed economies of the predominantly rural Communist strongholds favored small scale factories and handicraft and other types of cooperatives. Within such small enterprises the discussion, participation, and political arousal techniques favored by the Chinese Communists were used, but their suitability for organizing large scale, mechanized urban industry remained to be tested.

In their post-1949 efforts to organize the urban working class and restore production, the Chinese Communists used a combination of policies based on Soviet and their own Yenan experiences. Within factories trade union organizations and Party and Youth League units were established, and activists were cultivated from among the ordinary workers. In some factories workers were organized into groups for discussion of their grievances against the old factory system and social order. Through discussions and meetings, fermentation and cultivation, the new leadership increasingly penetrated the social relationships of ordinary workers.

This penetration was furthered by the various campaigns of the period 1950–1952. During the "resist America, aid Korea" campaign, workers were mobilized to sign patriotic pacts (ai-kuo kung-yüeh) pledging to increase production and fulfill other tasks. Workers in some plants were organized to discuss work problems and criticize violators of work discipline. During the campaign against counterrevolutionaries, workers competed in denouncing Kuomintang agents and other "bad elements" in their midst. Sometimes production units organized current events study groups and newspaper reading groups for the workers.[4] In 1952 the Five-Anti campaign led to the dispatch into factories and work places of work teams trained to involve the workers in speaking bitterness against the bad treatment and the graft and corruption of

3. See K. H. Shih and J. K. T'ien, *China Enters the Machine Age* (Cambridge, Mass.: Harvard University Press, 1944).

4. See *Hsin-wen-pao*, May 18, 1951; *Ta-kung-pao* (Peking), Nov. 9, 1951; *Ch'ang-chiang Jih-pao*, September 10, 1951.

the private owners and management of their units, a tactic similar to that used in the land reform campaign described in Chapter 7.[5] Participation in these activities varied widely, however, reflecting differences in the new elite's control and influence in various work units during these early years.

Along with these typically Chinese Communist efforts to penetrate and involve the workers, initial steps were taken to introduce Soviet industrial policies. The most important of these were the "one man management" authority system, and the "responsibility system," whereby insofar as possible workers and work groups were assigned to specific locations, tasks, and equipment for which they could be held responsible, thus facilitating supervision of, and rewards for, their work.[6] Soviet material incentive policies were implemented, as was the Soviet emphasis on planning, output goals, and bonuses. However, these Soviet practices were not adopted without some Chinese modifications. In one article a worker who arrived five minutes late was subject to group criticism rather than administrative penalties or a fine meted out by factory authorities.[7] Although China in these years did boast of rate-busting miners similar to the Stakhanovites, individual production heroics were generally given less emphasis than in the Soviet Union.[8]

In spite of the increasing Soviet influence after the launching of the first five-year plan in 1953, efforts to fully involve workers in factory affairs and political activities do not seem to have been eliminated. For example, Wuhan authorities complained in 1955 that after-hours organized activities for workers were taking up too much time and harming the health and enthusiasm of the workers, in effect giving them a thirteen- or fourteen-hour day. To combat this tendency they passed a resolution stating that workers on an eight-hour shift could be subjected to no more than two hours of organized activities outside of work each day, and the limit for nine-hour shift workers would be one and a half hours. To aid factory officials they provided trial plans which would enable workers to participate in production discussions, newspaper read-

5. J. Gardner, "The Wu-fan Campaign in Shanghai: A Study in the Consolidation of Urban Control," in A. D. Barnett, ed., *Chinese Communist Politics in Action* (Seattle: University of Washington Press, 1969).

6. Franz Schurmann, *Ideology and Organization in Communist China* (2nd ed.) (Berkeley and Los Angeles: University of California Press, 1968), Chap. 4; and Barry Richman, *Industrial Society in Communist China* (New York: Random House, 1970).

7. *Tung-pei Jen-min Jih-pao*, December 11, 1949, cited in F. Schurmann, *op. cit.*, pp. 247–249.

8. Y. Gluckstein, *Mao's China* (Boston: Beacon Press, 1957), p. 231.

ing groups, political and current events study, technical training, literacy classes, union meetings, organized recreation, and Party and Youth league meetings without surpassing these limits.[9] Such a heavy burden of non-work activities went far beyond anything existing for ordinary factory workers in the Soviet Union. However, it is doubtful that this report is typical of the situation in China at this time. The political activities of workers in the many scattered handicraft cooperatives and other small enterprises were probably much less rigorous.

Trends in the organization and activities of workers after the early 1950's parallel those in other spheres and will only be mentioned briefly here. In the period 1955–1957 the socialization of even small scale enterprises and shops was carried out, and handicraft enterprises were amalgamated into larger cooperatives, more suitable to higher level command and control. The Soviet model for industrial management came under increasing attack after 1956. The Great Leap Forward of 1958–1960, which emphasized mass mobilization tactics rather than material incentives and bureaucratic coordination, marked the Maoist effort to find a different road to economic development. During this period discussion and mobilization meetings of various types were re-emphasized as keys to generating enthusiasm and improving production, and workers throughout the country volunteered for extra work and longer hours.[10] Although the failure of the Great Leap was due more to agricultural problems than to industrial disruption (although the latter did occur), when the Herculean efforts of the workers were not rewarded with the promised material prosperity, but rather with severe food shortages, morale problems set in. In the period 1960–1962 material incentives and piece rates were re-emphasized, political study activities were curtailed, and there was a general swing away from political mobilization as a method for improving production.

After partial economic recovery, the pendulum swung back again to a renewed emphasis on political mobilization in the period 1963–1966.[11] Workers, like students and others, were organized to study the

9. *Ch'ang-chiang Jih-pao*, July 18, 1955. See *Chung-kuo Ch'ing-nien Pao*, May 31, 1956, on the same problem in a Shenyang (Mukden) factory.

10. Work days of twelve or more hours were frequently undertaken during this period, with occasional high tides of workers continuing on the job for as long as three days and nights. See *Kung-pen Jih-pao*, November 20, 1958, November 27, 1958.

11. Details on the escalation of political activities and pressures among workers during this period can be found in *Kung-jen Jih-pao*, August 20, 1964, December 18, 1964, May 8, 1965; *Jen-min Jih-pao*, June 18, 1964, February 6, 1965, April 20, 1966.

People's Liberation Army and to emulate heroes. Trade unions were criticized for being too concerned with the workers' material welfare and not concerned enough about their political health. Workers were criticized for wanting to avoid political activities and for developing "bourgeois habits" in unsupervised free time activities.[12] Excessive reliance on material incentives as a technique for motivating workers was attacked, although initially the wage system was not substantially altered.

During the Cultural Revolution the broad range of industrial policies of the period after the Great Leap was attacked as "revisionist." Rebel organizations arose within the factories to attack those responsible for leading the country back down the road to capitalism. Many of the themes of the Great Leap Forward period resurfaced: more workers' participation in management, downgrading the authority of technical experts, encouraging innovations by ordinary workers, and utilizing political mobilization more than material incentives.[13] The extravagant promises of future prosperity and the marathon work sessions of this earlier campaign were missing, however.

In sum, penetration of the social groupings of ordinay workers, mass mobilization, and political involvement have always assumed greater importance in industrial management for the Chinese than for the Soviet leadership. However, over time there have been the same marked shifts in policy emphasis that we have seen in other realms between competing and generally contradictory strategies for organizing the supposed vanguards of the proletarian revolution.

LI KUNG-JEN: A FACTORY WORKER

Li Kung-jen, who was 25 years old when I talked to him in 1969 (he was interviewed three times, for a total of nine hours [14]), was born in Shanghai, but in 1950 his family moved to Canton. His father worked as a cook and was classified as a worker after the Communist victory.

12. *Nan-fang Jih-pao*, May 6, 1965, trans. in *Survey of the China Mainland Press*, no. 3467; *Kung-jen Jih-pao*, May 8, 1965.
13. For a brief summation of the "Maoist strategy" of industrial management, see Steven Andors, "Revolution and Modernization: Man and Machine in Industrializing Societies, The Chinese Case," in Edward Friedman and Mark Selden, eds., *America's Asia* (New York: Vintage Books, 1971).
14. In all I interviewed 15 non-agricultural manual workers. None worked in large fully modernized industrial complexes, but they came from a wide variety of less majestic concerns. Seven worked in factories of various types, five worked on construction projects, and three fall in the miscellaneous category.

Li admits to being one of the unruly students of the type described by Tai Hsiao-ai. He was never very interested in schoolwork and study, and he much preferred to spend his free time in athletic activities or other recreation with close friends. Apparently his working class background counterbalanced this fault to some extent and enabled him to join the Youth League in 1964. In the following year, not long before Li was scheduled to graduate from lower middle school, his father offered to arrange through a friend to get Li a job in a large automobile parts manufacturing and repair factory in Canton. Li knew that this job would give him a more secure future than trying to continue in school, and he eagerly accepted the opportunity. After starting work in the factory early in 1965 Li spent a year and a half working as an apprentice and was then promoted to grade one technical worker (the lowest of eight grades).[15]

The factory's work force of over 1,000 was divided into several major workshops, each headed by a chief and a few assistants. The workshops were subdivided into various work hsiao-tsu. Li was assigned to an arc welding group of twelve members within a small welding workshop of about thirty people. The hsiao-tsu had a head and an assistant head. Li is uncertain about the structure of the factory administration. He knows there was a factory director, a Party general branch, and a Youth League general branch. He says that in fact the Youth League was almost dormant in his factory. Although when he started work he filled out forms mentioning he was a League member, he was never organized into a League branch or participated in League organizational life.[16] There was also a trade union, but it, too, played a minor role. Li joined the trade union and paid regular dues, but there were no union meetings or organized activties. Union officials were mainly concerned with administering the welfare system for workers and putting up propaganda posters to spur production.[17]

---

15. Other informants mention longer periods of apprenticeship, often three years. Li worked under a set wage determined by his rank as a worker, but this was supplemented by monthly bonuses. Li is a little vague about just how the bonuses were determined and awarded. But they were separate from the prizes for advanced workers, which went to far fewer people. Li says his basic wage as a grade 1 technical worker was about 45 yüan a month, and that he could sometimes earn up to 10 yüan a month in bonuses (one yüan = U.S. $.40).

16. My other informants mention more active Youth League organizations in their factories. This makes me suspect that Li was not a Youth League member at all, wanted to claim he was, but wanted to play it safe by not trying to describe activities he knew nothing about.

17. On the welfare role of unions see Joyce Kallgren, "Social Welfare and China's Industrial Workers," in A. D. Barnett, op. cit.

When Li started work there was no regular routine of political study and mutual criticism among the workers. There was a weekly meeting of all the workers every Saturday after work in the factory dining hall. (This was a single shift factory, so all of the employees could be conveniently assembled at one time. In multiple shift factories organizing meetings is considerably more difficult.) At these meetings the factory director, Party secretary, or some other official would give a report. Generally these reports were on the current work situation, but sometimes they focused on current events or political themes. Sometimes an official passed on a report from some higher level conference he had just attended. The speeches often took up most of the roughly two hours allotted to these meetings, leaving little time for discussion. Occasionally a report was discussed within individual work groups scattered around the dining hall, but most of these discussions were cursory.

Other types of meetings sometimes occurred. Occasionally work was called off for the afternoon to hear a special report, often on a political topic, and generally there was work group discussion of such a report. There were also quarterly meetings to discuss and evaluate work perfomances during the preceding three months. For several evenings after work the results of the past period were reviewed and problems were discussed. Then each group nominated some of its number as advanced workers. A special evaluation committee (*p'ing-pi wei-yüan-hui*) composed of representatives of management, the trade union, the Party organization, and various workshops reviewed the nominations and approved them. Then the Party general branch gave its approval, and in a meeting of all workers the names of the advanced workers were read out and awards presented. The awards varied somewhat from time to time, sometimes including a t-shirt, a notebook, a small cash prize, or similar items. The criteria were strictly production excellence and skill at this time, and Li states that he was never selected for these honors.

There were few other meetings or organized non-work activities during 1965 in Li's factory. Workshop meetings were very rare, and the workshop was primarily a unit for facilitating the administration of production rather than an organizational base for non-work activities. (There was a workshop Party *hsiao-tsu,* however.) The workers did have frequent contact with the workshop chief, who came around regularly to inspect and criticize their efforts, in many cases pitching in and showing them how to do things. At this time there was no regular newspaper reading or political theory study for the workers in Li's factory. Nor were the work group head and his assistant very much concerned with the political attitudes of members of their group. They were very concerned with individual work problems, however. The work group head spent much of his time consulting with, helping, and correcting workers. Because of this constant contact it was not necessary to call special work group meetings to discuss work problems or assignments. Welding work on automobilies and auto parts did not entail large machinery, complex coordination, or frequent changes in work organization, and the work was fairly routine, with little prospect for innovation or short-cuts. Thus organized discussions to cope with such concerns were not required as they are in some other types of factories, and individual consultation could correct most problems.

Although generally little attention was paid to examining the political thoughts of workers at this time, Li feels that political errors were dealt with very severely. He recalls two workers who got into political trouble. One man of petty-bourgeois class origin was overheard complaining that he could not find enough food and consumer goods to spend his wages on, and that these shortages showed the lack of real concern of China's leaders for the workers. The factory Party authorities organized an all-factory struggle meeting against this fellow, but he refused to admit any errors. No criticism meetings in his work group preceded this session, and the matter was handled by factory Party officials. After the struggle meeting the man was turned over to public security authorities, and Li understood that he was sent for a year of labor re-education as a declared wrecker of socialist construction and of the Socialist Education campaign.

Another worker was doing volunteer work for the trade union during the Socialist Education campaign and, while joking around with fellow workers, he (apparently) inadvertently mixed up the order of the standard slogan to read "If you confess you will be treated harshly, if you resist you will be treated leniently" (t'an-pai ts'ung-yen, k'ang-chu ts'ung-k'uan). The Party general branch officers called him in for interrogation, and the next day he was sent off to an "employees, workers, and cadres thought reform study class" for three months of thought reform.[18] In this case no meetings were called to discuss this fellow's error. And so, according to Li, the political involvement of the workers was low while political control remained tight.

Li describes his own work group as fairly solidary, with little or no

---

18. In China there are a variety of kinds of punishment and reform which fall short of confinement in prisons or labor reform camps, and one of these is the study class. Study classes have been used from time to time to deal with a variety of kinds of individuals with various thought problems, but their nature, extent, and details are little known and deserve more research.

WORKERS AND POLITICAL RITUALS

tension between leader and led or between competitors for rewards and honors. Even the quarterly evaluations of workers involved more discussion and praise than criticism, and the importance of skill in winning the awards took some of the competitiveness out of the selection procedure. The main cleavage within the group was based upon age and skill levels. The work group head and his assistant were both around forty and of relatively high rank (the head was a rank six technical worker), while the ten other members were all in their teens and early twenties with none over rank three. There were no Party members in the work group, and two Youth League members played no special role and had no special prestige.

This age and skill differential did not lead to conflicts. In fact the work group head and his assistant were quite well liked. They took a lot of extra time helping new young workers adjust to job demands and teaching them various work skills. While the workshop head tended to be sharp-tempered and critical, the group head worked much more through advice and persuasion to improve work performance. The cleavage within the group was most apparent in free time activities. After work or on days off the younger members of Li's group sometimes got together to play basketball or to go swimming, but they rarely engaged in outside social activities with the two leaders. This factory had no workers' dormitories, and, except for such informally organized recreation, the workers generally dispersed to their separate homes at the end of the day. Li's closest friends were not in fact fellow workers, but neighborhood and school friends with whom he remained in touch. He spent much more of his free time with these outside friends than with fellow-workers, and he thinks this was generally the case for other workers in his factory.

Thus, during Li's first year in the factory the pressures for political participation were not very heavy, and the workers were able to maintain independent private lives and to avoid total involvement in factory life. They were sometimes exhorted in ideological terms to improve their work, and political errors were severely dealt with, but their actual work fell into a fairly stable routine which was not affected much by political events and activities.

At the time Li started work the Socialist Education campaign was just coming to a conclusion in his factory, and what little drama there had been had already come and gone.[19] Li knew that there had been

19. The Socialist Education Campaign had less impact in factories and many other urban organizations than in rural communes. Many of my informants describe the urban part of this campaign as a relatively mild propoganda and study campaign.

propaganda about the campaign and meetings organized to discuss whether factory officials had committed graft or other abuses. But apparently no serious problems were discovered (outside of the two errors already mentioned), and the campaign concluded quietly.

In late 1965 or early 1966, Li notes, changes in the daily routine were introduced. A new system of political study for all workers was instituted, with meetings every Monday, Wednesday, and Friday after work. Sometimes these meetings were similar to Saturday meetings of the past, with the entire work force gathering to hear reports from factory Party authorities. Usually, however, the work *hsiao-tsu* gathered at their work posts for about two hours right after work for political study. Most of these sessions involved the reading and discussion of Mao's quotations and analysis of the last few days work in light of Mao's ideas. The *hsiao-tsu* head and assistant head led the study and discussions and showed a new interest in raising the political consciousness of their work-mates. The other members of the group did not feel that this sudden shift in their behavior from production to political concerns was at all unusual. The change in the political mood within the factory was simply adapted to by all, as had been the case with similar shifts in earlier periods.

At first the study meetings were related fairly closely to work efforts. Mao's quotations were read and discussed in relation to current tasks, with the intent of finding some ideas in the Chairman's thought which would improve work performance. As time went on, however, the connection with the daily work became attenuated. Workers were expected to memorize three new Mao-sayings for each study session, and considerable time was spent simply going around the group listening to the recitations and drilling those who had not done their homework. There were also competitions among workers in memorizing the "Three Constantly Read Articles" written by Chairman Mao, as well as in learning and singing revolutionary songs.[20] Li feels that even the initial sessions had little effect on production, and later on factory authorities did not even seem too concerned about how work was affected by Mao study. Li feels that most of the members of his work group as well as other workers in the factory regarded these meetings as an onerous

---

20. The three constantly read articles are "In Memory of Norman Bethune," "Serve the People," and "The Foolish Old Man Who Removed the Mountains," all short pieces written by Mao Tse-tung in the anti-Japanese war period and included in his *Selected Works*. During the Cultural Revolution these three articles were used frequently as study materials, particularly among the workers and peasants.

addition to a hard working day. However, such sentiments were not openly expressed. Li did not complain about these meetings even to his closest friends within the work group, and no complaints were openly expressed to him. Only through occasional facial expressions and the general lack of initiative in study could such sentiments be detected. At this stage no new activists emerged in Li's group. The group head and his assistant were the most activist, but the other members of the group felt this was due to their belief that their leadership posts now carried this responsibility.

At about the same time, the worker evaluation system was altered. Instead of advanced workers, selections were made of "five good workers" who were judged good in politics, in study, in production, in work discipline, and in relations with co-workers. The judging procedure was the same as before; work groups discussed and nominated their members according to general criteria, and then higher levels approved and announced. Although the new evaluation procedure was supposed to place greater emphasis on ideological criteria, in Li's group, at least, the change made little difference. Everyone, with the possible exception of the group leaders, was at roughly the same level of political activism, so skill continued to be the main differentiation between those chosen and those not. The same people who had been picked as advanced workers were selected as five good workers, and Li still could not qualify. The awards had changed, however; sets of Mao Tse-tung's selected works replaced the clothing and money of earlier selections.

Li claims that after some months of these new routines relations within his work group grew somewhat strained. The increased amount of time they had to spend in each others' company during the week, plus an increased amount of mutual criticism of work and political thought, even though fairly perfunctory, led to more friction. Li gives as the main indication of this change the fact that on evenings when there was no organized study, workers did not get together outside the factory for sports or other joint leisure time activities as much as they had in the past. The tendency to disperse immediately to their homes increased, as workers tried to preserve as much of their private lives as they could.

From the autumn of 1966 events in Li's factory took a further turn with the onset of the Cultural Revolution. The complex events of this period cannot be reported in detail, but the major outlines will be sketched. At first the workers were outsiders to the new movement, looking on as students struggled with academic authorities and searched private houses for the "four olds" (described in Chapter 7). A month or so later the first student Red Guards started coming to Li's factory and conducting propaganda about the goals of the Cultural Revolution. Competing student factions came to proselytize, and although arguments and debates were stimulated, the workers tended to remain confused about the purposes of the campaign. They did not really begin to participate actively until about February 1967, after the Kwangtung provincial authorities had been overthrown.[21] At about this time workers in Li's factory started forming their own rebel groups, largely in imitation of outside factions whose ideas the workers found congenial. Initially these rebel groups spent most of their time making propaganda and trying to recruit members.

A major dispute erupted over the issue of who could participate in these rebel organizations, the same issue we saw dividing students in Tai Hsiao-ai's school in Chapter 6. Li claims that the workers who finally sided with the East Wind factions in Canton opposed the participation of workers classified as "the seven kinds of black" (hei ch'i-lei— the original five bad elements discussed in Chapter 7 plus the new demons and monsters and capitalist roaders). Those who favored more open participation eventually sided with the Canton Red Flag factions, as in Tai's school. Li joined with seven members from his workshop (four of whom belonged to his work group) to form a scarlet guard (ch'ih-wei-tui) organization. Li says he initially decided to get actively involved in the Cultural Revolution to protect his mother. She had a history of disputes with the residents' committee cadres in the area where she lived, and Li was afraid these cadres would use the opportunity of the Cultural Revolution to pin some charge on her and subject her to humiliation. He knew that if she had a son who was a Red Guard this would protect her, since neighborhood authorities would not want to risk a fight with a Red Guard organization. As time went on, however, Li found rebel activities exciting and adventurous, and protecting his mother became a less important motive.

Li's scarlet guard organization opposed the participation of the "seven kinds of black" elements. He had no personal quarrel with most of the workers who fit this label, but he felt that those who had exploited the population prior to 1949 should not be able to play a

---

21. Participation in the Cultural Revolution began earlier for some of my other worker informants. For details on more extensive worker involvement in the Cultural Revolution in Shanghai, see Neale Hunter, Shanghai Journal (New York: Praeger, 1969).

leading role in the new revolutionary movement. Li is not too clear about the bases for the various rebel groups which arose at the time. The original members of Li's scarlet guard organization were all about the same age and skill level and had developed close relationships through informal sports and recreation in the previous period. Li says in general those with similar ideas and friendship ties tended to band together. His group sided with the "ground command (*ti-ch'u tsung-pu*) factional alliance within the factory, which was in turn affiliated with the Canton East Wind Red Guard alliance.

Throughout the spring and early summer of 1967, the workers' Red Guard organizations competed with each other in attacking factory authorities, largely in imitation of what they saw going on outside in Canton. Although the East Wind faction that Li adhered to was known as more conservative than the Red Flag faction, Li claims that within his factory if anything the East Winders were more vigorous and hostile in attacking the "power holders."

The workers' motivations for participating in struggle meetings against the factory manager and other officials were complex. Many workers participated mainly to avoid getting in trouble for not being active during the Cultural Revolution, although there were no direct threats against non-participants to support this anxiety. Li claims that few of the workers had substantial grievances with the factory officials or compelling convictions that these officials were seducing them back down the road to capitalism. The workers had little personal contact with the factory manager and knew little about him. In subjecting him to struggle, however, the workers could emulate the rebellion going on in other organizations, they could express their power vis à vis competing factions within the factory, and they could feel the exhilaration of throwing their weight around and seeing their former bosses reduced to humiliation. Perhaps there were other motives as well: getting back at personal enemies lower down in the hierarchy and gaining relief from the discipline of factory work.

Although at first the workers could think of few specific charges against factory officials, outside of the general "power holder" and "capitalist roader" labels, people who worked in management offices were coaxed into supplying information from the personnel dossiers and stories about the personal lives and past indiscretions of these officials. When the factory manager and his main subordinates refused to bow their heads and fully admit their errors, the workers added the charge of disrespect for the masses and failure to accept the Maoist line. So over time new disclosures, the resistance of the officials, and the competition between rebel factions led to increasingly strong emotions and animosity. Li confesses that he himself found the sensation of being someone important who could play a role in humiliating these former officials the most exhilarating part of the events of this period.

While the struggle with factory authorities was going on work continued much as before. Most of the struggle meetings were held after work, and during the day the work routine continued largely unaltered in spite of the lack of leadership from the factory manager. Then in June 1967, major battles erupted between competing factions in Canton and the rebels within Li's factory turned their attentions increasingly to these external events. Li found the new experience of roaming the city doing battle with competing Red Guard groups even more of an adventure than participating in factory struggle meetings. The battles of this period also disrupted the flow of repair work coming into the factory, so that at times workers reported in the morning to find only two or three hours of work to do. After finishing work Li and some of the younger, more adventurous workers set off to do battle, while most of the others went home. Only a "hard core" of those who had participated in the Cultural Revolution within the factory kept up their participation when these outside battles began.

There were no major fights within Li's factory at this time. Initially three other Red Guard groups had been formed in Li's workshop, and some of these groups ended up on opposite sides in later factional divisions. But an informal truce was maintained within the factory when active conflict broke out in the city. Li says that when he did show up for work during this period his relations with other members of his work group were much as before, and everyone accepted the fact that after work Li and several others would be spending the rest of the day in battle while others would simply go home and keep out of the way. Then beginning in August the factory was closed down completely, and Li was able to devote all of his energies to Cultural Revolution activities.

Li left China near the end of October 1967. He claims he had not contemplated escaping to Hong Kong when he was younger, and with a working class background and a job as a skilled worker he could have counted on a fairly secure future in China. However, in one clash with a rival faction in Canton there were some casualties, and Li was recognized and marked for revenge. In fear of his life, Li hid out for several days and then, with several middle school classmates, he set out for Hong Kong.

LIANG CH'ING-NIEN: A "PEOPLE'S WORKER"

I conducted two interviews with a 25-year-old man named Liang Ch'ing-nien. Liang was born and grew up in Kwangsi province. His family had been classified as landlords during the land reform campaign, and both his mother and father had passed away during the early 1950's. Liang lived with an uncle until 1960, when he moved to join an older married sister who lived in Canton. He finished his upper middle schooling there in 1961, but he was not able to gain admission to a university. He claims he had received good grades and even had tried to be politically activist, but his status as the son of a landlord excluded him. As a result, he became very discouraged about his prospects for the future. The authorities in his school urged him to go to the countryside to work in agriculture, but Liang was not interested. He stayed on in Canton, picking up whatever jobs he could find. He held one steady job for over a year, but because of its low pay he quit in 1963 to look for something better. He had little luck, and he spent most of the following year unemployed, except for occasional odd jobs.

At this time the residents' committee where Liang lived began organizing regular meetings to deal with the problems of the many unemployed youths who were drifting around Canton. Neighborhood youths were assembled for evening meetings, at which they were urged to accept jobs in various distant places. Liang and most of his friends were not too eager to work in distant Sinkiang or Inner Mongolia, even if the terms of employment were relatively favorable.[22] They much preferred staying near relatives and friends in Canton, even if it meant a relatively insecure existence. Finally word came of the demand for workers in a huge water conservation project along the East River outside of Canton. Liang signed up for a job on the project, hoping to salt away a little money and perhaps find some opportunity to escape to Hong Kong. In the following pages we examine the situation in a sector of this construction project where Liang spent almost a year, from late 1964 to late 1965.

Liang and his co-workers were called *min-kung*, a term meaning lit-

---

22. During the Cultural Revolution the practice of trying to entice youth to leave the city with promises of jobs with good conditions and fringe benefits was criticized. Also at this time youth who had gone to distant areas and then found that they had been misled, and that many of the fringe benefits were nonexistent, streamed back into the cities, sometimes attacking the residents' committee authorities who had been responsible for their exile.

erally people's worker or citizen worker.[23] A large number of construction projects have been carried out in China since 1949, and many of these have relied upon short term volunteer laborers, people working without pay as a way of fulfilling manual labor obligations. Liang's project was of a different sort. The unskilled physical labor on his and many similar projects was provided not by short term volunteers, but by *min-kung* hired for longer periods of time and paid a regular wage. Most of those who ended up as *min-kung* were in some way marginal, without (or discharged from) regular employment and forced to accept this kind of work. In Liang's project there were former factory workers, demobilized soldiers, unemployed students, and rural "four bad elements" and their children. There was also a large number of "boat people" who had formerly resided and eked out a living on the waterways around Canton, but who, due to the government's ambitious resettlement program, had been deprived of their sources of income. Marginal personnel from all these sources had been recruited to work together on Liang's project.[24]

In Liang's work sector there were over 1,000 *min-kung* organized into a brigade. The brigade was broken down into nine middle teams, and each middle team was divided into small teams, each with ten to twenty *min-kung*. Attached to each brigade were full time cadres as well as salaried technicians and skilled workers who provided the leadership and technical knowledge to supplement the physical labor of the *min-kung*. The middle team head and his assistant were also state cadres, but the small team heads were *min-kung* selected for this position by the middle team heads. In most cases relatively young and strong workers were picked to lead the small teams.

The relatively marginal nature of the *min-kung* is reflected in the absence of other organizations. Liang knew there was a Party and a Youth League organization among the cadres and skilled workers, and probably a trade union as well. But among the *min-kung* there was no Party organization, no Youth League, and no union. No *min-kung* was an active member of any of these organizations.

The *min-kung* lived in squat mud and bamboo barracks which they helped to construct at the work site. When Liang started work his

---

23. I interviewed four other individuals who had served as *min-kung*.

24. In some cases *min-kung* are recruited from one source, such as a rural commune, and organized into a team at that source. They stay together on the job, rather than being mixed in with other personnel. In a few cases, such as road construction projects, they may be able to live at home and commute to nearby work sites during the day.

team was assigned to unloading building materials at a nearby railway depot. He received a regular daily wage for this work, but when his team was transferred to earthmoving work they were shifted to piece-work pay, calculated by the area covered. The *min-kung* worked a three shift system and had irregularly scheduled days off about once a month.

When Liang came there were no regular political study meetings for the *min-kung*. Once a month the brigade head convened a large meeting to discuss work results and goals, and at the end of a day's work each small team sat around for a few minutes to discuss work problems and assignments. But there were no specifically political meetings or activities. Supposedly there was labor competition between teams, but in practice this was a formality. Each middle team had a bulletin board where work results of each team were posted, with a red flag beside the name of the team which had done best the previous week. However, there were no meetings to discuss the competition results, and for the most part the *min-kung* ignored the entire matter. With no regular meetings or political activities, the *min-kung* simply went to bed after the evening meal (for those on the day shift), or washed and mended their clothing. Occasionally friends went off to the nearby town for an evening of recreation, and twice a month a movie team came to the project to show films.

In the late spring of 1965 this lax political atmosphere began to tighten. The brigade head announced that henceforth Tuesday and Thursday evenings would be political study periods. For about two hours or so each time the small team met to read and study newspaper articles, Mao's quotations and other materials as in *hsiao-tsu* in other organizations. These meetings were not very well run because of the fatigue of the *min-kung* and their relatively low educational levels. At least one-third of the *min-kung* in Liang's team were illiterate, and some of the rest were barely literate. Only one other team member besides Liang had attended middle school. Because of this distinction, these two "intellectuals" played a key role in political study, reading newspaper articles out loud and acting as recorders (*chi-lu-yüan*), taking notes on discussions for later inspection by the middle team head. Liang found himself in a new position. No longer was he felt to be among the most backward politically, as had generally been the case in school. Now his ability to handle the study materials placed him somewhere in the middle of the group politically. The backward position was dominated by some boat people and former workers who refused to open their mouths in meetings unless directly called upon and criticized. Liang felt that there were no real activists in his group to compare with those he had known in middle school, although the small team head and one or two others did say a lot in these meetings. Thus in mid-1965 political study became a regular activity for these *min-kung,* but their meetings were far from the ideal of general participation and enthusiasm described in Chapter 4.

At about this time the wage system was altered as well. When Liang started work various *min-kung* had worked under a daily time wage or a piece rate remuneration system. Now the system changed. Monthly team meetings were held to classify *min-kung* into five wage grades. In these meetings each team member was expected to state which grade he felt he deserved, based on his recent work performance, and then others would agree with or criticize his evaluation. After the grades were set in this fashion, they were approved by the middle team and brigade authorities and announced. A *min-kung* in the top grade earned about twice as much per day as a *min-kung* in the bottom grade.[25]

This new wage evaluation system was similar to the *Tachai* work point system described in Chapter 7, and it was supposed to have many of the same benefits.[26] Primarily this meant that *min-kung* would be led by the new system to pressure each other to work harder and to criticize slackers. In fact, Liang says, this did not occur. Mutual criticism, which had not been developed before, did take place to some extent in the evaluation meetings. However, it tended to lead to acrimonious disputes between team members. The *min-kung* came from such varied backgrounds and had so little in common that they had no sense of group loyalty and obligation. In addition, all knew that their jobs were temporary, that after a few more months their project would be finished, and they would disperse to look for other work. As a result there was very little team solidarity, and small cliques of friends within the team argued with each other about wage decisions. All criticisms of work performance came to be interpreted in terms of these intra-team disputes, rather than as a disinterested effort to improve overall team performance.

While the small team was not a solidary unit, the *min-kung* over time did develop individual close friendships. Liang became close

---

25. Liang says the five grades received .80, 1.00, 1.20, 1.40, and 1.60 yüan per day. When Liang had started work he received the set wage of 1.49 yüan per day. (One yüan = U.S. $.40)

26. Liang claims that there was no criterion of political thought or attitude used in the judging, as there is in the *Tachai* system, and that the *min-kung* judged each other solely on work performance.

friends with two other young *min-kung* in his team, both former workers and of more favorable class origins than himself. Liang got to know the attitudes of these two friends and found that they shared many of his dissatisfactions with life and his pessimism about the future. Over time he was able to reveal more and more of his own feelings to these friends, even discussing the possibility of escaping to Hong Kong. What little free time these friends had they spent together, and in wage evaluation meetings they supported each other against criticism from others.

Late in 1965 Liang's stage of the construction project was concluded, and the workers were dispersed. Some went home to look for other jobs, but Liang and some other *min-kung* were offered a transfer to another construction project. He accepted the offered but only stayed at his new job for a little over a month. Then his brother came to visit him, and together they planned and carried out an escape to Macao.[27]

GENERAL PATTERNS AND CONTRASTS

In comparing these two case studies we find certain obvious differences. Although the details are not as rich as might be desired, it is apparent that the political atmosphere in Liang's project was more lax than in Li's factory. Some *min-kung* resisted participation in political study in any but a minimal way, and the work groups lacked the solidarity necessary to make mutual criticism effective. Liang feels that little ideological "progress" was in fact expected of the *min-kung*, and that part of the reason for political study meetings was simply to occupy the time of the *min-kung* and keep them from drinking and carousing.

A number of features of the project Liang worked on seem to explain this lax political atmosphere. The *min-kung*, as people without regular jobs or schooling elsewhere who were forced to accept this low prestige form of employment, could be expected to come to their work with a variety of grievances and negative attitudes which would interfere with political study. The relatively short-term nature of the jobs, the high turnover in personnel, the relatively low levels of literacy, and the heterogenous backgrounds of the *min-kung* could all be expected to make a strict study routine difficult to establish. There were prob-

---

27. Macao, the Portuguese colony a few miles down the coast from Hong Kong, was a frequent haven for refugees up until 1967, partly because it was easier to escape to than Hong Kong. In 1967 the Macao riots led to strengthened Chinese Communist control within the colony, largely eliminating Macao as a way place for those escaping from China.

lems of leadership as well. The sharp gap in status and remuneration between the *min-kung* and their superiors and the failure of the *min-kung* to participate in the Party and other organizations of these superiors could be expected to impede the development of mass line interpersonal relationships and loyalty of the *min-kung* to these superiors and to the overall project. Those given the immediate leadership positions, the team heads, were generally poorly equipped to lead political study sessions. However, in spite of these differences between Liang's project and Li's factory, it is important to note that when political pressures were increasing in other organizations, they increased for the *min-kung* as well. Although political study was not particularly well run, higher authorities did have sufficient control over the lives of the *min-kung* to start regular study meetings and to keep negative attitudes from being openly expressed. Other *min-kung* informants generally confirm Liang's account of the relative distinctiveness and the lax political atmosphere in this kind of construction project.

The accounts of my other informants differ in certain respects from these case studies. One problem is the great diversity in types of manual non-agricultural work. I was unable to interview any workers from large mechanized national or provincial run factories, no mine workers, and no dockyard workers. One would expect that the size and modernity of the work unit, the composition and stability of the labor force, the incentive system, the nature of the work process, the presence or absence of work unit-run dormitories, the level of governmental supervision, and no doubt other factors would affect the political atmosphere within a given work unit. There seems to be a great deal of variation which the interviews do not allow me to examine adequately. Nonetheless, a few comments about the general patterns and contrasts represented in the accounts of other worker informants may be relevant.

Other informants confirm that there had been a relatively low emphasis on political activities among workers in the early 1960's, but several claim to have had more regular activities than those described by Li and Liang. Several mention at least a weekly political study meeting even during the years 1960–1963. Also several mention more factory-organized spare time activities, such as organized recreation and spare time schooling, than are described by either Li or Liang. There is also some mention of more vigorously organized work competitions in other factories in the 1960's. Even where work competitions were given greater emphasis by factory authorities, however, my informants feel that they had little impact on production—much less, at least, than in the hectic days of the Great Leap Forward. Work process differences may help explain why some units apparently had no work competitions during the 1960's (such as Li's factory) while others conducted them regularly.[28]

Other informants lend general support to Li's views that in the 1960's unions played only a peripheral role in factory life, mutual criticism was not emphasized as a way of motivating workers, and workers maintained some privacy in their non-work activities. However, the workers' political attitudes were not completely neglected in pursuit of production goals, and their involvement in political meetings and organized production discussions contrasts with the more rigid bureaucratic emphasis in Soviet factory management.

Workers in some ways seem to be under less pressure to conform to rigid political study demands than other sectors of the population. In part this may be because workers have a privileged status in China today, as the supposed vanguard of the revolution. They are not expected to harbor the kinds of negative attitudes that some other groups might. Also the relatively low levels of worker education (compared to other urban organizations), particularly in the smaller and more traditional enterprises, make it difficult for many work units to mount any very complex study ritual.

A basic problem in establishing a strict political atmosphere in such work units is presented by the demands of the work situation itself. My informants generally agree that individuals are selected for basic level leadership positions because of their work skills and experience (or, in the case of the *min-kung*, perhaps simply because of their strength), rather than for their skill in organizing political meetings or conducting ideological work on individuals. Work group heads may be firm supporters of the Communist Party or Chairman Mao or both, but they will not have been picked for this position because of their skill in communicating this attitude to others. When political pressures increase, as they did in the mid-1960's, these work group heads are the ones who have to lead the group political meetings, and my informants feel they often did so rather poorly. One informant mentions that during 1966 the Party leadership in his factory tried to cope with the poor quality of basic level political leadership by appointing enthusiastic young workers from each group as propagandists to lead

28. A production competition involves setting goals, throwing out production challenges to others, competing, and then evaluating the winners. The mere posting of advanced work groups or picking advanced workers can be based upon general work results over a period of time, rather than a specific competition.

political study. (Note the similarity with the introduction of study advisers and a political commander in the first rural case study in Chapter 7.) However, some of these youths were low in skill and experience (some were only apprentices), and the resulting conflicts over status within the factory had an overall negative effect upon the way political study meetings were run.

In spite of these problems the political atmosphere in these work units seems stricter than in most rural communes, at least in the sense that deviant attitudes and complaints cannot be expressed so openly. The greater ease of supervision, the absence of complicating kinship ties, and the danger of losing a good job and fringe benefits (this last is not, of course, applicable to the *min-kung*) may all contribute to the greater stifling of dissent in factories and other work places when compared with rural communes.

In sum, political activities and rituals seem to be generally less elaborate than in some other settings, particularly when compared with schools and government offices. Political meetings tend to be somewhat more routinized and regarded as somewhat extraneous to the main business of workers, which is production. However, even during the slack political periods, such as that in the early 1960's, there are some political meetings and a variety of other forms of worker discussion and participation which distinguish Chinese work units from those in many other societies. During the high tide of political campaigns the regular infusion of political activities into daily work makes the contrast with other societies even sharper. It is clear that during most periods these political activities are supposed to stimulate more and better work efforts, rather than to interfere and take time and energy away from work. The periodic shifts away from this emphasis on politics taking command over production in the past indicate that there has been some feeling within the leadership that political activities were not in fact stimulating production but were interfering with it. As in other organizations the Cultural Revolution witnessed attempts by other portions of the leadership to place politics more firmly in command, to build political activities permanently into the life of workers and prevent them from seeming extraneous. Again we will have to wait to see whether these new efforts will be continued and whether they can overcome the problems we have described.

IX

CORRECTIVE LABOR CAMP
INMATES AND
POLITICAL RITUALS

Hsiao-tsu in every setting are involved in reforming the thought and behavior of their members. The task of reform is perhaps most difficult when those members are inmates of penal institutions, people whose errors are considered serious enough to require isolation from society. This difficulty is attested by the literature on Western penal institutions.[1] The harsh nature of prison life, the inmate's loss of individuality and self-respect, the constant indignities and restrictions which he confronts daily all combine to produce hostility to prison authorities and the external society, and a desire to find protection and solidarity among fellow inmates. The result is an inmate subculture with its own structure, leadership (often the most hardened criminals emerge as leaders) and norms (the "inmate code"). Attempts by Western prison authorities to reform and rehabiliate inmates are continually frustrated by the existence of this inmate subculture, which perpetuates hostility and transmits criminal behavior to new arrivals. In other words, the coercive nature of the Western penal institution gives rise not only to individual hostility and alienation

---

1. See Richard A. Cloward, Donald R. Cressey, George H. Grosser, Richard Mc-Cleery, Lloyd E. Ohlin, Gresham M. Sykes and Sheldon Messinger, eds., *Theoretical Studies in Social Organization of the Prison* (New York: Social Science Research Council, 1960); Lawrence Hazelrigg, ed., *Prison within Society* (Garden City: Doubleday, 1968).

but also to an informal social structure which encourages and hardens such hostility and obstructs reform. Thus penal institutions represent in some sense the most severe test of the organizational model of which *hsiao-tsu* and political rituals are key aspects.

The origins and early development of corrective labor camps in the Chinese Communist movement remain obscure. Mao Tse-tung in a 1934 report praised reforms in the penal system of the Kiangsi Soviet which outlawed corporal punishment and emphasized reformatory education and labor discipline.[2] Documents from later in the same year, during the crisis produced by the Kuomintang's Fifth Encirclement campaign, convey a slightly different impression. Chang Wen-t'ien, Chairman of the Council of People's Commissars of the Soviet area, denounced the indiscriminate sending of landlords, rich peasants, and others to forced labor in areas removed from their homes as a policy which was causing widespread resentment among the population.[3] The fragmentary evidence we have indicates that after they established their new headquarters in Yenan the Chinese Communists continued to use a combination of forced labor and political re-education to deal with offenders, as did their Nationalist opponents.[4] However, much of the development of a widespread network of penal institutions occurred after 1949. Statutes and regulations were published in the first years of national power specifying the kinds of offenses, both criminal and political, which would result in imprisonment, and in 1954 the statute on labor reform (*lao-tung kai-tsao*) was promulgated, specifying the regulations for the operation of penal institutions.[5]

In his speech introducing the labor reform statute, Lo Jui-ch'ing credited Soviet legal experts with advice in drafting the code, but the extent of Soviet influence is by no means clear.[6] Under Stalin all

2. Translated in Victor A. Yakhontoff, *The Chinese Soviets* (New York: Coward-McCann, 1934), p. 262.

3. Chang Wen-ti'en in *Red China*, no. 208, June 25, 1934, translated in Tso-liang Hsiao, *The Land Revolution in China 1930–1934* (Seattle: University of Washington Press, 1969), pp. 285–6.

4. Gunther Stein, *The Challenge of Red China* (New York: McGraw-Hill, 1945), Chaps. 4, 29, 30.

5. The labor reform statue appears in *Jen-min Jih-pao*, September 7, 1954. Various translations are available. In Albert P. Blaustein, *Fundamental Legal Documents of Communist China* (South Hackensack, N.J.: Rothman, 1962), this and several of the earlier penal regulations are translated.

6. Lo's speech is contained in a New China News Agency dispatch from Peking, September 7, 1954. See also *Current Background*, No. 293, September 15, 1954. At the time in the Soviet Union the 1933 criminal code was supposedly still in effect, although recent sources verify that it had long since been supplanted by a variety of internal (i.e., secret) regulations. The 1933 code is available in translation in Hsinwoo Chao, *The Labour Correction Code of the Russian Socialist Federated Soviet Republic* (London: Sweet and Maxwell, 1936).

pretense of re-education for labor camp inmates was abandoned, and the main obligations of Soviet prisoners were to meet their daily work quotas and not to cause disturbances. Expressions of political loyalty were not called for or expected, and in fact some refugees from Soviet camps have said that the freedom to complain and curse their rulers was much greater than that existing in outside society. Common criminals were given positions of control over political inmates and allowed to exploit them cruelly. The evidence we have on Soviet camps suggests that inmate subcultures did develop, particularly among the common criminals, and that criminal attitudes and resistance to reform were fostered among those lucky enough to survive the camp ordeals.[7] In contrast, in the Chinese prisons of the 1950's there was a strong emphasis on political study reinforced by group criticism as a technique for reforming offenders of various types.[8] Other contrasts will be noted in our case studies, but it should be clear at least that whatever the advice received from Soviet legal experts, the Chinese incorporated heavy doses of their own ideas and early experiences in establishing a penal system.

The available information about penal policy in China is also rather scanty. Chinese officials seem to have vacillated between periods of pride in their penal institutions as organizations whose experience should be publicized, and periods of secrecy in which the public fear of these institutions prevented much from being said about them. The 1954 labor reform statute specified the existence of prisons, detention houses, juvenile corrective settlements, and labor reform teams or camps. Figures published at this time revealed that the great majority of prisoners (more than 83 per cent) were taking part in labor during their confinement, rather than spending all their time in intensive prison thought reform.[9] It appears that even in 1954 the sort of intensive thought reform which received the most attention and study in the West was a rather atypical experience. For most offenders punishment meant a brief stay in a prison or detention house and then the

7. For a general discussion of forced labor in the Soviet Union see David J. Dallin and Boris I. Nicolaevsky, *Forced Labor in Soviet Russia* (New Haven: Yale University Press, 1947); also Viacheslav P. Artem'ev, *Rezhim i Okhrana Ispravitel'no-trudovykh Lagerei MVD* (The regimen and security in the corrective labor camps of the MVD) (Munich: Institute for the Study of the USSR, 1956). On the question of the inmate subculture, see Donald R. Cressey and Witold Krassowski, "Inmate organization and anomie in American prisons and Soviet labor camps," in *Social Problems*, 5, Winter 1957–1958.

8. Robert J. Lifton, *Thought Reform and the Psychology of Totalism* (New York: Norton, 1961); Edgar H. Schein, *Coercive Persuasion* (New York: Norton, 1961).

9. *Jen-min Jih-pao*, September 7, 1954.

bulk of their terms in a corrective labor camp. These labor camps, rather than the prisons, are the focus of this chapter.

Those assigned to penal institutions under the 1954 labor reform statute, whatever their offenses, all had some form of legal sentencing and were considered criminals in the legal sense. At this time, as in later periods, other elements of the population were assigned to periods of study or manual labor or both without such formal sentencing or designation as criminals, and in many cases without any recognition that punishment was involved. Debate about what is punishment and what is a criminal may be left to the philosophers and legal scholars. It is clear at least that during the 1950's other corrective labor institutions (besides labor reform camps) were created to give quasi-penal reform to pick-pockets, prostitutes, errant cadres, and a variety of other minor offenders.[10] In the wake of the Anti-Rightist campaign of 1957 this second network of camps was institutionalized and expanded. The August 1957 State Council decision which formalized the establishment of these labor re-education (*lao-tung chiao-yang*) camps specified the kinds of people for whom they were designed:

1. Those who do not engage in proper employment, those who behave like hooligans, and those who, although they steal, swindle, or engage in other such acts, are not pursued for criminal responsibility, who violate security administration and whom repeated education fails to change;
2. Those counter-revolutionaries and anti-socialist reactionaries who, because their crimes are minor, are not pursued for criminal responsibility, who receive the sanction of expulsion from an organ, organization, enterprise, school, or other such unit and who are without a way of earning their livelihood;
3. Those persons who have the capacity to labor but who for a long period refuse to labor or who destroy discipline and interfere with public order, and who receive the sanction of expulsion from an organ, organization, enterprise, school, or other such unit and who have no way of earning a livelihood;
4. Those who do not obey work assignments or arrangements for getting them employment or for transferring them to other employment, or those who do not accept the admonition to engage in labor and production, who ceaselessly and unreasonably make trouble and interfere with public affairs and whom repeated education fails to change.[11]

---

10. For a discussion of these antecedents of labor re-education, see Jerome A. Cohen, *The Criminal Process in the People's Republic of China 1949–1963* (Cambridge, Mass.: Harvard University Press, 1968), Chap. 4.

11. Translated in *ibid.*, p. 249. It should be noted that no detailed regulations

After 1957 this new network of camps absorbed rightists and a wide variety of other offenders whose errors were not serious enough to warrant confinement in labor reform camps. No formal court procedure was involved, and administrative decisions (by the individual's unit and by the public security bureau) could result in a term in these camps. There is no reliable information about how many camps of both types there are, or how many inmates are confined in them.[12] The author's guess is that together these two kinds of camps confine at least many hundreds of thousands (some individual camps are reported to contain over 10,000 inmates) but do not rival in scale the labor camp network of Stalinist Russia. The size of the camp network seems to fluctuate over time, with expansions following major campaigns (such as the Anti-Rightist campaign) and contractions during the lulls between campaigns and following major pardons.[13]

In the 1950's the Chinese press carried occasional accounts of the successful reform of large numbers of offenders and claims that the atmosphere in the new penal institutions was markedly different from that existing in prisons in other societies.[14] There is some corroboration for this view from individuals who spent time in Chinese prisons during these years. Witness the observation of the French priest Father Bonnichon:

I was very suprised in the beginning to observe the following: that not a single one [of my cellmates] seemed to complain, nor seemed to feel at one with his fellow-prisoners against the government which arrested us. On the

comparable to the labor reform code have ever been published for labor re-education. This 1957 document is merely a general decision of the State Council and leaves many questions unanswered.

12. A Taiwan source claims that in the period up to 1967 almost 80 million people had spent time in forced labor, with 12 million confined at any one time, and that 5.3 million had died as a result. See Institute for the Study of Chinese Communist Problems, *1967 Yearbook on Chinese Communism* (in Chinese) (Taipei, 1967), p. 464. No sources for these estimates are given, and needless to say the estimating agency can be suspected of biases. Earlier studies, such as *Kung-fei nu-kung chih-tu chih yen-chiu* (Research on the communist bandit slave labor system) (Taipei, n. d.), include in such estimates large numbers of personnel not actually confined to forced labor camps, such as the *min-kung* discussed in Chapter 8 and former landlords working in their own villages under mass supervision. Earlier Taiwan estimates are discussed and disputed in Edgar Snow, *The Other Side of the River* (New York: Random House, 1961), Chap. 47.

13. Apparently in 1956 some of those dealt with during the *su-fan* campaign of the previous year were rehabilitated. In 1959 Liu Shao-ch'i signed amnesties covering certain categories of offenders. Jerome A. Cohen, *op. cit.*, pp. 268, 629, 631.

14. See, for example, *Nan-fang Jih-pao*, December 17, 1951; *Hsin-hua Jih-pao*, November 5, 1951; Wen Hui Pao (Hong Kong), December 15, 1951; *Liaoning Jih-pao*, January 27, 1957; *Ta Kung Pao* (Hong Kong), March 10, 1957.

contrary, everyone spoke as a fervent and enlightened Commuist, and everyone accused himself of crimes.[15]

Observations such as these lead to crucial questions about penal institutions in China in the 1960's: Does the emphasis on group rituals and political re-education Father Bonnichon and others experienced in the early 1950's continue? Are Chinese penal authorities really so successful in preventing the formation of hostile inmate subcultures? What sort of political atmosphere does, in fact, develop within penal institutions? In an effort to shed light on these questions, we shall examine accounts of both of the major types of corrective labor camps.

HU YU-P'AI: A LABOR RE-EDUCATION CAMP INMATE

I talked with Hu Yu-p'ai on two occasions for a total of six hours.[16] He was 36 at the time of our talks, and he came from a family of large landholders who lived in a *hsien* capital in Kwangtung province. Hu's father was executed during the land reform campaign of 1951, but a year earlier Hu had falsified his name and background and joined the army. During the next several years he ran afoul of authorities several times in minor ways. After he was demobilized in 1953 he enrolled in a university, but during the 1955 *Su-fan* campaign against hidden counterrevolutionaries his true identity and class status were discovered, and only by faking illness was he able to drop out of school and avoid serious trouble. Then, using the connections of a friend, Hu got a job teaching in a spare-time school. During the "Hundred Flowers" campaign in 1957 he imprudently raised complaints and criticisms and was branded an "extreme rightist" in the ensuing Anti-Rightist campaign. After several struggle meetings in which Hu's errors over the past several years were recited, he was expelled from his unit and assigned to labor re-education.

Hu then spent a week of study in a detention house in Canton, and during this time labor re-education officials (from the Ministry of Pub-

---

15. Cited in Commission Internationale Contre le Regime Concentrationnaire, *White Book on Forced Labour and Concentration Camps in the Peoples' Republic of China* (Paris, 1957), Vol. 1, p. 61.

16. In all, fourteen former labor camp inmates were interviewed, eight of whom had served in labor re-education camps, the rest in labor reform camps. Twelve of the fourteen had served time in camps in Kwangtung province, the other two in Heilungkiang and Inner Mongolia. I do not know how serious this regional bias is, because my informants cannot agree on whether labor camps in more remote areas had a more severe regime than those in Kwangtung. In terms of weather, at least, this would be the case.

lic Security) explained the rules and policies governing this form of punishment. The rightists were told that they did not have definite terms, and that as soon as they gave evidence of having reformed properly they would be released and could come back to work in their original units. Then in early 1958 Hu was assigned to a large labor re-education farm in southwestern Kwangtung province. He estimates that this farm held over 5,000 inmates during his stay there, although it was somewhat smaller when he first arrived. The farm had formerly housed labor reform inmates who had been transferred elsewhere. The primary crops were sugar cane and rice.

At the farm the inmates were divided into five middle teams *(chung-tui)*, each with its own land and housing facilities. One of the middle teams consisted entirely of women, the others all of men. Middle teams were generally split into four branch teams *(fen-tui)*, each of which was in turn divided into roughly four large groups *(ta-tsu)*, and then further into *hsiao-tsu,* each with about fifteen inmates. The middle team was led by two public security cadres, a middle team head, and a political education officer *(cheng-chih chiao-tao-yüan)*, the latter responsible for leading the political study of the inmates. Each branch team was headed by a single leader, also a public security cadre. The large group and *hsiao-tsu units* had inmates appointed by camp authorities to lead them.

Hu is uncertain about the structure of the camp administration. He mentions that there was a farm head at the top who doubled as secretary of the farm Party committee. There were a number of staff departments dealing with finance and production, but Hu can not specify them all. The section with which inmates had the most contact was the correctional work section *(kuan-chiao ku)*, which planned the political study routine for inmates and assisted the middle team political education officers in carrying out inmate study. Hu also mentions that a contingent of public security troops guarded the camp. There was also a group of free employees at the camp who were organized into two teams and lived separately from the inmates.[17]

When Hu first arrived he and about a hundred other new inmates were assigned to the second middle team, where they were dispersed among the existing *hsiao-tsu,* two or three in each. This middle team contained an assortment of inmates—not only rightists but rural cadres who had committed errors, people who had tried to escape to

---

17. These free employees received a regular wage, were not under guard, and were for the most part former inmates themselves.

Hong Kong, peasants who had streamed into Canton and had refused
to return to their villages, and many others. The inmates already there
did not fill in the new arrivals on camp routine, and in fact there
was much mutual avoidance between old and new inmates at first,
which the authorities encouraged. Only over time, through instruction
from the cadres and trial and error, did the new arrivals learn the
ropes, and only subsequently did they begin to form friendships with
those who had entered the camps earlier.

In 1959 there was a reorganization of the camp in which the inmates
who had held cadre or employee positions in the past, such as Hu,
were transferred to the first middle team, leaving only peasant-origin
inmates in the second middle team. The rationale was not announced,
but Hu feels that the previous mixing of inmates of different backgrounds had resulted in constant disputes and tension. Forming more
homogeneous groups might make it easier to develop political rituals
properly.[18] After this there were no other large reorganizations, but
inmates were often shifted from group to group, sometimes only temporarily, to adjust to changing work needs. Some groups were split up
for other reasons. An exemplary *hsiao-tsu* might be split up and its
members assigned to head other groups, replacing less able heads. An
inmate who labored poorly or caused trouble and did not respond to
group criticism was sometimes shifted out of his group and assigned
to labor under the supervision of a more activist *hsiao-tsu*. The activist group was expected to prod and criticize the troublemaker until
he corrected his ways.

The daily routine varied by season, as might be expected. During
slack agricultural seasons there was roughly a ten-hour working day
and a two-hour political study session in the evening. During busy
seasons the work day was lengthened, and this cut into the time allotted to meals, rest, and study. Inmates were supposed to receive two
days of rest a month, but this regulation was rarely adhered to. During the most arduous period of labor, in 1958–1959 during the Great
Leap Forward, the inmates often spent fourteen or fifteen hours a
day in the fields. In all of these activities—labor, meals, study, and
sleep—the small group was the organizational unit, and only limited

---

18. Recall from Chapter 4 that the ideal is a *hsiao-tsu* which is neither too
homogeneous nor too heterogeneous. My informants disagree about how inmates
were grouped together in the camps. Some claim that it was the general policy
to mix inmates of different types together to create dissension and make control
easier, while others say that inmates were grouped by offense or by social background in order to facilitate thought reform. Apparently there was no set policy
in this regard, and there were variations over time and by camp.

opportunities for fraternization with other inmates existed (during rest periods after meals and sometimes while dispersed in the fields).

During the latter part of Hu's stay in the camp a cultural work team was organized with more than fifty inmates participating, including Hu. The members of this team put on skits and songs in various parts of the farm, activities designed to encourage reform and to whip up enthusiasm for labor.[19] While he was in the second middle team Hu had never received particular notice for his work efforts, because he was in competition with experienced peasants. But he picked up some work techniques from these peasants which he put to good use. After his transfer he was consistently picked as a model worker, and perhaps because of this he was chosen by camp authorities to be a *hsiao-tsu* head. When the cultural work team was organized, Hu was promoted to serve as head of its large group (composed of four *hsiao-tsu*).

Although labor and production were very important to camp authorities during this period, political study was not neglected. Generally, as mentioned, the inmates met for two hours of study every evening, although in the busy seasons these sessions were somewhat abbreviated. Occasionally study consisted of going to an all-farm meeting to hear reports from the camp's leading cadres, often at the initiation or conclusion of some campaign. Some of the campaigns of the outside society penetrated into camp life, for instance the Great Leap Forward, but the inmates were isolated from others, such as cadre rectification campaigns. There were also special campaigns run only within the camps. For instance, once or twice a year the camp authorities launched campaigns against escape attempts, and for several evenings inmates were expected to examine their thoughts to reveal whether they had notions of fleeing.

Middle team meetings were much more common than all-farm meetings. Before the busy seasons all of the inmates in a middle team would assemble to listen to mobilization reports urging them to work hard in the fields. After the busy season concluded a middle team meeting would be convened to initiate the selection of labor activists and the more exalted "model soldiers" (*piao-ping*). In these meetings criteria for selection were announced, and then within *hsiao-tsu* the self-report mutual-evaluation procedure was carried out to arrive at nominations. Nominees were in turn approved and announced in mid-

---

19. The work of a similar cultural team is described in Lai Ying, *The Thirty-sixth Way* (Garden City, N.Y.: Doubleday, 1969).

dle team meetings. The middle team was also the forum in which the writing of the annual individual summations was initiated. Hu feels, however, that these summations were less important than in organizations outside the camps, and they tended to be brief (100 to 200 characters) and void of any revelations. Middle team meetings were also called to struggle inmates who committed serious errors, such as trying to escape, fighting, or stealing.

When there were no special matters requiring larger meetings, nightly study was carried out entirely in the *hsiao-tsu.* At the designated time inmates assembled in their groups in various corners of the barracks, sitting on adjacent beds. One night they might discuss current production results or problems, another national and world events, and still another individual progress toward reform. Sometimes they simply read and discussed selected articles from the newspaper (each *hsiao-tsu* had a subscription to *Southern Daily,* the Kwangtung provincial Party committee newspaper). Once a week the evening session was devoted to a livelihood self-examination meeting, where group members discussed their conduct during the past week, as in other organizational settings.

It is important to note that the inmates did not spend a great deal of their time criticizing the errors they had committed in earlier days. In fact, Hu claims, inmates were specifically advised by camp authorities to avoid talking about their pre-camp lives, their family backgrounds, and similar topics.[20] The standard against which personal reform was supposed to be gauged was not pre-camp behavior, but prior conduct within the camp. Inmates discussed how their attitudes toward manual labor had changed as a result of the recent harvest campaign, or how they had ridden themselves of thoughts of escaping they had had only a few weeks before. This present orientation of camp mutual criticism activities contrasts markedly with the confessions and examinations of past activities which took place in the earlier prison thought reform situation.[21]

The inmates' political study was not run as well as the foregoing comments might imply. Most of the evening study meetings were rather listless, with little real debate or enthusiasm. When Hu was in

---

20. My other informants generally confirm that there was little discussion of pre-camp lives and behavior.

21. Studies of early prison thought reform emphasize that the self-criticisms of earlier life and conduct are extremely powerful psychological components of the thought reform process, vital in the "death and rebirth" identity change which is supposed to take place. Without this activity we should expect thought reform in labor camps to be less effective. See Robert J. Lifton, *op. cit.,* Chap. 4.

the second middle team, mixed in with inmates from peasant backgrounds, discussions were almost never well run. The peasant inmates rarely spoke and often dozed off, leaving the group head with "cold floors" in which he had to do all the talking himself. When they did speak, most of the peasants could not be held to the assigned topic, and most needed help from other inmates to cope with any study tasks requiring reading and writing. When group members did doze off the *hsiao-tsu* head and the group recorder sometimes made up false discussion notes to turn in to the middle team cadres, although they would have been in serious trouble if this deception had been discovered. In the first middle team discussions were more orderly, since ex-cadres were all accustomed to these political rituals, but even among the former cadres slacking was not uncommon, especially during the periods of the heaviest work. Slacking and the padding of discussion notes were made possible by the fact that camp cadres made only spot checks on inmate study activities, since they had their own evening group study to attend.

Even if political rituals were not well run, it may seem strange that they could be maintained at all among inmates who had just completed strenuous work in the fields. The extensive system of supervision, sanctions, and rewards made this possible. Supervision was carried out not only by the cadres and guards, but by the inmates themselves. The *hsiao-tsu* study notes were regularly turned over to middle team cadres. In addition, *hsiao-tsu* heads had to report on a regular basis (about once a week) to branch team and middle team cadres on the problems of *hsiao-tsu* members. There was also a great deal of informal cadre-small group head consultation in which day to day problems were discussed. The cadres tried to pick *hsiao-tsu* heads who would be fairly diligent in reporting the misbehavior of fellow inmates, but in practice these reports were not fully reliable. Hu illustrates with his own situation. As a *hsiao-tsu* head he did report regularly on others, but he toned his reports down to protect members of his group, and he also gave individual members confidential advice on how to stay out of trouble. He feels that the cadres did not expect him to report everything, because to be so diligent would have meant alienating himself from others in the group. The group would not then have done so well in production activities, and the cadres were concerned about production results as well as about thought reform and social control. So they permitted *hsiao-tsu* heads to be less than totally diligent in their reporting.

However, because they could not depend fully on *hsiao-tsu* heads for information, the cadres maintained a network of informers among the inmates. The presence of informers limited the extent to which *hsiao-tsu* heads could conceal misbehavior, although from Hu's discussion of the "padding" of discussion notes we can see that even the informers were not completely diligent or effective. The presence or danger of informers affected the group atmosphere and kept most inmates from being open in expressing their feelings to others. It is interesting to note that at least some of the informers were known to other inmates and yet escaped the kind of retaliation we would expect in an American prison or Soviet labor camp. Other inmates did try to avoid the informers or to get them in trouble with the authorities, but there were no acts of violence against them that Hu was aware of.[22] Apparently there was no "prison code" to encourage such retaliation, and the informers and the other inmates lived together in an uneasy coexistence.

Cadres used a broad range of rewards and sanctions to influence the behavior of inmates. Rations were given out in three levels, which were set by the self-report mutual-evaluation procedure within groups, and then revised and approved by middle team authorities. The rations were mainly set according to the labor power of the individual, but inmates who constantly caused trouble were given a lower rank or suffered a temporary ration cut.[23] Inmates also received wages, which were awarded in five grades ranging from 30 yüan down to 16 yüan per month (one yüan equals U.S. $.40 at the official rate). Both labor and progress in reform were supposed to be considered in the self-report mutual-evaluation procedure which established these ranks.[24] Evaluations for both rations and wages took place irregularly, roughly at three-month intervals.

The inmates' privileges were also manipulated by the cadres. Inmates were supposed to be allowed two visits from relatives a month, each for not more than two hours. The visits were not automatic,

---

22. My other informants confirm the openness of some of the informers, and their relative immunity to retaliation.

23. Some of my other informants say that there was a regulation that rations could not be cut in their camps as a punishment.

24. As in Soviet labor camps the wages of inmates are not given to them to use freely. First a deduction of 10 to 20 yüan is taken out each month to pay for the food, clothing, and shelter the state is providing. Then another portion may be sent to help support the dependents of the inmate outside the camp. If there is any left it is kept by camp authorities, and the inmate can request that purchases of soap, writing paper, and other items be made for him. The maximum pay in this and other labor re-education camps corresponds roughly to the wages of an unskilled factory worker.

however, and had to be applied for. Cadres withheld their approval
from the applications of troublesome inmates, and they also inter-
cepted packages intended for them. Hu claims that in 1960 a new
privilege became available. Special housing was constructed so that
the wives of a few inmates could come for an overnight visit. Prior
permission was required, and only the most trustworthy received this
privilege. Some trusted inmates, usually those whose terms could be
expected to be over soon, were also allowed to leave camp for a day's
visit home. This was also a very rare privilege.[25]

The cadres also manipulated labor assignments. Troublesome inmates could be assigned to supervised labor, and an entire *hsiao-tsu*
which was classed as "backward" could be shifted to more difficult
work (such as earth moving and water conseravtion work). Exemplary
groups, on the other hand, could be given lighter work, such as light
weeding or rowing the boats used to transport the farm's sugar cane.
This reward did stimulate some mutual criticism within the group, as
inmates encouraged each other to work better in order to receive
choice work assignments. However, this practice also was in direct
contradiction to the elite's claim that labor in China is not used as
a form of punishment.

The inmates who were selected periodically as labor activists and
"model soldiers" received only public praise (along with a T-shirt, in
the case of the model soldiers). But they had the additional knowledge
that they might be promoted into positions of camp leadership and
trust, and might even further their chances for an early release. Thus
there was a certain amount of interest surrounding the competition
for these titles.

Inmates who caused trouble might receive heavier penalties than
group criticism, such as cuts in their rations and privileges, and a shift
to more difficult work. For serious errors they could be subjected to a
struggle meeting which could result in a longer sentence or, in extreme
cases, even in death. Hu gives an example of a struggle meeting which
affected his life. The cultural work team in which he served near
the end of his stay performed in various areas of the camp, and this
mobility provided more escape opportunities than other inmates
possessed. Hu, as the large group head within the team, had been
instructed to keep a special eye on several members whom cadres

---

25. My other labor re-education camp informants do not mention these last two
privileges. Those who served in these camps later than Hu claim that labor re-
education had become more punitive over time, with stricter controls over inmates
and fewer special privileges.

suspected of wanting to escape, but he did not take this warning seriously. One day two of them attempted an escape but were caught and returned to the camp. They were interrogated for several days by camp authorities and then turned over to the middle team for struggle. In a large meeting the middle team head described the circumstances of the case, and the two escapees, sitting up front, were asked to justify their actions. Their explanations were followed by inmates rising from the floor to denounce them. Most of those who participated were *hsiao-tsu* heads, who had been briefed in advance. At the conclusion of the meeting the middle team head announced the penalty, which clearly had been decided in advance. Both escapees were sentenced to terms of labor reform and were shipped out of the camp. In the same meeting Hu was criticized by the cadres for his lack of vigilance, and he was removed from his post as large-group head.

The control that camp authorities exercised over the lives of the inmates in Hu's camp was quite impressive. Nonetheless, the result was not the desired strict political atmosphere. Hu feels inmates were mainly concerned with staying out of trouble and serving their time, rather than with pressuring their peers to reform themselves. There were no "naïve activists" in this camp as there are in other organizational settings—individuals who unselfconsciously work hard, study hard, and urge others to reform. Rather, there was a strong element of calculation in the behavior of all the inmates. Mutual criticism within groups was not very effectively developed, and Hu feels inmates were more concerned with the sanctions controlled by cadres than with the criticism they received from other inmates. Minor kinds of deviance, such as the padding of discussion notes, did continue to exist, and inmates were not completely isolated from all unorthodox opinions. Over time they were able to develop some close friendships and to confide their alienation to friends in private conversations. Hu says that he made friends with about half a dozen other inmates, mostly rightists in other *hsiao-tsu*. He gradually built up trust and an ability to confide his bitterness and fears to these friends. Through such confidential talks Hu gained the impression that his feelings of alienation were widely shared. But such sentiments were never expressed beyond these small nodes of friendship, and a general sharing of grievances could not occur.

Hu feels that little real thought reform was produced by camp experiences, and in fact the predominant tendency was toward increasing resentment. Policy trends in this period contributed to these negative results. As mentioned previously, Hu and the other inmates were at first told that their terms were not set and that they could be released as soon as they had demonstrated reform. They were led to believe that releases might be granted after as little as six months of confinement. As time dragged on and few were released, however, the mood of some inmates changed from one of hope and determination to a feeling of having been misled and cheated. Hu claims that the first releases were granted to peasants whose error had been to move to the city and refuse to return home. Hu feels that those released had not distinguished themselves by their activism or personal reform and did not deserve to be the first to leave. Even later, when rightists and others started to be released, the pattern of those chosen, in Hu's estimation, bore no clear relationship to conduct within the camp. Hu had generally been cooperative, had frequently been chosen as a labor activist, and had served in leadership positions, but he was not released for three years. And his release came shortly after he got in trouble for not being sufficiently vigilant against potential escapees. He and his friends developed their own explanations for the pattern of releases. One theory was that release depended not on how well one was reforming, but on how serious the original error had been, and that inmates did have fixed sentences proportional to these errors which were simply not revealed to them. Another theory was that one's original work unit had a major voice in his release, and if authorities there didn't want his services back he would be kept for a longer period of time. Whatever the true explanation, the gap between the originally announced policy and the reality contributed to a growing bitterness among inmates. Perhaps because of this problem, in 1961 there was a change in official policy to make labor re-education carry fixed sentences.[26]

In 1961 Hu was finally released and sent back to his original unit. When he arrived, however, there was no job for him, and he was sent down to the unit's cadre farm. In 1962 he tried to escape to Hong Kong but failed. He spent a period of time unemployed, living off relatives and friends, and then he worked for a while as a substitute teacher in a commune primary school. In 1964 he made a second escape attempt and successfully reached Macao.

26. Jerome A. Cohen, op. cit., p. 269; 1967 Yearbook on Chinese Communism, op. cit., p. 469. There is no official confirmation of this shift, but a general argeement exists among other sources that in late 1961 or early 1962 the Ministry of Public Security started using set terms, generally ranging from six months to three years.

WANG LAO-KAI: A LABOR REFORM CAMP INMATE

Wang Lao-kai is a 32-year-old male from a rural area in Kwangtung province whom I interviewed twice for a total of six hours. His family had been classified as landlords at the time of the land reform campaign, and his father had been executed, leaving a large and embittered family. Wang and his nine brothers were constantly at odds with the local cadres, and in 1961 Wang was sentenced to six years of labor reform as a "counterrevolutionary bad element." He claims he committed no specific crime to earn this sentence, but perhaps he is not being completely frank about his troubles. The sentence was announced in a brigade struggle meeting with a representative of the local people's court present, rather than in a formal courtroom procedure. After sentencing Wang spent one month in a local supervision station (k'an-shuo-so), and in the following years he served time in four different labor reform institutions, all in Kwangtung province. Wang claims that frequent transfers of inmates are part of labor reform policy, designed to prevent inmates from building up friendship ties and arranging escapes.[27] Here we will discuss the labor reform camp in which Wang spent the largest part of his sentence, from 1961 to 1964.

In this labor reform camp both mining and farming were carried on. There were two brigades (ta-tui) of inmates, one for each main economic activity, and a total of 6,000 inmates. The mining brigade contained the inmates who had committed the most serious crimes and were serving the longest terms, such as former Kuomintang military officers, counterrevolutionary landlords, and rapists. The second brigade, which engaged in farming, included less serious offenders with shorter terms, including Wang. In this brigade the inmates were further divided into three middle teams, each of which was divided into from six to eight small teams. These were finally divided into hsiao-tsu, each with about fifteen members. (These terms differ somewhat from those used in Hu's labor re-education camp, but the differences are not significant. There is a great deal of variation in the organizational terms used for both types of camps.) As in Hu's camp there were separate teams of free employees, most of them former inmates.[28]

---

27. Several other inmates agree that frequent transfers were part of official penal policy. However, other informants claim this was not so, that transfers were primarily due to shifting work needs and the expansion and contraction of various camps.

28. Measures accompanying the 1954 labor reform code contain stipulations that

Wang mentions that the brigades, middle teams, and small teams were all led by public security cadres, while the *hsiao-tsu* heads were inmates appointed by the camp authorities. There was no political education officer in Wang's camp; instead, members of the correctional work section were assigned to work with particular middle teams on a regular basis. (Again, there is no special significance to this difference.)

In many respects the features of camp life reflect those described by Hu. The work day was roughly ten hours long but varied seasonally. Every evening, six days a week, the inmates participated in political study sessions, usually in their *hsiao-tsu* units. In Wang's camp, as in Hu's, outside campaigns sometimes penetrated into the camp routine. Wang mentions that the Four Cleanups campaign of 1964 was adapted for use within the labor reform camp. The "four uncleans" under scrutiny were peculiar to the camp situation; each inmate was expected to confess to his group whether he was dissatisfied with his sentence, whether he had thoughts of escaping, whether he was participating in any oppositional cliques within the camp, and whether after his release he would get into trouble again. The range of incentives and sanctions available to camp authorities was also similar, including ration cuts, good or bad work assignments, struggle meetings, and early release or lengthened sentences.

The evening study routine was also similar to that discussed by Hu, with meetings in the barracks, note-taking, and reporting by *hsiao-tsu* heads. These group discussions were often poorly run and listlessly engaged in, and mutual criticism tended to be superficial or directed only from the *hsiao-tsu* head to other members. Wang never served as *hsiao-tsu* head, and he has a somewhat less favorable view of those who held this position than does Hu. He feels that many group heads were hypocritical and nasty, that they got other inmates in trouble as a way of easing their own suffering. Wang mentions, as does Hu, that inmates were discouraged from bringing up and discussing their past lives and relationships outside the camps.

So while in theory there was a sharp difference between labor reform and labor re-education camp inmates, with the latter not considered criminals and not deprived of all of their civilian rights and occupational ties, in actuality camp life was similar for both types of

---

labor reform inmates can be kept on to work as free employees after their release if they desire to do so and are needed, if they have no home or job to return to, or if they have served time in a sparsely settled area where settlers are needed. Jerome A. Cohen, *op. cit.*, pp. 634–635. No comparable provisions have been published for labor re-education inmates, but similar criteria seem to apply.

inmates.[29] But Wang mentions frequent roll-calls and body searches, while Hu does not. Wang received no wages, but only small amounts of pocket money (*ling-yung-ch'ien*) each month, ranging from 60 cents to 1 yüan, depending upon monthly group evaluations of individual conduct. Wang says that his fellow inmates were often denied visiting and mail privileges, and were allowed no overnight visits from wives or visits home. In Wang's camp there were also solitary confinement cells where troublesome inmates could be isolated on reduced rations, but these were missing in Hu's camp. Wang also claims that camp cadres occasionally resorted to beatings to enforce their will, while Hu says that physical punishment was not allowed and would have brought punishment upon any cadre attempting it. The major difference between the two types of camps seems to be that there were more restrictions and a somewhat harsher regimen in the labor reform camp described by Wang.

While the range of incentives and penalties available to the cadres are similar in the two accounts, there seems to have been more reliance on negative sanctions in Wang's camp. It is apparent from Wang's account that the authorities in his camp had more severe control problems than did the people running Hu's camp. There was a sizeable contingent of very bitter inmates, many of whom were under long sentences and had no hope of release. Some inmates also simply considered themselves bitter and eternal enemies of the Communist regime, and Wang would place himself in this category. Some of these especially bitter inmates openly declared their defiance and put up with constant abuse as a result. Some demonstrated their resistance in other ways, through anti-communist graffiti on latrine walls or through suicide. In this situation camp authorities could not hope to rely heavily on group criticism to maintain control, and instead they emphasized struggle meetings, solitary confinement, and other penalties. They also seem to have relied very heavily on informers, since even the diligent *hsiao-tsu* heads were not very effective in uncovering and reporting on the behavior of the most bitter inmates.

Wang describes the *hsiao-tsu* in which he spent the most time in this camp: the only activist was the group head, and he was heartily disliked by the others. In most meetings this fellow did much of the talking, giving his views on the study materials and berating the poor reform of his peers. Because of his diligence there was little slacking in study and no "padding" of discussion notes. In spite of the general

29. There is a brief discussion of rights and privileges retained by labor reeducation inmates in Peiching Jih-pao, June 28, 1958.

discontent with the group head there was little confiding of grievances among the others. Wang claims that there was too much risk in being frank with others in the group, since one could never be sure when a fellow inmate would report him in order to "establish merit" with camp authorities. (Wang did make some friends with inmates outside of his group, but he did so very cautiously, testing these friends by revealing his true feelings little by little over a long period of time.) The group head was able to maintain control of most group activities, but he was never able to achieve anything like general involvement in, and enthusiasm for, study and reform. Wang says the cadres in his camp were more concerned with controlling inmates than with production results, so that inmates could do little to undermine an activist group head by working poorly.

Wang himself was constantly in hot water for his poor behavior, although he managed to avoid major errors. He worked poorly and did not always hide his bitterness. He was regularly given the lowest level of pocket money within his group, but the differences were so small he did not care. He was constantly warned to behave himself, both by his group head and by the small team head, but he changed little. He also failed to respond to the generally low ration rankings he received. He managed to toe the line just enough to avoid serious trouble, and the most severe penalty he received was a ration cut and a demand that he work three extra hours a day for a short period.

In sum, control problems were more severe in Wang's labor reform camp than in Hu's labor re-education camp. The façade of general thought reform broke down much more, and alienation was more openly communicated. Nonetheless the supervision, sanctions, and group structure did make communication of such feelings difficult, and no real inmate subculture or informal inmate hierarchy developed.

After six years in various labor reform camps Wang was released on schedule early in 1967, in spite of his spotty record of reform. He mentions that in his last labor reform camp there was at the time of his release no discussion of the Cultural Revolution, although rumors about turbulent events had reached inmates from visiting relatives and from new inmates. Upon release Wang was ordered to return to his home village, where he engaged in agricultural labor as before his sentencing, but under mass supervision.[30] In 1968 he and five friends took advantage of the confusion of the Cultural Revolution to steal a boat and escape to Hong Kong.

---

30. See Jerome A. Cohen, *op. cit.*, Chap. 5, on supervised labor.

GENERAL PATTERNS AND CONTRASTS

The basic features of labor reform and labor re-education camps are echoed by others interviewed. My informants did not believe they were surrounded by enthusiastically reforming inmates, in contrast to the impressions of Father Bonnichon and others who underwent prison thought reform in the early 1950's. Insincere confessions were not immediately criticized, and for the most part inmates, and probably cadres, accepted the fact that such hypocrisy was a necessary part of adapting and surviving within the camps. In other words camps of both types seem to have had a much more lax political atmosphere than the thought reform prisons of the immediate post-1949 years.[31]

There are a number of important differences between the camps and the early prisons which contribute to the different atmospheres. In the prisons the inmate's entire day (and often much of the night) was spent in study and thought reform activities, while in labor camps this activity is confined to two hours or so daily. Both cadres and inmates have to be concerned somewhat more with production, then, and less with pursuing thought reform. Control and supervision are also simpler within a prison than in many labor camps, where inmates are dispersed at their work posts or in the fields. In the early 1950's there was also an atmosphere filled with great changes and new opportunities, in which many people were undergoing various forms of thought reform and re-education. This atmosphere sometimes penetrated into prison life and contributed a spirit of hope to inmate activities.[32] In the 1960's, with society more stabilized and fewer opportunities opening up, inmates in corrective labor camps were perhaps more pessimistic and aware of their status as outcastes. The crucial difference between the two situations, however, is the fact that participants in prison thought reform had not, for the most part, had their sentences set, while labor camp inmates (with the partial exception of labor re-education camp inmates prior to 1961) had definite terms to serve. The cases of inmates undergoing prison thought reform were still under investigation, and they were led to believe that the progress of their reform was a life or death matter. If they fully confessed their past errors and showed real repentance they might receive a light sentence, even for a serious crime. But if they resisted confessing lesser

---

31. The reader should refer to the descriptions in Robert J. Lifton, *op. cit.*, and Edgar H. Schein, *op. cit.*

32. Allyn and Adele Rickett, *Prisoners of Liberation*, (New York: Cameron Associates, 1957); Harriet C. Mills, "Thought Reform: Ideological Remolding in China," in *Atlantic Monthly*, Vol. 204, December 1959.

offenses they might receive very serious penalties. True repentance was to be displayed, among other ways, by taking an active interest in pressuring others to confess. Sometimes only after several years of intensive thought reform was a prisoner's case brought up for legal decision and sentencing.

Labor camp inmates, in contrast, have undergone an abbreviated version of this ritual in prisons or detention houses, but then their cases have been decided and they have received a sentence. In the camps confession of past mistakes is no longer stressed. Sentences have been set, and only the most heroic acts or the most serious errors will alter those sentences in any major way. The day-to-day political study rituals are not a life and death matter, though they may affect the level of an inmate's rations and his access to camp privileges. Without the intense examinations of past lives, the active and enthusiastic pressure of other group members, and the anxiety and hope surrounding one's future, the corrective labor camps must be much less effective in changing political attitudes than were the early prison thought reform experiences.

Nonetheless, *hsiao-tsu* political rituals have not been abandoned behind the screen of secrecy that surrounds these institutions. Political rituals for labor camp inmates have been vigorously maintained by camp authorities. Although they may not be very effective in changing anti-social elements into activists, these rituals do, apparently, make it easier for camp officials to control their charges. They obstruct the development of an inmate subculture and inmate loyalties which arise as a matter of course in Western and Soviet penal institutions. And by obstructing the development of an inmate subculture, they may contribute to reform in a less ambitious sense. They may at least make it possible for Chinese authorities to prevent their penal institutions from becoming "schools for crime" (or political opposition) where new inmates are rapidly trained and indoctrinated into deviant ways by hardened offenders.

The Chinese have developed corrective labor camps which are distinctive in many ways from their Soviet counterparts, particularly in the heavy emphasis given to political re-education efforts and the reliance upon group manipulation more than on physical force and incentives tied to work performance.[33] The atmosphere within Chinese camps is also fairly distinctive when compared with that in organiza-

---

33. A recent Soviet text says 50 minutes *a week* are allotted to political work among prisoners. *Ispravitel'no-trudovoe pravo* (Corrective labor law) (Moscow: Iuridicheskaia literatura, 1966), p. 217. This source was brought to my attention by Walter Connor.

tions discussed in earlier chapters. Control and restriction of inmates and pressures to reform are strong, and there is little of the open complaining and ignoring cadre criticisms which we saw in the rural political rituals. At the same time, the initial alienation and negative reactions to the harshness of camp life makes inmates unlikely to respond enthusiastically to the demands of authorities. *Hsiao-tsu* and political rituals do contribute to a fairly effective control over inmates' actions, but they are unable to achieve the general enthusiasm and pressures for reform and the strict political atmosphere which are desired.

X

ORGANIZATIONAL SETTING
AND POLITICAL ATMOSPHERE

We have now examined five organizational settings: offices, schools, rural communes, factories and other work units, and corrective labor camps. In analyzing our case studies, we have tried to discover what it was about a particular organization that led to either a relatively strict or a relatively lax political atmosphere. Our task in this chapter is to draw together and summarize the insights gained from the comparison of case studies in order to specify the critical structural properties of organizations which may affect the political atmosphere which can be developed within them.

Before we begin our analysis, we should reiterate what we mean by the term "strict political atmosphere," as described in Chapter 4. First, all activities of members of an organization will be judged by official standards of thought and behavior, and all deviations from those standards will become public knowledge and the focus for group political rituals. Second, effective social pressure will be mobilized in support of official norms in each case of deviation. This implies that social pressure within the group against the deviant is unanimous, that the deviant is unable to find social support for continued deviance either from within or from outside the group, that the deviant is unable to impute ulterior motives or insincerity to his critics, and that he feels ties to his group (and to the larger organization) and desires to avoid its criticism. In other words, there are two basic characteristics of a strict political atmosphere: that vigorous social pressure in support of official norms will develop in the first place, and that social pressure, once it has been mobilized, will have the desired effects upon its targets. Structural properties of an organization can affect both of these basic characteristics.

Whether official standards are applied rigorously to all thoughts and behavior and whether deviations result in vigorous social pressure will be influenced by the nature of the activities carried out within the organization, by the quality of leadership of that organization, and by the ease of supervision within the organization. Each of these three major organizational features has several aspects which are relevant to our problem. Let us consider them one at a time.[1]

An organization seems more likely to develop a strict political atmosphere if political rituals are at the center of organizational life than if these activities are in some way extraneous. Ideally, organizational leaders should try to see that, as the slogan goes, "politics takes command" in all organizational activities, even when the political relevance of some activities is not immediately apparent and has to be explained to the participants. The organizational leaders, their superiors, and regional and national Party programs should all stress the importance of political rectitude and political aspects of work, study, and other activities. Political rectitude and performance in political rituals should be given primary emphasis in decisions about promotions, wages, rations, demotions, and job and school placement.

We have already seen in some of the case studies that organizations do not always successfully put politics in command. In our five settings, in fact, people ordinarily spent most of their time in activities other than political rituals, primarily in work or academic study. Only during major campaigns are political activities and rituals the focus of organizational life; the rest of the time they are important, but clearly secondary activities, in terms of the time and energy devoted to them. To state the obvious: people in China cannot spend all of their time in political study and thought reform. Most energies have to go into such activities as work or training for future work.

If political rituals and evaluations are not the central activities within an organization, the danger is that they will be seen as ex-

---

1. The discussion that follows is based upon insights gained from comparison of all of the interview accounts, not simply those presented as case studies. From time to time generalizations will be supported by references to some of the case studies, but to do so in every instance would make the text unwieldy. In sum, all of the general statements have some basis in the interview materials, although the crude nature of qualitative comparison leaves the validity of these generalizations open to some question.

traneous or as an added burden. To prevent this from happening, the other activities have to be well integrated with political rituals, so that participants see political activities as serving work needs and work results as having major political implications. There is clearly an effort to do this in all organizations in China, but this effort is not always successful. The integration of politics with other activities requires skillful leadership, something not every organization can command (leadership problems will be discussed shortly). In addition, it would seem that some kinds of activities, such as academic study, are inherently harder to integrate with political evaluations and rituals than others, such as work in the Party apparatus.

In sum, an organization's activities may detract from the creation of a strict political atmosphere, but these activities cannot simply be abandoned, or even be more than minimally or temporarily de-emphasized. Recurrent campaigns may temporarily place politics in the center of people's lives and relate politics more closely to other activities, but campaigns recur precisely because their effects tend to wear off in time.[2] In some rural areas there is a slack agricultural season when cadres can stress political activities, thus altering the traditional rural emphasis on work and family affairs. But as long as political activities are reserved for the slack seasons the danger remains that they will be seen as extraneous to production activities. If political study is emphasized during the busy seasons it may help to improve morale and work attitudes, but (especially if it is conducted poorly) it may instead be seen as a burden which takes important time and energy away from food production.

If there are other important activities within an organization besides political rituals, then there will also be other criteria for evaluating and promoting personnel. To stress technical skill, strength, academic performance, or other criteria can create obstacles to the desired political atmosphere in two ways. Individuals who are not politically activist may find security through meeting these other criteria, and thus may be able to show less concern for political rectitude than would otherwise be the case (recall the engineer Kung Ch'eng-shih). Also, individuals who do not meet these other criteria but who might be inclined to be politically activist may feel that the

---

2. The cycling of mobilization and normalization stages in the Chinese countryside is discussed in G. William Skinner and Edwin A. Winckler, "Compliance Succession in Rural Communist China: A Cyclical Theory," in Amitai Etzioni, ed., *A Sociological Reader on Complex Organizations,* 2nd edition (New York: Holt, Rinehart and Winston, 1969).

rewards to the skilled, the strong, the bright, and so on are greater than the rewards to the politically pure and enthusiastic, and may be discouraged from activism.

There is an additional problem entailed in evaluating personnel. Ideally, political evaluations should focus on attitudes and motivations—for example, whether an individual is diligently and sincerely rectifying his unorthodox attitudes and values. However, even with the aid of political rituals it is harder to assess a man's thoughts than to assess his background or behavior. If political behavior (e.g., political activism) is evaluated rather than political attitudes, there is always the chance that people can feign activism and find security or mobility without altering their underlying attitudes and values. Partly because of such difficulties, in practice background characteristics (such as class origins, or membership in the Party or Youth League) often stand as proxies for political attitudes; when this practice is followed, those who are favored gain an undesirable degree of security (recall the cadre Ma Kan-pu), while those not favored may feel pessimistic and poorly motivated to meet political standards (recall the rich peasant Chang Nung-min). Even if a concerted effort is made to emphasize political criteria in evaluating personnel this will often be a difficult task.

Strong political leadership is also critical in shaping the atmosphere within an organization. In official jargon, an organization should have a strong "political core"; this refers to both the quality and the distribution of leadership personnel. It is difficult to give a precise definition of high quality political leadership, but it should include leaders who are loyal and enthusiastic, who diligently apply mass line principles and try to work through and with their subordinates, who stress the political aspects of all activities, and who apply ideological criteria to the activities of their subordinates. A strong political core requires the distribution of high quality leadership at every level in an organization down to the *hsiao-tsu* heads, and in addition requires a healthy supply of activists within each group to aid the leaders in developing social pressure in favor of official goals and standards.

Many organizations may not be blessed with a strong political core, and may not be in position to do much about it. The leaders of some organizations may have undergone intensive training in leadership techniques or may have been tempered in early guerrilla struggles (remember that the desired style of leadership is modeled to a considerable extent on the leadership patterns within guerrilla organizations during the Yenan period). Other organizations, however, may have to make do with local personnel promoted from below (as in many rural production teams and brigades) or with individuals who received their leadership training in pre-1949 Kuomintang institutions. Since organizations have other goals and activities besides political indoctrination, leadership posts may be awarded for reasons other than political quality (recall again the work group headed by the engineer Kung Ch'eng-shih). Organizations may also have difficulty in extending the political core to the lowest levels. *Hsiao-tsu* heads may be of low quality, either because the better people have been promoted (as in Tai Hsiao-ai's technical school), or because they owe their positions more to skill than to political enthusiasm (recall the worker Li Kung-jen's account). In some organizations it may be difficult to assemble and organize a large number of activists, and then leaders of high political quality will not be able to work through their subordinates as much as they would like to. To some extent the supply of leadership is increased through a variety of long and short term political training institutions and through campaigns designed to develop activists within various organizations. But the training institutions have varied over time, both in their numbers and their quality, and the effectiveness of these measures can be debated.[3] In any case may of these matters are largely outside the control of leaders within a given organization, (for example, a corrective labor camp official cannot demand that he be sent only activist inmates), and clearly the strength of the political core does vary from organization to organization. In an organization without a strong political core orthodox standards are less likely to be diligently applied to all activities and attitudes of members than in an organization which is more favorably endowed.

Some organizations also have more serious supervision problems than others. In organizations where daily activities are dispersed (e.g., communes, agricultural corrective labor camps) it is inherently more difficult for superiors to supervise the activities of their subordinates than in organizations which are more centralized (e.g., schools, factories). Other limitations on supervision occur when members spend considerable time outside of the organization. Some organizations (e.g.,

---

3. The extensiveness of leadership training facilities, particularly for low level leadership positions, has varied widely over time. During the Great Leap Forward there was an effort to disperse rural Party schools and other training facilities into the villages, so that team and brigade cadres could receive training, but by 1961 this effort seems to have tailed off. See *Jen-min Jih-pao*, January 13, 1960; *Shang yu*, February 10, 1960; *Jen-min Jih-pao*, May 4, 1961; *Jen-min Jih-pao*, August 10, 1961.

corrective labor camps) are nearly "total" in scope; that is, all a person's activities are carried out within the organization. Some other units, such as the factory and the non-boarding school, govern only part of a person's activities. It is more difficult for organizational authorities to apply official political standards to outside activities than to activities conducted within the organization. Besides physical dispersal and scope, organizations may differ in their pervasiveness, that is, the extent of application of official norms to all activities within the organization. Unsupervised contacts between friends or activities within the privacy of the home (in the case of communes) may escape official supervision, and may result in undesirable influences. In our case studies, individuals found some people to whom they could confide private thoughts, people whose sympathy and support could break the unanimity of organized social pressure.[4]

In other words, problems of physical dispersal, low scope, and low pervasiveness may result in pockets of privacy and de-politicization. Even if individuals do not gain or strengthen politically hostile views in unsupervised associations, these associations still obstruct the elite's desire to develop vigorous and unanimous social pressure to confront all deviants (recall the cadre Ma Kan-pu's account of the sympathy he received from his friend Ch'en during the Cultural Revolution). Leaders have only a limited ability to effect solutions to these problems. The labor of rural peasants cannot easily be centralized in one location, nor do sufficient boarding schools exist to house all students. In the wake of the Cultural Revolution, some efforts are being made to cover the existing "dead spots" in the politicization of society. After-school political activities have been set up for students in some areas, and peasants have been increasingly drawn out of their homes for political study meetings and also have had political rituals brought

---

4. In the famous Asch conformity experiments, in which confederates of the experimenter gave false judgments of the length of lines presented to them in an effort to get experimental subjects to go along with these false judgments, it was found that a single person besides the subject who judged the lines accurately could effectively negate the social pressure of many false judgments and lead to a correct judgment by the experimental subject. S. Asch, "Effects of Group Pressure upon the Modification and Distortion of Judgments," in H. Guetzkow, ed., *Groups, Leadership and Men* (Pittsburgh: Carnegie Press, 1951); and S. Asch, "Studies of Independence and Conformity: A Minority of One against a Unanimous Majority," in *Psychological Monographs*, Vol. 70, whole no. 416, 1956. In the Asch experiments subjects who gave false judgments did not apparently become convinced that their eyes were deceiving them. In other words not even a single ally was necessary for most subjects to preserve the feeling that the majority was judging the lines incorrectly.

into their homes in the form of family Mao Tse-tung's thought study classes. These efforts clearly are not final solutions to the supervision problems; final solutions would require at least major structural changes rather than simply the addition of more political activities.[5]

So far we have been discussing the conditions that affect whether or not general social pressure will be mobilized to confront individual deviants. The other major aspect of a strict political atmosphere is that such pressure will be effective in influencing its target (which may be any individual in the organization at any time). Individuals will feel the effects of mobilized group pressure if they have strong ties and a sense of solidarity in their *hsiao-tsu*, ties and concern over their place in the larger organization, and loyalty and gratitude to the na-

---

5. In this discussion the implicit assumption is that increasing organizational control over members facilitates building up a strict political atmosphere. But we can consider a more complicated relationship. It is possible that the relationships between organizational scope and pervasiveness and the political atmosphere are not linear; that at some point individuals will feel so oppressed by the control an organization has over their lives that they will more actively resist attempts to influence them. Studies in Western organizations point out that participation in any structured organization gives rise to tensions, and that there has to be some mode of tension release if these tensions are not to intolerably disrupt the organization. For organizations with high scope and pervasiveness the generation of such tensions should be great, and many would have to be released in some way within the organization (rather than by "blowing off steam" outside the organization). See Talcott Parsons, R. F. Bales and E. A. Shils, *The Working Papers in the Theory Action* (Glencoe: The Free Press, 1953), pp. 185 ff.; Hanan Selvin, *The Effects of Leadership* (Glencoe: The Free Press, 1960); and the discussion in Amitai Etzioni, *A Comparative Analysis of Complex Organizations* (New York: The Free Press), pp. 162–3. Chinese organizations are generally higher in scope and pervasiveness than their Western counterparts, and political rituals both generate tension and depend upon a certain amount of tension in order to be effective. If correctly run these rituals should end up by relieving tension, as individuals make self-criticisms and are then reintegrated in the group. But if these rituals are poorly run they should generate tensions and then not properly relieve them, and just how those tensions would be relieved remains somewhat of a puzzle. Organized recreation and sports, activities much emphasized in Chinese organizations, may contribute to tension release. Tensions may accumulate over time, and then be released in the hectic activity of major political campaigns. But I would expect that the high scope and pressures of organizational life in China would result in periodic efforts to release tensions outside, such as the "binges" noted in the military units analyzed by Selvin. From what little information I have, however, outside binges seem to be relatively rare in Chinese society, in spite of the high pressures of organizational life. Is this because of a cultural factor connected with the Chinese emphasis on self-discipline and concealing basic emotions? Is this because organizations reach outside of their boundaries to monitor to some extent the private lives of participants? Do organizations release the tensions of their members internally more effectively than I have given them credit for? Or is the whole notion of tension generation and release a faulty one? At this point I can only speculate, and I invite the reader to do the same.

tional political system. These ties and loyalties can in turn have a variety of sources.

A high turnover in personnel and the prospect of future changes were credited with interfering with group solidarity by my labor camp and *min-kung* construction project informants. The cadre Ma Kan-pu, in contrast, credited the general personnel stability in his unit with contributing to a highly developed group solidarity. Solidarity can also be fostered by personnel homogeneity (in regional origins, education, class origins, Party membership, clan membership, and so forth), while heterogeneity will introduce the potential for disputes and cleavages (recall the student Tai Hsiao-ai's discussion of regional cliques and the peasant Liang Hsia-chung's discussion of clan conflict). Group and organizational solidarity can be promoted through cooperative activities, or obstructed by highly competitive activities.[6] (Recall Tai Hsiao-ai's description of the competitions in his technical school.) If personnel cleavages do exist, it is particularly important that they not coincide with and reinforce other divisions within the organization (particularly the division between leader and led), since this would interfere with identification with the larger organization.

We have stated some considerations for organizational personnel and how to distribute them. But, as was true in the earlier discussion of the political quality of personnel, it may not be easy to arrange things so neatly. Leaders of corrective labor camps and *min-kung* construction projects cannot request homogeneous personnel, and considerations of work needs or social control may override the desire for homogeneity and stability when groups are formed. (As we noted in Chapter 4, a homogeneous group without a strong political core or ties to higher leadership is less desirable than a heterogeneous group with such features). Individuals in both labor camps and construction projects will easily notice that there is a great status gulf between themselves and their superiors which cannot be eliminated simply by frequent vertical contacts and communications. Similarly, efforts to decrease the haughtiness of teachers and to eliminate formal military ranks do not completely eliminate the obstacles to close vertical ties in schools and the army. (In the case of teachers who are too "bour-

---

6. Western social science has extensively explored the importance of cooperation in building solidarity. See Morton Deutsch, "The Effects of Cooperation and Competition upon Group Process," in Dorwin Cartwright and Alvin Zander, eds., *Group Dynamics,* 3rd Edition (New York: Harper & Row, 1968), Chap. 35; M. Sherif, et al., *Intergroup Conflict and Cooperation* (Norman: Oklahoma University Press, 1961).

geois," close vertical ties may not be all that desirable.) In rural communes leaders have to deal with a pre-existing social and residential structure, with cohesion and cleavages based upon hundreds of years of local development and history. Even when new organizations and activities are successfully introduced into rural villages, they constitute an overlay upon, rather than a replacement of, the existing social structure. Thus in a variety of organizational settings heterogeneity and cleavages may be unavoidable.

While cooperative activities may do the most for organizational solidarity, there are a number of reasons why competitive activities may be stressed. By now the reader should be aware that China in the 1960's was by no means a society which de-emphasized individual competition. The emphasis on competition is of a different sort than in the West or in the Soviet Union, but it clearly is an important aspect of life in China. Groups play an important role in discussing and judging the relative merits of competing individuals, but purely group competitions and rewards are comparatively rare, for a number of reasons. Some activities are inherently difficult to organize on a group basis (e.g., academic study). Some kinds of rewards may not be suitable for entire groups (such as release from a labor camp). Group cooperative activities and rewards may not be as effective in certain circumstances as individual competition and incentives,[7] and they may be seen as unfair to both the best and the worst members of the group. In addition, so long as some positions in society are higher in status than others and more people desire to occupy those positions than there are positions available, then some sort of selection and individual advancement has to take place. For example, in primary schools cooperative activities seem to be emphasized, but in higher schools, where advancement is more selective, individual competition is increasingly stressed. To reiterate a conclusion drawn from the school case studies in Chapter 6, even when individuals compete for scarce political honors rather than for grades or material rewards, the likely result will be an undermining of group solidarity. Competition based upon politics rather than upon economics or academics is still competition.

Ties to the organization and loyalties to the national political system may stem from a variety of sources. If individuals find their daily

---

7. If group pressures are not fully effective in supporting official demands, then sanctions and rewards for individuals and individual competition may have to be used to channel behavior. In the process the competitive atmosphere developed will make it less likely that effective social pressure will be developed in the future, creating a sort of vicious circle.

activities rewarding, they are likely to feel closer ties to the organization than they would if they found activities tedious or punitive. If an organization has high national or local prestige, members are likely to value their place in it more than if the organization has low prestige. An organization which is more complete in scope not only is able more easily to supervise its members, as discussed earlier, but also is likely to be seen as more salient to the lives of members than organizations low in scope, and this salience may lead to personal involvement. If an organization offers attractive mobility opportunities or a life that is markedly improved, then the members are likely to feel ties and gratitude to it. If, in contrast, an organization offers few mobility opportunities or only undesirable mobility opportunities (recall peasant ambivalence toward serving as a cadre), or if it is the bottom of the heap (as in the case of labor camps), then the organization is likely to be seen in a less favorable light. All of these sources of ties to an organization can affect individual responsiveness to organized social pressure.

Leaders have only limited means of changing their organizations, to create stronger feelings of identification among subordinates. There are only so many highly desirable activities to go around, and in spite of vigorous efforts to convince those doing boring and tedious jobs that their contributions are just as noble and important as those of everybody else, there does not seem to be a complete elimination of the feeling that such jobs are less desirable. Similarly, strenuous efforts to convince the public that certain work units are as important as others does not completely eliminate the feeling that some units (e.g., the military, government offices) have higher prestige than others (e.g., communes). And organizational leaders generally cannot control the past mobility of their members, or offer more than a limited number of opportunities for mobility within the organization. The various honorary titles that are created from time to time as alternatives to occupational or other forms of mobility may or may not be seen by the members as meaningful alternatives.

Ties to an organization and to the national society can also be influenced by events and policies occurring in the larger society, as well as by memories of past events and policies. If the lives of members of an organization have generally improved since 1949, if the local economy is expanding and prospering, if friends and relatives outside of the organization are similarly enjoying more rewarding lives, then indivduals are likely to show faith and gratitude and to be relatively responsive to social pressure. If individuals or their outside friends have fallen on hard times since 1949, or if receptiveness to official policies in the past has been followed by disappointment or suffering, then individuals are more likely to feel ungrateful or even hostile.

Many of these factors are again outside the control of organizational authorities. The economy is subject to natural disasters as well as to the results of shifting national campaigns. Campaign excesses which cause resentment may be the result not so much of the zeal or poor judgment of the organizational leaders, but of the severe pressures they receive from their own superiors. Organizations of course generally have no control over the range of experiences their members have had since 1949, nor over the successes or problems of loved ones outside of the organization.[8] Even organizations which are nearly total in scope, whose members are isolated from undesirable outside contacts and communications, still cannot eliminate the influence of memories of the past, which may be either positive or negative.

No doubt other conditions affect the political atmosphere within an organization. For instance, organizational leaders should certainly have sufficiently powerful rewards and sanctions to gain compliance if social pressure is not effective (this is particularly a problem in primary schools, and to some extent in rural communes). We do not claim that we have considered every possible feature of an organization which might affect the political atmosphere which develops within it, only that we have dealt with the most important structural problems which emerge from the comparison of case studies.[9]

In these pages we have tried to summarize the conditions which affect the development of a strict political atmosphere. These include conditions affecting how well social pressure gets mobilized in the first place (the centrality of political activities, the quality of the political core, the nature of supervision problems) as well as conditions influencing whether pressure, once mobilized, will be effective in influenc-

---

8. During the "three bitter years" following the failure of the Great Leap Forward, there were severe morale problems in the army. Although the soldiers were in some ways shielded from the suffering that affected the rest of the population, they maintained correspondence with relatives and learned of the severe food shortage in the rural areas. This bad news from relatives led to severe complaining by the soldiers themselves. See J. Chester Cheng, ed., *The Politics of the Chinese Red Army* (Stanford: Hoover Institution, 1966).

9. There is one remaining set of variables which has been left out of the analysis. I have been comparing organizations to see how social pressure will be developed to confront any deviant member. It is possible that organizations will also vary in the modal personality characteristics of their members, with some having individuals who are more incapable of change. In other words, because of age, upbringing, or other differences, the participants in equally strict political atmospheres in two organizations may still react somewhat differently. A complete test of the ideas presented here would have to take personality variables into account.

ing the attitudes of group members (ties to the group, to the organization, and to the national political system). We have seen that each of these conditions can in turn be broken down into other structural features of an organization, all of which will have some impact on the kind of political atmosphere which will develop. These structural features in turn interrelate and interact in complex ways. An organization which has high prestige may be able to get higher quality leaders and personnel and to offer its members an improved life. Organizations which lack interpersonal solidarity may be able to build it up in time if they have skilled leaders and can emphasize cooperative activities.

Our analysis suggests that the advice offered to organizational leaders in the pamphlets described in Chapter 4 was too simplistic and too optimistic. These pamphlets seem to assume that if the prescribed forms of political rituals are diligently followed, then a strict political atmosphere will develop. The analysis here suggests that there are many structural obstacles to the development of a strict political atmosphere, so that in many organizations no matter how faithfully the leading cadres follow the advice in the pamphlets, the desired atmosphere will not result. Moreover, many of the structural obstacles are such that, even if organizational leaders turned their attentions to attacking them directly, many of the problems would be outside their capacity to solve, or would defy easy solution. In this respect the analysis here is more Marxist (i.e., structural determinist) than Maoist (i.e., when "politics takes command" material and structural obstacles can be overcome).

To the sociologist, the ideas emphasized here—that the structure of an organization and its environment affect how successful group political rituals can be—may seem obvious. For example, some of the generalizations derived here from a comparison of Chinese case studies overlap with generalizations arrived at by Amitai Etzioni from Western organizational comparisons.[10] Etzioni found that organizations could be classified as coercive (e.g., prisons), utilitarian (e.g., factories) or normative (e.g., religious orders), and that these types tended to vary systematically in regard to a number of variables (e.g., goals, elite structure, pattern of communications), as well as in the expected orientation of lower participants (alienation in coercive organizations, calculative involvement in utilitarian organizations, and moral commitment in normative organizations). In these terms the Chinese ideal is to use

---

10. Amitai Etzioni, *A Comparative Analysis of Complex Organizations* (New York: Free Press, 1961).

primarily normative power and achieve moral commitment in organizations of all types, and Etzioni outlines a large number of ways in which organizational requirements make this difficult to accomplish. For example, Etzioni finds, as we do, that in coercive organizations a sharp status gap and low vertical cohesion is unavoidable between leaders and inmates,[11] while in utilitarian organizations production goals contribute to a tendency for instrumental leaders (work leaders and technical specialists) to dominate expressive leaders (political activists in the Chinese case).[12] Thus, while our method in this study has been generalization from case studies rather than the testing of Western-derived hypotheses, the results should contain few real surprises for the student of Western organizations.

This is not to say that Chinese organizations are just like their counterparts in the West, or that they are rigidly fixed in form and cannot be altered by the introduction of political rituals. Throughout this study we have noted ways in which Chinese organizations and life within them are quite different from Western ones, in part because of *hsiao-tsu* and political rituals: greater explicit politicization of all activities, less autonomy for groups of subordinates, more organized spare time activities, etc. We have seen much evidence of organizational changes in our case studies, and Skinner and Winckler, working with Etzioni's categories, provide an analysis of the cyclical changes in the political atmosphere in rural China which have occurred ever since 1949.[13] The point is not that Chinese organizations are unremarkable or that they are set in concrete, but that they still vary systematically in ways which are of consequence for the effectiveness of small groups. A rural production team is very different from a Western farm or even a Soviet collective farm, and at some times political rituals are more effectively developed within it than at other times. But there is only a certain amount of flexibility possible in any given organization, and a rural production team cannot, by the addition of political activities and rituals, eliminate or override all of the things which make its political atmosphere different from that in a school or a government office.

If many of the generalizations presented in this chapter seem obvious, why belabor them? The emphasis is necessary because in many studies of contemporary China such structural considerations are ignored. Some assume that, as soon as the older generation which grew

---

11. Ibid., pp. 96–102.
12. Ibid., pp. 113–125.
13. G. William Skinner and Edwin A. Winckler, op. cit.

up before 1949 dies off, the leadership's problems in mobilizing their (now fully indoctrinated) population will be eliminated. The Cultural Revolution is sometimes portrayed as a campaign to bring the Chinese cultural superstructure into agreement with the socialist socio-economic based created in 1955–56, thus eliminating the remaining source of such undesirable sentiments as elitism and bureaucratism.[14] According to a related argument, the thrust of the Cultural Revolution was to attack and replace post-1949 leaders who, though dedicated communists, retained or had been contaminated with traditional or bourgeois bureaucratic and elitist mentalities, and recruit new leaders and institutionalize a new style of leadership based upon participatory activism and controlled struggle.[15] Others focus on the issue of the "malleability of human nature" and see many developments since 1949 as a great human contest to see whether the Chinese people can be made more selfless and public-spirited.[16] All of such arguments, which are of course stated with much greater complexity and sophistication by their proponents, are oversimplifications insofar as they overlook the influence on individuals of the immediate social structure in which they operate. The new generation does not get processed ideologically on some sort of uniform assembly line. Rather, youths start out from various places in the social structure, they have varying experiences with the official instruments of education and indoctrination, and they end up in a variety of social positions, some of which may be more conducive to political activism than others. Selfish or other undesirable sentiments are not simply the product of a culture which is out of tune with the socialist base of society, for socialism does not remove all the structural sources of such sentiments. People continue to live in individual families and compete with others for scarce goods and services (unlike, say, the situation on the Israeli kibbutz), and the interests of people in different social positions (not just in different classes as in classical Marxism, but in different occupational, political, and residential positions) still conflict to some extent.[17] Similarly, bu-

14. One version is presented in Gerald Tannenbaum, "China's Cultural Revolution: Why it Had to Happen," in Richard Baum and Louise Bennett, eds., *China in Ferment* (Englewood Cliffs: Prentice Hall, 1971).

15. See Richard H. Solomon, *Mao's Revolution and the Chinese Political Culture* (Berkeley and Los Angeles: University of California Press, 1971).

16. One aspect of the malleability argument is addressed in Donald J. Munro, "The Malleability of Man in Chinese Marxism," in *China Quarterly*, no. 48, October–December 1971.

17. Mao Tse-tung provided important tools for the recognition of such conflicts within socialism in his conception of "contradictions among the people." (See Mao

reaucratic mentalities are not simply the product of "surviving" elitist orientations, but of the division of labor and organizational demands of the huge bureaucracies which, as Max Weber emphasized, state socialism must create.[18] And the obstacles to changing human nature may reside as much in the varying immediate social environments of individuals as in either the pessimism of elitist ideologues and pedagogues or the resistance of the human mind itself. This is a plea then, for future research on China to focus more on concrete social structure and how it affects individuals and groups, and less exclusively on national cultural, political, and ideological trends.

May not the Cultural Revolution have invalidated much of this analysis by creating throughout society a new upsurge of ideological fervor? If the ideas advanced here are correct, the answer is clearly negative. We have been saying that there are a number of structural features of organizations and their environments which must be changed in order for substantial change in their political atmospheres to occur. The Cultural Revolution, for all of its sound and fury, has had a decidedly mixed effect upon these "things that matter." On the one hand political activities and political criteria for personnel evaluation have increased in all organizations, and some mobility opportunities have been opened. On the other hand, factional conflicts have heightened organizational cleavages, and the net effect of these events has been a large increase in downward mobility (due to purges, pruning of administrative staffs, and large movements of personnel to the countryside). Future research will have to examine how these and other trends have affected different types of organizations. For the moment, the conclusion is that leaders of organizations in the post-Cultural Revolution period still face most of the same difficulties in creat-

Tse-tung, "On the Correct Handling of Contradications among the People," [1957], translated in Robert R. Bowie and John K. Fairbank, eds., *Communist China 1955–1959: Policy Documents with Analysis* [Cambridge: Harvard University Press, 1962], pp. 273–294.) However, Mao's analysis of contradictions has not led his supporters in the Cultural Revolution or enough of his analysts abroad to the realization that structural problems require structural solutions. Cultural or ideological solutions (e.g., increased political indoctrination) can at best ameliorate such problems, but they cannot eliminate them.

18. Max Weber, *Economy and Society* (New York: Bedminster Press, 1968), Vol. 1, 1968, p. 225. The classic statement of the way organizational requirements undermine the egalitarian ideals of socialist parties is Robert Michels, *Political Parties* (New York: Free Press, 1962) (first published in 1911). The seminal treatment of the effect of bureaucratic office on the personality of incumbents is Robert K. Merton, "Bureaucratic Structure and Personality," in Robert K. Merton, Ailsa P. Gray, Barbara Hockey and Hanan C. Selvin, eds., *Reader in Bureaucracy* (Glencoe: The Free Press, 1952).

ing a strict political atmosphere which have been pointed out in our pre-Cultural Revolution case studies.

It is our contention that the structural properties outlined in the preceding pages are critical for the development of a strict political atmosphere and for the reform of the values and attitudes of participants in organizations. These structural properties emerged from a detailed comparison of a large number of interviews, and the specific generalizations are still at the level of hypotheses. Ideally these hypotheses should be put in the form of concepts which could be directly measured, and then tested against the reality of organizations in China, to answer questions such as the following: Does each of these structural properties really make a difference in an organization's effectiveness in changing attitudes? How do these properties interact and reinforce or cancel each other out? Which of these properties are the most important or powerful? Given any two organizations, would the measurement of these properties allow us to predict with any accuracy which would be more effective in influencing the attitudes of its members? Unfortunately it still is not possible to conduct the kind of research in China which would be required to refine and test our ideas, and the hypotheses must remain hypotheses for the moment. But perhaps the discussion of the relationship between structural properties and political atmospheres can help us to analyze more systematically the differences among the five settings we have been considering throughout this book. Let us turn back to these five types of organizations.

Corrective labor camps of both the reform and re-education variety possess favorable characteristics for developing a strict political atmosphere primarily in their large organizational scope, and the resulting limitation on outside communication and contacts. The inmates' activities are also relatively easy to supervise, although this varies to some extent according to the type of labor being performed. The quality of leadership (meaning camp cadres and their superiors) is also relatively high, reflecting the rigorous political standards used in recruiting public security personnel. However, corrective labor camps rate quite low on most other conditions which affect individual motivations, group solidarity, and identification with the larger organization. The work is harsh, past mobility has been downward, the personnel and groupings are unstable, the backgrounds of personnel are diverse, competitive activities are emphasized, and the general political quality of inmates is low. The political quality of inmate *hsiao-tsu* heads is questionable, and there is a sharp cleavage in status, background, etc., between inmates and cadres. As a result, corrective labor camps seem to be typified by poor relationships within groups, unconvincing support of official standards, ineffective group pressure, and negligible or negative attitude changes.

Production teams within rural communes possess favorable conditions for a strict political atmosphere primarily in the homogeneity, stability, and common backgrounds and ties of organizational personnel. Leaders of production teams are likely to have close ties with their subordinates, and in some areas common ordeals in guerrilla warfare and land reform may reinforce these vertical ties. On the other hand, kinship rivalries and clan conflict may disrupt this unity, and in some areas campaign experiences may have aggravated internal cleavages (e.g., if in a past campaign there had been violence among strong factions). Other aspects of the rural commune tend to be relatively unfavorable for the development of a strict political atmosphere. The peasants tend to be of relatively low political quality, unaccustomed to political rituals, and conservative in many ways. Rural leaders also tend to be of relatively low political quality, and their close ties with subordinates can result in ineffective support for official norms and demands. Production teams are not as pervasive as our other organizational settings, and many rural activities escape official supervision. *Hsiao-tsu* comparable to those in other organizations have not been the rule in rural areas, and many teams may lack a strong political core. Political rituals are not the primary activity and have been emphasized only intermittently in the countryside. The emphasis on agricultural production has tended to promote and reinforce the competition of skill and strength with political quality as criteria for personnel evaluation. Past experiences in mobility and economic improvement have varied from place to place, with gradual but often erratic improvement, present status is fairly inflexible, and mobility into rural cadre posts has at times been unattractive. Individual communes rank low in national priorities (while agriculture as a whole ranks high) and are not generally able to recruit high quality leaders or to restrict their membership. Thus political rituals are less salient to peasants than they are to participants in other organizations, and when attempted they are rarely very vigorous. As a result, it is difficult to produce effective social pressure behind official norms and demands through these rituals unless such support already exists for other reasons.

Workers occupy a middle ground in this analysis, although, as mentioned in Chapter 8, there are important differences between work organizations of different types. In some ways the organizational situation of the *min-kung* workers is more like that of corrective labor camp inmates than like that of other manual workers. Factories and similar work units are generally easy to supervise, at least in comparison with rural production teams. However, a systematic emphasis on work activities and qualifications as more important than political criteria often undermines the political atmosphere. Production remains the major concern, skill and performance in work are given major consideration in mobility decisions at the lowest levels, and group leaders may lack desirable political qualities or the support of a core of activists within their work groups. If leadership is of poor quality, political rituals may be poorly integrated with work activities. And the work unit is generally less than total in scope and pervasiveness, giving individuals opportunities for unsupervised activities and for outside communication and contacts. The result seems to be fairly routinized political activities and ineffective group pressure behind demands for changes in political attitudes, but more effective group pressure behind work demands.

In schools there are also important subtypes which make generalizations difficult. The most important divisions are those between primary, middle, and university levels, with the last most important in prestige and national importance and more selective in terms of both leaders and participants than lower level schools. Schools generally possess favorable conditions for a strict political atmosphere in the way they provide mobility opportunities, in the common past activities of participants (as students) and their similarity in age, and in the relatively enjoyable nature of school activities. Some things have varied markedly over time, such as the general emphasis on political activities and the emphasis placed upon political vis à vis academic criteria in school advancement. Schools, like factories, are limited in their scope and the claims they make on their participants, and this is particularly true for students in non-boarding schools and in the lowest levels. There have also been recurrent problems in recruiting and training immediate leadership personnel (teachers) of high political quality. In sum, the political atmosphere in schools tends to be somewhat stricter than in the labor camp, commune, or factory settings, but because of the shifting policies and the turnover in students the political atmosphere in schools is subject to more marked fluctuations over time than is the case in our other organizations.

In units made up almost entirely of cadres, political rituals seem to be the most fully developed, and the political atmosphere the strictest of all our settings. In general, cadres tend to be of high political quality, to have undergone special selection and training for their posts, and to work in organizations with strong political cores. Cadre organizations also tend to rank relatively high compared with our other organizational settings in the emphasis placed upon political activities and rituals, the satisfaction gained from the work, the opportunities for upward and downward mobility, and in the emphasis placed on political criteria in promotion decisions. But cadre organizations vary in their prestige and national importance and in the proportion of "old intellectuals" and "white expert" cadres who may undermine the political atmosphere. In other words, in general cadre organizations have a relatively strict political atmosphere, but this is less true of, say, a county land reclamation office than of the central Propaganda Ministry.

Not only, then, are there a large number of organizational properties which may affect the internal political atmosphere, but also these properties pose more problems and obstacles in some organizations than in others. While there is much variation within organizations of a single type, we may reasonably expect that schools and cadre organizations will be able to develop stricter political atmospheres than labor camps, communes, or factories, and that as a result they will be able to influence the attitudes of their members more effectively.[19]

---

19. The reader will note once more the parallels with the analysis by Etzioni. Again this does not mean that Chinese organizations are just like Western ones, only that the systematic differences between organizations of different types in China are in many cases like the differences between comparable types of organizations in the West.

Due to these similar differences Chinese authorities, like their Western counterparts, must emphasize coercion more in penal institutions than in other organizations, and material incentives more in factories than in other organizations. *Hsiao-tsu* and political rituals may minimize the extent to which authorities in different types of organizations need to use different compliance strategies, but they do not eliminate this need.

XI

CONCLUSIONS

In 1949 China's new leaders took power with a determination to rad-
ically alter their society. The existing social structure was simply not
suitable for establishing socialism or pursuing rapid economic development. China's history provided ideas about how to preserve social
stability, but little in the way of techniques for mobilizing the population for change. The Soviet Union served as a model for many of
the post-1949 Chinese institutions, but, aided by experience and experimentation in the decades of struggle for power, the Chinese pupil
eventually outdid the Soviet teacher. A new conception of organization and leadership emerged which departed in important ways from
the Leninist -Stalinist model. A key feature of this new conception is
the encapsulation of individuals in all walks of life into *hsiao-tsu*, and
then the manipulation of interactions and emotions within these
groups through political study and mutual criticism.

Under this new conception of society, each individual will be constantly aware of the new ideas and goals set by China's leaders and
will feel that his own ideas and contributions are of value to society.
He will work harder and improve his skills not in order simply to earn
more or to avoid losing his job, but in order to earn the respect of
those around him. He will refrain from stealing or loafing not in
order to avoid the punishment of higher authorities, but in order to
avoid loss of prestige within his group. He will volunteer for new and
difficult assignments not out of a personal desire for advancement,
but out of a desire to join the ranks of others who are leading the

way toward a new society. He will be concerned not only with his own progress and position, but also with aiding, pressuring, and cajoling those around him to become more activist. In the process the individual's attitudes and values will be gradually transformed, as will those of others around him.

The organizational ideal involves an emphasis on trying insofar as possible to base social change and economic development on the unified labor, energy, and determination of every member of the population, rather than on the differential contributions of various strata in society. True mass mobilization is desired. The Soviet model was not fully suitable for achieving this ideal, and the Chinese Communists grafted on their own ideas, in particular the notion of extending the Party's discipline and rituals outward until they enveloped the entire society. The extension of this model to the population progressed rapidly after 1949, although even now many peasants are only intermittently involved in political rituals. During the Cultural Revolution the *hsiao-tsu* network atrophied when the political structure which supported it fell apart, but since then the *hsiao-tsu*-political study-mutual criticism complex has been resuscitated and extended still further, in some cases down into individual families.

How successful have *hsiao-tsu* and political rituals been? To a large extent the answer to this question depends upon which *hsiao-tsu* goal is being discussed. The most ambitious goal of group rituals is to create organizational environments throughout society that are capable of transforming the attitudes and values of participants. We have argued that this goal of thought reform often goes unrealized. In some organizations individuals do feel pressure from peers whom they respect to change their attitudes, and find the prospect of "falling behind" hard to bear. But in some other organizational settings individuals feel they are surrounded by opportunists waiting to criticize their slightest misstep in order to gain favor with superiors. In other settings individuals look upon political rituals as a bothersome but unavoidable routine, and save their energies and emotions for activities outside the group. In these and other ways the ideal strict political atmosphere is not achieved, and the psychological impact of group activities is reduced, or even reversed.

Hsiao-tsu rituals were originally conceived in part as a device for institutionalizing in-service thought reform; Chinese in various walks of life would, in the course of their regular organizational routines, be moved gradually by group pressure toward greater political purity and activism. The first exposure to such rituals after 1949 may have had such an impact on many people,[1] but in later years the novelty seems to have worn off. *Hsiao-tsu* rituals in most organizational circumstances seem to be highly routinized, performing primarily "maintenance" functions. In other words, they are valuable for maintaining present levels of activism and promoting the influence of existing political activists over other elements within an organization, but generally they are not so effective in producing day-by-day attitude change. The periodic mounting of campaigns and special intensive thought reform institutions serves as testimony to the elite's continuing frustration with the pace of popular attitude change. And the opening up of new opportunities and activities and participation in campaign struggles seem to be much more important in inducing individual change than the routine of *hsiao-tsu* study.

We have argued that much of this failure to transform attitudes is due to the structural properties of organizations. Depending upon the nature of an organization, it may be difficult to get individuals fully encapsulated in *hsiao-tsu,* to mobilize group pressure well, or to create the kind of group ties that would make that pressure effective. This conclusion can be looked at in terms of our discussion of primary groups in Chapter 2. Western primary group research orients us toward assuming that the individuals among whom a person carries out his daily activities will have an important influence on his attitudes, an influence often stronger than that of his organizational superiors. But just as organizational elites are not free to manipulate the political atmosphere within their organizations at will, so group ties that develop among subordinates are the product of the organizational environment that surrounds them. In other words, the autonomy and importance of primary groups cannot, in the Chinese context at least, be simply assumed, and the influence that *hsiao-tsu* and political rituals have on the attitudes of participants is highly problematic, depending on the variety of organizational factors discussed in the previous chapters. In a number of circumstances individuals may develop their most meaningful primary group ties outside of the *hsiao-tsu* structure, or outside of the organization itself.

The problematic nature of *hsiao-tsu* influences on attitudes should not lead us to assume that in a lax political atmosphere these groups and political rituals are of no consequence. These organizational innovations still make the life of a citizen in China very different from

---

1. See, for example, William G. Sewell, *I Stayed in China* (London: George Allen & Unwin, 1966); Harriett C. Mills, "Thought Reform: Ideological Remolding in China," in *Atlantic Monthly,* Vol. 204, December 1959.

that of his counterparts in other societies. Even when the atmosphere is lax and thought reform is ineffective, other goals may be advanced. Let us analyze why this is so.

Hsiao-tsu are expected to contribute to preventing deviance and maintaining social control. In this regard they seem to be generally effective even when little thought reform takes place. As long as the political structure remains intact, as long as even one loyal activist can be located within each group, and as long as effective sanctions are available, supervision and control of activities within the organization can be maintained. In our interview materials there are few instances of individual deviance or open opposition within organizations, and even fewer instances of overt group resistance. In an organization which has a lax political atmosphere, an individual may conform merely to stay out of trouble, but the group structure still makes effective supervision and control possible. Orders, threats, and physical coercion have by no means been eliminated from Chinese life, but the new organizational model does seem to make it possible to keep these techniques of control in the background.

Hsiao-tsu are also expected to get people to work harder and to volunteer for new and difficult tasks. In this regard, as well, most of the evidence indicates success. In the interview materials there are many instances of campaigns in which individuals who secretly opposed participation joined in with even an appearance of enthusiasm. Again, as long as the political structure, the activists, and the sanctions are available, the ability to mobilize people for new tasks remains, even if the desired levels of belief and commitment are not internalized. What is more problematic is the sustaining of these new levels of effort. *Hsiao-tsu* rituals may become routinized, activists may not be prodded to prod others, and the initial mobilization may not be self-sustaining. The Chinese Communists seem to be more successful in getting people to drop old habits and to undertake new tasks through political rituals than they are in maintaining these changes. In sustaining high commitments and efforts, the elite still relies upon material incentives and sanctions more than it would apparently like to.

Hsiao-tsu are also expected to contribute to effective communications, to getting official ideas down to ordinary citizens. In theory all citizens, even if illiterate, are supposed to understand new goals and policies, reflect upon their implications for their own lives, and conscientiously put them into practice in their daily activities. If the political atmosphere is lax, individuals may not understand every aspect of new policies or become as reflective and purposeful as desired, but they will at least be reached by communications and have to respond to them. Thus a lax political atmosphere only marginally affects the usefulness of small groups in downward communications. Upward communications may be more seriously affected if individuals feel that voicing objections and reservations might get them into trouble.

Hsiao-tsu are supposed to provide a forum for bringing personal disputes into the open and resolving them, creating a warm and supportive atmosphere for participants. In a lax political atmosphere this may not happen, and tensions may even be aggravated in the heat of mutual criticism. Even in such cases, however, individuals can usually find emotional support from others within or outside of their organization. In the case studies there are many instances of unmanipulated friendships that developed in spite of the small group controls. While these friendships might be called a failure of *hsiao-tsu*, since they show that these groups do not always effectively "capture" primary ties, this failure may actually contribute to organizational success, since these unmanipulated ties may give people the emotional support necessary to endure the discipline of *hsiao-tsu* life. Even if *hsiao-tsu* activities fail to resolve or even aggravate personal tensions they provide a means for noticing conflicts and at least keeping them below the boiling point.

In conclusion, even in organizations which are not working as they are supposed to, *hsiao-tsu* and political rituals still make important contributions to organizational effectiveness. Although individuals may not feel caught up in a contagious spirit of enthusiasm and attitude change, the *hsiao-tsu* network does help insure that they become aware of official goals and demands, that they will have difficulty expressing or finding support for opposition, and that they will have even more difficulty avoiding compliance. Only minimal organizational conditions (pressure through the Party hierarchy, enough activists in *hsiao-tsu*, the availability of backup sanctions) are necessary for *hsiao-tsu* to be effective in communication, social control, and political mobilization. Therefore *hsiao-tsu* and political rituals have an important place in organizations in China even when they are not very effective in reforming bad thoughts. To put it another way, *hsiao-tsu* and political rituals may not seem as appropriate a technique for changing attitudes and values in every organizational context as the elite thinks they should be. But without them life in Chinese organizations would be very different, and no doubt the elite would have much more difficulty in organizing and mobilizing their citizens.

What has happened to the "sheet of loose sand" that was China in the early part of the twentieth century? Certainly the metaphor is no longer appropriate to the China of the 1960's and 1970's. An impressive organizational apparatus, and early record of military and economic success, a large cohort of dedicated believers, and the sophisticated application of group political rituals have combined to produce a relatively high unity of action in pursuit of national goals since 1949. But underneath this unity there is a complex social reality. Characterizations of the Chinese population as a uniform mass of conditioned and unthinking blue ants, or terrorized anti-communists, or revolutionary zealots miss this complexity. The elite has been relatively successful in producing a unified and organized populace, but they have been less successful in transforming and unifying the varied hopes, fears, needs, aspirations, and loyalties of their citizens. At times when hierarchical political controls have for one reason or another been weakened (1957, 1960–1962, 1966–1969), old and new problems and divisions in Chinese society have come to the surface. On the scale of human history the changes in the Chinese social structure and way of life have been drastic and rapid, but the creation of a true unity of thoughts and wills, a unity which does not require constant control and manipulation, will be a much longer and infinitely more difficult undertaking.

Appendix I:

METHODOLOGICAL NOTES

The primary source of information about China used in this study is accounts of refugees interviewed in Hong Kong. In this appendix information about how these refugees were located, the nature of the interviews, and the ways in which the interviews were used will be discussed.

The difficulties in locating and interviewing refugees in Hong Kong are considerable, in spite of the fact that several thousand leave China for the British colony each year.[1] Most of them cross the border illegally, often in small boats or by swimming, and it is in their interests to "lie low" for awhile and establish themselves in Hong Kong before they register with the authorities or make their presence publicly known in other ways.[2] Formerly the nearby Portuguese colony of Macao was a convenient place to contact and interview "fresh" refugees, but since the riots of 1967 Macao has become too sensitive politically for such research. In my study it was not extremely important that those interviewed be very recent arrivals, and some of those I talked to had left as early as 1962.[3] But earlier arrivals are still more difficult to locate. There is no central register or clearing house established for the convenience of academic researchers. A variety of techniques have been used by others in finding people to interview. There are in Hong Kong a number of relief and welfare organizations which aid refugees from China, and some of these are willing to aid Western researchers in finding people to talk to.

---

1. In 1968 the Hong Kong Director of Information estimated that 5,000 to 8,000 illegal immigrants enter the colony from China each year, although some estimates are still higher. *Hong Kong Standard*, September 16, 1968.

2. For information on the problems of refugees see Perry Link, "Refugees in Hong Kong," in Harvard University *Papers on China*, Vol. 22B, December 1969. A Hong Kong newspaper estimates that 90 per cent of the illegal immigrants escape detection by the authorities. *Hong Kong Standard*, August 16, 1968.

3. The main problem with informants who left several years ago is simply that they have had more time to forget details that I wanted to know.

There are also in Hong Kong at any given time other researchers working on interviewing projects who can provide introductions to people they have interviewed. The researcher can also ask those he interviews to help him to find other refugees. And he can hire people especially to go out and find interviewing subjects.

All of these methods have advantages and disadvantages, and each was used in this study to some extent. It takes time and effort to cultivate contacts within relief and welfare organizations, and often officials in these agencies are too busy or have no particular desire to help visiting researchers. I did not have too much success in cultivating this source, although about one-third of the students I interviewed were introduced to me through the kind auspices of the Chinese Cultural Association, an organization with Taiwan ties which helps students from China continue their education in Hong Kong. Some of my most interesting informants were steered to me by friends and by other researchers in Hong Kong. And for many of my interviews I relied upon the introductions of people I had already interviewed, or upon hired go-betweens. The main defect of the latter procedure is that the researcher has little control over those referred to him and is usually not able to check out their backgrounds, as he is often able to do with individuals supplied by friends or agencies. The main merit of this procedure is simply that it is an established practice in Hong Kong, and that it permits the researcher to concentrate on the interviews and their analysis rather than on locating refugees himself. The use of a wide variety of sources of interviewees at least assures that whatever biases are introduced by one source will not appear systematically throughout all of the interviews.

Each informant was interviewed in a special apartment designed for this purpose. The apartment is an ordinary one in an upper-middle class apartment building, with furnishings as politically neutral as possible—simple desks and chairs and prints of horses and chariots from Ancient China. During the course of my research I was assisted by three very able Chinese assistants. Most of the interviews with Mandarin speaking individuals I conducted myself, with notes taken by both myself and an assistant, who helped whenever language confusions arose. The standard interviewing period was three hours. After each session I compared my notes with the Chinese notes of my assistant, discussed any discrepancies, and typed in English a report of the information supplied. I did not use a tape recorder, because (a) it might have created anxieties among some informants, (b) the two way check with an assistant could satisfactorily clear up ambiguities and uncertainties about what had been said, and (c) translating and transcribing entire interviews would take too much time and would not yield much more information.

Occasionally this procedure was not followed. Some refugees spoke no Mandarin at all, and they were interviewed by one of my assistants by himself, using topics and methods discussed in advance. Then I relied solely on my assistant's notes and comments in typing my report. Occasionally I had to interview an informant without the aid of an assistant, and again my report was based upon a single set of notes. Since I used a loosely structured interview format rather than a closed questionnaire, these variations should not be the source of major methodological concern.

Most of the interviews were conducted on a rather impersonal cash basis; the going rate for a three hour interview at the time was $20 Hong Kong (about $2.33 U.S. at that time). In some cases, particularly with informants who were well educated or who had good jobs, no remuneration was given, or some sort of gift was presented. It might have been desirable, especially given the Chinese cultural context, to establish more personal relationships with my informants and to avoid the use of cash and the negative connotations this involves. However, since my research plan entailed interviewing a fairly large number of people, most of them only once or twice, the development of a personal relationship was generally not possible. Furthermore, paying for interviews has become a fairly standard practice in Hong Kong and seems to be viewed by many not as degrading, but as a good way to pick up a little extra income. This attitude has its drawbacks, since the use of cash can encourage the proverbial "professional interviewee" who lives off retelling his experiences in China (real or imagined) to various scholars. My research was designed to make this problem less serious than it has been in other interviewing studies. It was not necessary that my informants have any special expertise or that they not have been interviewed by others. My research was designed to find out about matters which are part of the everyday mundane experience of most citizens in China, and those who had been interviewed before would still be of use to me providing I could convince them there was no need to embellish their pasts.

It should be noted that economic concerns also applied to the go-betweens who introduced refugees to me. These go-betweens were not reimbursed on a "cash per head" basis, but were paid sums periodically in some rough proportion to their diligence. The problem of dishonest go-betweens was combated by using a large number, each of whom was asked to supply a few people, and by making it clear that their services would no longer be required if I had doubts about the genuineness of informants they had steered my way.

It should be clear at the outset, then, that the primary reason for informants to consent to these interviews was the desire to earn a little money. There were other motivations, such as the desire to tell "the world" about China, the emotional catharsis of spilling out the events of the past, the desire to help a go-between friend, the hope I could assist them in finding a job or in securing a visa to America, and so forth. At the same time there were a variety of sources of threat in these interviews. Except for those interviews set up by personal friends or public agencies, my informants had only my own assurances that I was a scholar with no connections with any government or intelligence service, and that I would keep their identities a secret and would do nothing to harm them or their loved ones back in China. If they did not accept these reassurances they might worry about how what they were telling me might affect loved ones, or might even influence their own future in some undetermined way. It should also be made clear that those who consented to interviews are probably not representative of the total refugee community in Hong Kong. The hazy line between research and intelligence work leads many refugees who retain feelings of loyalty toward China to want to avoid being interviewed by foreigners, for fear of bringing harm to the image of their homeland. On the other hand, I talked to some individuals whose patriotic sentiments toward China were still strong, and who consented to interviews precisely in order to correct the distorted view of China they felt I must have been getting from other refugees.

In sum, it is clear that the interviewing situation is not ideal, that people may come to the interviews for undesirable reasons, and that the anxieties produced may lead to various kinds of concealment and distortion. In spite of such problems, I feel that a relatively relaxed atmosphere and a certain amount of rapport did develop, particularly in follow-up interviews. Only one informant refused to return for a second interview, apparently because of concern for his family and friends in China.[4] The ways I have dealt with various kinds of bias which occur in this non-ideal interviewing situation will be discussed shortly.

In the initial stages of my field research I worked out a list of topics to be covered in the interviews (see Appendix II). The bulk of the questions on this list concern a single organization in which the informant had spent some time, preferably recently. Informants were asked to describe the structure of one such organization, the political study and meeting routine, how problems were solved, how political campaigns were carried out, and so forth. The people I interviewed thus served as informants much like in an anthropological study (although at a distance) rather than as respondents in a questionnaire-type survey. This format makes quantitative analysis difficult, but such analysis would be of dubious value in any case, since my informants are very unrepresentative of the population remaining in China.

The topic list was designed to tap information that would be relatively unaffected by the political biases of the individual informants. The focus was on objective features of the organizational situation (for example, how many members in the small group, how often meetings were held) rather than on more subjective matters. Informants were constantly prodded to stick to concrete details rather than to reveal their general feelings and impressions. In some cases I tried to find out about more subjective matters in an indirect manner in an effort to avoid biased replies. For instance instead of asking how well the informant got along with others in his organization, I asked him with whom he spent his spare time, and doing what. In spite of these efforts to remain objective and concrete, informants did make

---

4. Some other informants could not be located for follow-up interviews, and it is possible that some of these also did not want to return.

many evaluative and subjective comments, and these were noted. Even seemingly objective details can of course be embellished or distorted to present a biased picture, and only skeptical probing and comparisons with other sources of information can place these biases in perspective. In sum, the topic list was designed to require more memory of objective reality and less subjective judgments than is often the case in refugee interviewing projects, but the latter could not be totally eliminated.

The topic list was also flexible, suitable for use in interviews of various levels of intensity. About half of my informants (48) were interviewed only once, either because they were hesitant to return or unlocatable (about 8 of these) or because I decided that they were not very good informants and could provide little other useful information. In the first interview with all informants an effort was made to cover at least the first three sections of the topic list in order to find out the basic background facts about the informant, the structure of one organization he had spent time in, and the study and meeting routine within that organization. Only after these sections were covered did we move on to other sections dealing with interpersonal relationships, campaigns, changes over time, and so forth. If an informant had a fuzzy memory or seemed unable to discuss an organization with much insight only these initial sections might be covered, and he would not be asked to return. Responsive informants, on the other hand, were sometimes interviewed eight or ten times, covering all of the topics on the list and perhaps discussing a second organization as well. The order of the topic list was not followed strictly; if the informant started on a topic of interest we often turned to discuss it, and then returned to where we had left off. In fact, one informant was interviewed a grand total of 42 times, although she is not quite comparable to the others since she served as a general resource person, fielding my questions about a wide variety of aspects of Chinese society.

Thus in spite of the fact that almost half of the informants were interviewed only once, in all we talked to 101 people and conducted 260 three-hour interviews, or on the average slightly more than two and a half interviews per person. I have certain kinds of basic information from everyone, and then other kinds of information from increasingly smaller subsets of the interviewees. Obviously it would have been preferable to have more detailed information from everyone, but the variation in the ability of informants to recall and discuss their pasts made this sort of flexibility seem advisable.

As mentioned in the introduction, I had originally planned to conduct interviews about every organizational setting in which hsiao-tsu occur. However, I was not able to locate enough former soldiers or urban housewives, so the military and the residents' committee hsiao-tsu are not included.[5] This

---

5. A good discussion of small groups in military units, although based on an earlier period (the Korean War) is contained in Alexander George, *The Chinese Communist Army in Action* (New York: Columbia University Press, 1967). No comparable source exists for urban neighborhood small groups, but some details are

leaves five organizational settings: the school, the office, the factory or similar work unit, the rural production team, and the corrective labor camp. The number of individuals supplying information about each organizational setting varies from 14 (for the corrective labor camps) to 23 (for the production teams). A list of basic background facts about each informant is included in Appendix III.[6]

We turn now to some basic kinds of problems in the use and interpretation of information provided by refugees. The most serious danger is of course connected with outright falsification, the notion that some "bogus refugees" (who may never have been to China at all) will make up false stories about life on the Mainland. As mentioned previously, my research design, involving as it did interviewing people from ordinary walks of life about mundane group activities, should have made me less likely to run up against this problem than those researching more esoteric topics.[7] Each person interviewed was told initially that I was interested in ordinary information about daily activities and would not be displeased if they had nothing to report about Chinese missile development or Mao Tse-tung's sex life. In addition each informant was told at the start that there would be at most two or three interviews, no matter how varied and interesting a life an individual had led. All of these steps were taken to try to discourage outright falsification or embellishment of past activities.

The interview itself then provided further checks on accuracy and truthfulness. My three assistants had all lived in China for long periods themselves and were able to ask probing questions about events and activities which seemed dubious. The responses could also be checked with information supplied in other interviews, and the conflicts probed. After a while the patterns of experiences of my informants began to emerge so clearly that I, too, could spot odd replies and start probing. Questionable information could also lead to searches through the Chinese press for confirmation. Where my assistant and I detected such information we often tried to schedule a later interview with the same informant, sometimes after several weeks, to see whether he had forgotten what he had told us and would contradict information

---

contained in F. Schurmann, *Ideology and Organization in Communist China* (Berkeley and Los Angeles: University of California Press, 1968), Chap. 6; and Jerome Cohen, *The Criminal Process of the Peoples' Republic of China 1949–1963* (Cambridge: Harvard University Press, 1968).

6. It should be noted that some of my informants were interviewed about two kinds of organizations and are included under both organizational headings in Appendix III. Thus from a final total of 93 informants I have information about 101 distinct organizational settings. (Actually the real total is still somewhat larger since some informants, like the student Tai Hsiao-ai, described more than one organization, but of the same type.)

7. This problem is especially serious when one is searching for refugees with very specific histories, such as past work as a judge. See Jerome A. Cohen, "Interviewing Chinese Refugees: Indispensable Aid to Legal Research on China," in *Journal of Legal Education,* October 1967.

supplied in an earlier interview. Finally, in some cases we could check information with other researchers who had interviewed the same informant.

Using a variety of such checks for outright falsification we eliminated eight of the original 101 informants as "bogus." However, I am not positive that everything the remaining 93 informants said was true. Individuals with some anxiety about the safety of their families and friends in China would have good reason to falsify their names, the names of their home villages, the schools they had attended, and certain other kinds of information. These kinds of minor falsifications would be extremely difficult to detect without knowing certain facts about the informants' real families, home villages, schools, etc. In other words, an unknown proportion of my 93 "good" informants probably falsified parts of their background information to protect people. Fortunately, most of these minor falsifications would not affect my analysis. Background items were asked in order to get some rough idea of from what corner of the Chinese social structure the individual had viewed the events he was recounting. Thus I wanted to know whether an individual had grown up in a village and whether he had attended school, but I was not too concerned about knowing the specific village or school. There would be some kinds of falsification, however, such as claiming to be of poor peasant status while really from a landlord family, which would be almost as hard to detect, and which would more seriously affect my interpretations.

While some of the background information on the 93 informants may have been falsified, the rest of the information they supplied seems to have been consistent both internally and with information supplied by other informants. However, there are a number of other potential difficulties in using refugee data besides the outright falsification issue, and these concern various kinds of biases. There are several standard criticisms of refugee interviewing studies. One criticism concerns the sample bias problem, the fact that the people interviewed are not representative of the remaining Chinese population. A related comment is the claim that the people who come to Hong Kong are those for whom "the system failed," i.e., they are an atypical group whose organizations did not tend to their needs or their indoctrination and thus should not be used to learn about organizations from which people did not flee. A third comment concerns simple political bias, the fact that the act of leaving China represents a rejection of Chinese Communist institutions, and that a refugee could only give a distorted picture of those institutions. All of these criticisms are substantially accurate, and yet it is not impossible to utilize information from refugees if this is done carefully.

In regard to the sample bias problem reference to Appendix III will show that among the 93 individuals interviewed there were only 9 females, only 18 outside of the age span of 20 to 35, and only 11 who described organizations outside of Kwangtung province. In addition, class backgrounds such as landlord, rich peasant, and capitalist were heavily overrepresented in comparison with the population remaining on the mainland, and my informants were a relatively well educated lot. At the same time, former Youth League (15) and Communist Party (4) members were also somewhat overrepresented in comparison with the total population in China. So it is clear that my informants were different in many ways from the population of China. However, I have not tried to quantify my results and project them back on the remaining population. Instead, I have used a form of qualitative analysis which permits me to take the group of, say, student informants and look at the information described by males versus females, by students of poor peasant background versus those of landlord background, and so forth, in order to judge in some rough way the extent to which the unrepresentative nature of my sample was distorting the information I received.

On the question of "system failure," it is certainly true that a majority of my informants had strong grievances about how they were treated within organizations in China, grievances which accumulated for some time and which contributed to the decision to leave for Hong Kong. There were no refugees who had landed in Hong Kong as a result of forces beyond their control, as was the case with some of those interviewed in the Harvard Russian Refugee Interviewing Project.[8] However, there were some individuals in my sample who had left in order to join relatives in Hong Kong or to look for better economic or educational opportunities, and who lacked any strong sense of grievance about the way they had been treated in the organizations they described. Even if the "system" had failed an individual, his information would not necessarily be useless to me. In fact in some sense the views of "system failures" are just as valuable as the views of those who had regrets about leaving China. My study concerned the circumstances under which an organization carries out political rituals well or poorly, and those who reported poorly run political rituals could (and did) help me to identify the features of their organizations that made them "fail" for them.

Finally many of the people I interviewed did have a variety of anti-communist sentiments which might bias their responses. As previously mentioned, some attempt was made to ask questions about relatively objective matters, but even so one cannot avoid the influence of political biases completely. The basic way to deal with potentially biased information is again to find people who don't share the same bias, ask them similar questions, and then compare the answers. Thus I tried to find individuals who had left China legally, individuals who came from favored worker and poor peasant backgrounds, and so forth, in order to supplement information I got from, say, the alienated children of former landlords. And in fact I did find seven individuals who had left China legally, twenty-five who claimed favorable class backgrounds, and several who left China because of family obligations or a sudden turn in personal fortunes and who retained a strong sense of respect for many of the achievements of the Chinese Communists. The ac-

---

8. See Alex Inkeles and Raymond Bauer, *The Soviet Citizen* (Cambridge: Harvard University Press, 1959), Chap. 2.

counts of these individuals, who did not fit the stereotyped image of the anti-communist refugee, were used to check information supplied by individuals who fit that stereotype more closely. This does not mean that the views of the former pariahs and the alienated were simply discounted. The view of a commune held by a former landlord is certainly not the entire picture, but it is some part of that picture.

Unfortunately for the reader, most of the comparison of accounts of refugees of different types took place in my head and cannot be fully reconstructed within the narrow confines of this volume. One example may help illustrate the reasoning process used. Among my peasant informants some reported that former landlords and rich peasants and their children were not awarded equal work points for equal work in comparison with other peasants in the early 1960's. Other rural informants, on the other hand, reported that class background made no difference in awarding work points. Were the reports of the first group simply the product of political bias? I checked the backgrounds of the two groups. It turned out that some poor peasant informants reported work point discrimination against former landlords, while some children of landlords reported that they received equal treatment. From this I concluded that the disagreement over how fairly former class enemies were paid was not due simply to the biases of the former class enemes themselves, but was probably "real," reflecting variations in the way the work point system was administered in different places. The disagreement was more the result of local variations than of sheer political bias. Through comparisons such as these (including comparisons with published information) I tried to weed out false information and place negative impressions in the perspective of the categories of people who had expressed them. Of course this kind of qualitative comparison is rather crude, and there were not enough informants to support all of the kinds of comparisons which would have been desirable. For example, I interviewed no women labor camp inmates, and no peasants from outside of Kwangtung province. In spite of such limitations I have made a variety of generalizations based upon my interviews, using this internal comparison process. These generalizations seem to me to be the best possible given the current shortage of information.

There are a few other problems in the use of refugee interviews that should be mentioned here. One is the problem of memory. I had originally planned to focus my research on the internal dynamics of *hsiao-tsu* and to ask informants to describe specific group meetings. However, this proved impractical because most informants were unable to recall in clear detail many specific *hsiao-tsu* meetings. For the most part individual meetings were not of great importance to them, and tended to blur together in their memories. Poor memory is also a more general problem, and many of the informants I did not ask back for a second interview were people who could not recall basic facts about the organizations in which they had worked and lived, or who could not keep events straight chronologically.

Another basic problem is simply ignorance. There were many facts about their own organizations that my informants did not know. When asked who decided on promotions, who set rations, who fixed penalties for deviance, etc., many informants replied with terms such as "the Party," "higher levels," "leading cadres," or simply "they." In part this fuzziness about decision making is the result of the conscious leadership policies advocated in China since the split with the Soviet Union, policies which emphasize spreading authority and including various levels of an organization in any important decision. But simple lack of knowledge is a factor here as well. Most of my informants were ordinary participants who viewed the structure and operation of their organizations "from below." As such their judgments about the operation of the top leadership within their organization cannot be accepted uncritically. For this reason most of my questions focused on the details that ordinary participants could be expected to be familiar with, and when I have dealt with issues further removed from direct experience I have tried to insert phrases such as "the informant claims . . ."

Given this variety of problems the reader may wonder whether there is enough value in refugee-supplied information to justify making these interviews the core of a research project. My answer is "definitely yes." Refugee interviews do add to our information about China. They are a source of information about aspects of China which cannot at present be fully studied in any other way. No other source of data could have provided me with all of the kinds of information I sought—not only unavailable facts about the internal life of corrective labor camps, but details of ordinary life in other settings, how meetings were run, the patterns of interpersonal relationships, and so on. Until researchers can go into China and study organizations and social units first hand in an intensive way,[9] no other source will be able to provide the rich insight into complex human experiences, the vivid detail, and compelling drama that at least the best refugee interviews can provide. Moreover, informants are a much more efficient source of information about China than most at our disposal. They can be asked questions, while, say, a newspaper has to be scanned and searched for information relevant to a given topic. And in spite of a variety of biases, most informants are not completely closed-minded and negative about everything in China. Many show an ability to look at various sides of an issue and give replies which are quite at variance with what one might expect from the stereotypical ardent anticommunist. Finally, most other sources of information about China in recent years have been subject to serious bias problems as well and must be used with caution. Research based upon sources such as the mass media or the

---

9. A very few foreigners have been permitted to visit China and gather some kinds of data. See W. R. Geddes, *Peasant Life in Communist China* (Ithaca: Society for Applied Anthropology, 1963); Jan Myrdal, *Report from a Chinese Village* (New York: Pantheon Books, 1965); Barry Richman, *Industrial Society in Communist China* (New York: Random House, 1969).

reports of travelers to China has to cope with somewhat different, but equally thorny, bias problems. The best approach is obviously to try to combine information from various sources, and this I have done to some extent by checking in the mass media for confirmation of things told me by interviewees. I believe, then, that refugee interviews represent an extremely rich and valuable source of information which, if used with caution, can yield many insights into Chinese society.

In selecting the case studies which are used in Chapters 5 through 9, I first formed a pool of the most intensive cases, those in which several interviews had yielded a fairly full description of a given organization. Then I looked within this pool for the "best" interviews, those in which the informant had shown a fair amount of insight into his own experiences. From these I selected the ones which showed interesting contrasts which would highlight the analysis. The other interviews were not then ignored, but were consantly used as checks on the information presented in the case studies, as the reader will have noted. At the close of each of these five chapters there is a brief attempt to summarize the ways in which the cases presented differed from the experiences of other informants in the same kind of organization. In each case study the names and some of the specific information about each informant have been changed in order to preserve his anonymity. The reader will also notice that these studies are not full cases in the sense of telling us everything we want to know about an organization. In the interests of focusing on the central issue of the operation of *hsiao-tsu* and political rituals, certain kinds of information which was collected (See Appendix II) has not been included in the case studies, or has been relegated to the status of footnotes.

Appendix II:

INTERVIEW TOPIC LIST

I. Background Information:
   a. Original home of family
   b. Where born and grew up
   c. Family's social class categorization (respondent's *chia-t'ing ch'u-shen*)
   d. Composition of family respondent grew up in
   e. Any family members in serious trouble with CCP while respondent growing up?
   f. Respondent's present age
   g. Educational history—when, where, and what type of school?
   h. Respondent's personal status classification *(ko-jen ch'eng-fen)*
   i. Job history—when, where, doing what, within what work unit, and with what status and pay?
   j. Whether and when participated in Youth League or Party
   k. When left China, with whom, legally or illegally, and if the latter, how had he gotten to know his fellow escapees?
   l. How long had respondent been considering coming to Hong Kong and why?

At this stage, based on the personal history given, one period and one institutional affiliation of the respondent must be picked as the focus for further questions, the preference being for a fairly recent and fairly lengthy affiliation, except in cases where an earlier or briefer affiliation is of particular interest due to its rarity among refugees—e.g. in the army. The following questions deal with the unit selected.

II. Basic Organization:
   a. What is the name, function, and size of the overall unit (school, factory, commune, etc.)?
   b. What are the leading organs and leadership offices within this overall unit?

c. Describe the basic administrative structure of the overall unit, including the number of subunits at each level, their functions, and the leadership positions within them.

(These questions are asked to determine the basic structure of the overall unit. For the following questions, the basic level unit in which the respondent was situated is the focus. In most cases the basic level unit means the unit one level larger than the *hsiao-tsu,* such as a school class, a factory workshop, or a rural production team.)

d. What was the basic level unit in which the respondent was situated, how many people were in it, and what was the basis for membership?

e. Within the basic level unit how many were Youth League or Party members, what were the rough percentages from different family class backgrounds, of different ages, different regional origins, occupational grades?

f. In the period respondent there, how many people left the basic level unit, how many new people came in, were there organizational changes in the overall unit which affected the membership of the basic level unit?

g. What were the cadre positions within the basic level unit, what were their responsibilities, and how were they selected? What was the turnover in these positions while respondent there?

h. Was respondent ever a cadre in the unit—circumstances?

i. Relationship of Party and Youth League organization to the administrative structure—were there branches or *hsiao-tsu* of either in the basic level unit? And how did higher level Party and Youth League units correspond to the administrative structure? What was the changeover in officers in these organizations while respondent there? Did some hold administrative posts as well?

j. Did members of the basic level unit participate in other organizations, such as trade unions, militia, women's association, etc.?

k. If so, how many members of basic level unit partitcipated in each, what was the basis for participation, and how did the structure of these organizations correspond to the administrative structure of the unit, what were the leading officers, did they hold administrative or Party or Youth League posts as well, and what was the extent of turnover in these posts?

l. Did respondent ever hold cadre positions in these organizations?

m. Within the basic level unit how were members divided into *hsiao-tsu* —how many *hsiao-tsu,* the basis of division, who decided on the division, how many in each group, what leaders in each *hsiao-tsu,* how were they chosen, and the extent of turnover in *hsiao-tsu* heads over time?

In the following section, the purpose is to find out what meetings the respondent regularly participated in, and to a certain extent other meetings participated in by those around him. It is necessary to ask and get an inventory for meetings of different kinds of organizations within the overall unit (e.g., Party branch, administrative basic level unit, trade union, etc.) as well as to find out within any kind of organization the variety of meetings held. The questions below must be asked for all of the organizations and levels of those organizations that members of respondent's basic level group participated in (thus administrative *hsiao-tsu* meetings, administrative basic level unit meetings, larger administrative meetings; Party *hsiao-tsu* meetings, Party branch meetings, larger Party meetings; etc.)

III. Meeting Routine:
    a. When no campaign or special circumstances, is there a set meeting routine for (organization and level specified)?
    b. If so, on what day(s), at what times, for how long, and what factors lead to minor variations in these things?
    c. Are there several types of basic meetings of (organization and level specified), or are all such meetings more or less the same?
    d. If several distinct types of meetings, for each:
        1. How often and when is it held?
        2. Who chairs the meetings, and what is his function as chairman?
        3. What kinds of preparation are there for such a meeting?
        4. What is the distinctive feature of such a meeting?
        5. In general what is the format—who speaks, what reference materials are used—do people speak in turn, only a few speak, free discussion, etc?
        6. What kinds of matters are discussed—work (or academic study), political study, individual errors, etc?
        7. Is criticism and self-criticism regularly used at such a meeting, and if so how is it carried out?
    e. If not a set meeting routine—in general how often are such meetings held, who decides to call them, and in what circumstances are they called, variations in the frequency, and in how long the meetings last?
    f. For these irregularly held meetings, what is their nature—as in IIIc and IIId, above.
    g. For either set or irregular meetings, does respondent know to whom the meeting chairman reports on the meeting—if so to whom, how often, when, and how? Are official notes taken at the meeting—if so by whom, and what happens to these notes after the meeting? Do higher cadres or outsiders sometimes sit in on these meetings, and if so who, why and how often?
    h. When a campaign comes along what happens to this meeting routine?
    i. How did the meeting routine described above change over time, and if major changes, does the respondent know why, and what was the nature of the change (frequency, type of meeting, format, study materials used, etc.)?

j. (If not already mentioned) Was there a regular system for making self-examinations *(chien-t'ao)*—if so in what group, how often, written or oral, what was the format of the meetings, how much preparation for the meetings, and does respondent know what happened with the results of the self-examinations?

k. Was there a regular system of individual summations *(ko-jen tsung-chieh)*—if so, when were they made, in what kind of group, what was summed up, what was the format of the meeting, and what happened with the results of the summations?

IV. Individual Error Handling:

a. While respondent was there, were there individuals who committed serious errors of any type ("thought errors," graft, violation of policies, etc.)? If so, who, and the nature of the errors?

b. How was one of these instances handled—give a concrete account from start to finish including such things as:

1. How and by whom was the error discovered? How many people were aware of the error before it became an issue?

2. What individuals or divisions within the unit took charge of dealing with the error?

3. What methods outside of meetings were used—individual cadre talks, writing self-examinations, deliberation by leading cadres?

4. If meetings were called—called by whom, of what organizations, how many meetings, extending over what period of time, what was the format of the meetings, roughly what was said by those directing the meetings, by the person being criticized, and by those attending the meeting?

5. Were meetings termed struggle meetings, or less serious, and does respondent know who decided on the degree of seriousness?

6. What was the respondent's relationship to the person being criticized and his personal reaction to the proceedings?

7. What was the type of participation in the meetings of those individuals in the unit who were closest to the person being criticized?

c. What sanctions were applied to the criticized person as a result, and does the respondent know who decided and how?

d. Was the respondent himself ever severely criticized for some error during the period in question—if so use the questions under IVb, but add:

1. What was the respondent's personal reaction to the criticism of him in individual talks, in meetings?

2. While criticism was in progress, how did his relationship with individuals in his unit differ from before the matter was brought up—in particular how isolated was he, and did those closest to him in the group come covertly and express sympathy?

3. After the matter was concluded, if respondent was still in the

unit, how had his relationship with individuals in that unit changed from before, if at all?

V. Mobility and Livelihood:

(Substantial adaptation must take place in these questions, due to the very different nature of such organizations as schools, production teams, and factories. However, the main goals of the following questions are to find out what kinds of vertical mobility there were both vocationally and politically, who decided such things, to what extent basic *hsiao-tsu* discussions were a part of the decision process, and the rough extent of various kinds of mobility. As much as possible the respondent should be asked to give concrete examples, either from his own experience, or about others in his basic level unit).

a. Who determines what occupational grade people have when they come into the unit? Who determines subsequent raises and demotions? Insofar as the respondent has concrete knowledge, how are such matters decided, what are the criteria used, and what are the procedures used?

b. What advances in occupational grade took place in the respondent's basic administrative *hsiao-tsu* while he was there?

c. How many transfers into and out of the basic *hsiao-tsu* were there, and, to the extent of the respondent's personal knowledge, what were the procedures and criteria used for such transfers (include school advancement and job placement from schools here)?

d. Were people from respondent's unit sent down (hsia-fang)—and if so how many, when, and, as above, how were these decisions made?

e. Are there ways to earn extra income above the standard level for one's grade—and if so what are they, how many get such income and, as above, how are decisions affecting such extra income made?

f. If someone feels they deserve a higher occupational grade, greater income, a bonus, etc.—to whom can they appeal, how does such an appeal work, and give concrete instances of what happened in such appeals.

g. Were there instances of people in the basic level unit who had their incomes reduced, their rations cut, or were demoted or fired—and if so the reason, and how the decisions were made.

h. What sorts of organized competitions were there in labor or work—including such aspects as:

1. How often did such competitions take place, and what determined their frequency? What was the nature of the groups and individuals who excelled in the competitions, what were they called?

2. How were those who excelled picked—including the role of *hsiao-tsu* discussions and nominations or higher level decisions?

3. What kinds of awards were given to those who excelled?

4. Were those who did poorly sanctioned or criticized?

5. Could excelling in such competitions be connected with subsequent occupational or political mobility?

6. Were those who excelled usually the same people, or did most of the personnel get picked sooner or later?

7. How did such competitions change over time?

i. Did the unit have opportunities for spare time study or comparable ways of increasing occupational skills? If so what was the system, who determined which group members had access to such opportunities, how many in fact did participate and who were they, and could such activity be connected with subsequent changes in occupational status or income?

j. If faced with economic hardships—what opportunities for assistance or loans were there, what was the procedure for getting assistance, and give examples of people who got such assistance and how and why?

k. Did the unit have some sort of on-the-job study or training groups to prepare people to assume leadership positions in work? If so what was the system, who ran such groups, how were individuals picked for training, give concrete examples of people so trained, and how the training affected their subsequent position?

l. Taking the major basic level unit cadres, does the respondent know how long they had held these posts, and what they did before assuming these posts? Also for new people assuming these posts while respondent was there, what had they done previously? And for those replaced, what happened to them subseqently? Ask for similar concrete examples for higher administrative cadres in the unit.

m. How many people in respondent's basic level unit were accepted into the Party while he was there? Into the Youth League? Were any people expelled from either organization, and if so why?

n. Did respondent's unit have organized study groups or training classes for those being prepared for entering the Party or the Youth League? If so how many people participated, how were they chosen, and what was the training system? If not, were there other, less formal, ways of training prospective members?

o. Give concrete examples of the role played in work and in meetings of various types by new members of the Party or Youth League before and after their acceptance.

p. Was there any system within the unit for training Party or Youth League members to become cadres within these organizations, and if so what was the system and who participated?

q. For basic level Party and Youth League officers, give information comparable to that in V.l. for administrative officers. Also concrete examples for higher level officers.

r. Did the unit have organized competitions for political honors or in political study? If so what were the details, as in V.h. for work competitions?

    s. Did any individuals from the unit attend outside political training courses or schools? If so, who were they, what was the nature of their training, and, if respondent knows, how were they picked, and what was the difference in their status and activities after their return to the unit?

VI. Problem Solving and Grievances:

(This section is intended to find out how miscellaneous problems and grievances were dealt with in respondent's unit if they were dealt with at all. The main concerns are both minor forms of individual misconduct and individual grievances. The questions asked are in hypothetical form, but the respondent must give concrete examples in reply, rather than stating how such things would be done or were generally done. If some topics have already been covered from earlier sections, then omit here.)

    a. What is done if a person works poorly, comes to work late, is lazy, etc.? (or doesn't study, skips class, etc.)—who concerns themselves with such behavior, what methods are used to deal with this, are meetings called to criticize, etc?

    b. What if an individual in the unit has a conflict or a fight with someone else, either within or outside the unit—similar details?

    c. What about defects in spare time activities—drinking, gambling, practicing religion, etc?

    d. What if an individual in the unit has conflicts with his family—beats his wife, constantly argues with his parents, etc?

    e. What if an individual does poorly in political study—misses meetings, falls asleep, doesn't prepare properly, doesn't participate actively, etc?

    f. What about minor crimes and sins—petty theft, cheating on an exam, minor graft, etc?

    g. What if you feel you deserve more income—how could you get it improved, who would you go to, etc?

    h. If you feel work assignment is poor or unfair, how could you get it changed?

    i. If you have been falsely criticized, how could you counter that criticism?

    j. If you were given a transfer order or sent down—could you appeal, and if so how?

    k. If you were subjected to other kinds of unfair treatment from leading cadres in the unit, how could you appeal?

VII. Leaders and relations with the masses:

(This section is designed to find out more about those basic level and leading cadres who were most important in their influence over the respondent. Just which cadres will be asked about will depend upon the position and the unit the respondent was in, but in most cases it should include the *hsiao-tsu* head, the head of the administrative basic level unit, Party and Youth League branch secretaries and perhaps other influential leaders, such as the class chief (*pan chu-jen*) for students and the personnel office head for cadres. The following questions should be asked about each such cadre. But if respondent was in the unit for a long time and there was substantial turn over in these positions, then try to focus on one or two incumbents of relatively long tenure.)

  a. What sort of person was this cadre?
    1. Age
    2. Family class backgroud
    3. Provincial origin—and *hsien,* if known
    4. Party or Youth League membership, and tenure in these organizations
    5. Revolutionary experience (service before 1949) or not.
    6. Educational level—and schools, if known.
    7. Level of intelligence and professional skill.
    8. How activist was he relative to others in political activities?
    9. How diligent in work was he?
    10. Personality—especially arrogance and commandism vs. friendliness and comradely concern.
    11. Personal relations and ties with higher cadres.
  b. What were his ties with his subordinates?
    1. How close was respondent personally with this cadre? Nature of contacts? Any joint social life?
    2. What was respondent's personal feelings toward this cadre—respect, no special feeling, dislike and why?
    3. What was this cadre's relationship with other subordinates? Did he often seek people out for individual talks, did he inquire about problems, did he mingle with them during the day or keep aloof? Did he have certain people in the group he was closer to than others and relied on— who and what was special about these people? Did he have joint social activities outside with others in the unit?
    4. What was the general attitude of others in the unit toward this cadre—respect, fear, etc.—and how does the respondent know?
    5. Did this cadre ever make off-the-cuff remarks that differed from current policies? Or sympathize with those who had been penalized for errors?
    6. Any romantic ties with subordinates? Any kinship ties?
    7. Any major changes in relations with others over time, and why?
  c. If there was a change in this cadre position, how did the change affect relations within the unit and work progress?
VIII. Peer relationships—within and outside the unit.
    a. Were respondent's closest friends inside the unit or not? Inside the basic level unit or not? The *hsiao-tsu* or not?
    b. For those people within unit whom respondent was closest to:

1. What was their background—as in VII.a?
2. Did respondent have social relationships with these friends when outside of the unit—if so describe?
3. Could respondent speak completely openly with these friends—give examples of what was and what was not discussed?
4. If an instance where respondent being seriously criticized, or such a friend within the unit—what part did the other partner play in the meeting—if criticize, how severely—and was there informal communication of sympathy between the two?

c. Were there cliques or groups in conflict within the unit—if so what was the social basis of the cliques, and what was the nature of the conflict—were steps taken to resolve the conflict?

d. Any romantic ties within the unit?

e. Nature of kinship ties, if any, within the unit.

f. How many within the basic level unit could generally be considered to be activists—what kinds of people were they, what was their role in meetings and in work, what was their relationships with others, both while in the unit and outside. Does the respondent feel that they were genuinely activists (thoughts the same as actions, no opportunistic calculation), and how did he judge such a matter?

g. Were there any real outcasts within the unit—if so who and why, and what was their relationship with others? Were they subjected to special supervision, study, ostracism, etc?

h. Did personal feelings and kinship ties affect relations within the unit and criticism rituals—give concrete examples?

i. How many in the group would share grievances—re work load, food shortage, meeting load—with the respondent—concrete examples?

j. When males and females in the unit committed mistakes, were they criticized equally severely? In criticism meetings, were males and females equally severe in their criticism of others?

k. Within the basic level unit—were there subgroups whose members never criticized each other severely—mutual protection relationships? Was there a norm that if a close friend committed an error you should be the first and the most outspoken in criticism of him? Were there instances of informing on close friends within the unit?

l. Within the unit, who were the individuals most disliked by the respondent—what were their social characteristics—why were they disliked?

m. For those in unit outside of closest friends—did respondent have social relationships with them outside of the unit—avoidance?

n. For closest outside friends of respondent
1. How had he gotten to know these people?
2. Brief background as in VII.a.
3. How often together with these friends, and what activities?
4. Could respondent speak completely openly with these friends?

    5. Did respondent discuss events in his own unit with these friends?

    6. If an instance when respondent under serious criticism—did he discuss his troubles with outside friends—with what reaction—were there any instances of his unit seeking out such friends to try to get them to inform on him?

    7. What was the nature of comments from such outside friends about these events in his unit?

  o. For family members respondent living with or close to, ask questions VIIIn3–VIIIn8. And if married or met spouse during this period, ask also about how got to know spouse, and whether events in his unit were discussed at home.

IX. Political Campaigns:

(The preceding sections have been designed primarily to find out about the organization and study routine in respondent's unit over the long run and when not disrupted by campaigns. In this section one major campaign that occurred while respondent was in the unit is focused upon, to try to find out how it was carried out within the unit.)

  a. Pick one major campaign which took place during the period under examination.

  b. What was the rough duration of the campaign, what were its stages, and what things differentiated these stages?

  c. Did any outside people come in to direct or influence the campaign? If so who were they, who sent them, and what role did they play in various stages of the campaign?

  d. What kinds of meetings were held with what frequency in various stages in the campaign? In particular for the various kinds of meetings mentioned in response to section III, what happened during campaigns—intensified or fell off in frequency?

  e. Within the unit was there any reorganization or forming of new groups as part of the campaign? If so what were the new groups, how did they get formed, who was in them in relationship to the original organization, and what was their role in the campaign?

  f. What was the nature of the respondent's participation in the campaign and of other members of his *hsiao-tsu?*

  g. Did targets for criticism emerge during the campaign? If so at what stage, what were they criticized for, how were they treated, and how were their errors dealt with?

  h. How were relations between the respondent and other members of the basic level unit affected by the campaign—also relations with close friends within the unit, with major basic level cadres, and with outside family and friends?

  i. After the campaign concluded were there changes in personnel, in organization, in interpersonal relations, in the status of specific individuals (e.g. acceptance into the Party after a campaign)—or to what extent did these things return to their pre-campaign state?

Appendix III:

BASIC BACKGROUND INFORMATION ON INFORMANTS

KEY:

1 = Age at time of interview in 1969
2 = Sex
    M = male
    F = female
3 = Party or Youth League Membership
    CCP = Chinese Communist Party
    YCL = Youth League
    N = Neither
    Ex = Expelled
4 = Individual or family class origin
    Cap = capitalist, bureaucratic capitalist
    Pet = petty bourgeois: teachers, doctors, small traders, etc.
    Ll = landlord, bureaucratic landlord, industrial-commercial landlord
    Rp = rich peasant, small land lessor
    Mp = middle peasant, upper middle peasant, lower middle peasant
    Pp = poor peasant, hired peasant, or poor fisherman
    Os = Overseas Chinese
    Rev = revolutionary martyr
    Wor = worker
    (Con) = concealed true status, claimed poor peasant or worker
5 = Province of origin
    K = Kwangtung
    Os = Overseas
    Other provinces name specifically
6 = Province of organization described—same key
7 = Educational level
    LP = lower primary (generally 4 years)

UP = upper primary (6 years)
LM = lower middle school (9 years)
UM = upper middle school (12 years)
Univ = University
+ = some additional schooling
− = level of schooling indicated not completed
8 = Year left China (L after year indicates given permission to leave)
9 = Participation in Cultural Revolution
    Y = yes
    N = no
10 = Number of interviews (each interview equals three hours)
na = not available

The informants are presented by the category in which they were interviewed: students, cadres, peasants, workers, labor camp inmates, and the residual categories of urban residents and the military. Eight informants who were rejected from the study are not included. Those interviewed about two organizations are given a double symbol and listed under both categories (e.g., SC-1 was interviewed both about student experience and about cadre experiences). All the background information is self-reported and thus is subject to some falsification.

STUDENTS:

	1	2	3	4	5	6	7	8	9	10
S-1	24	M	N	Pet	Hunan	K	Univ−	1968	Y	3
S-2	22	M	N	Pct	K	K	UM+	1967	N	1
S-3	22	F	N	Cap	K	K	UM	1967	N	1
S-4	26	M	N	Cap	K	K	Univ−	1967	Y	3
S-5	29	M	N	Wor	K	Hupei	Univ−	1967	N	1
S-6	28	M	N	Os	Hong Kong	K	UM	1967(L)	N	1
S-7	31	M	YCL	Wor	K	K	UM+	1964	N	2
S-8	21	M	N	Ll	K	K	UM	1967	N	3
S-9	22	M	YCL	Wor	K	K	UM−	1967	Y	7
S-10	25	F	N	Pet	Hunan	K	UM	1962	N	2
S-11	20	M	N	Ll	K	K	UM	1968	N	1
S-12	22	M	N	Pet	K	K	UM	1969	Y	2
S-13	32	M	N	Os	Os-K	Shensi	Univ	1967	N	1
S-14	31	M	N	Os	Os-K	Hopei	Univ	1962	N	1
S-15	14	M	N	Mp	K	K	UP	1968	Y	1
S-16	22	M	N	Cap	K	K	UM	1968	Y	1
SP-1	23	M	N	Rp	K	K	UM	1967	Y	5
SW-1	25	M	N	Ll	Kwangsi	K	UM	1965	N	2
SC-1	32	F	YCL	Rev	Hopei	Hopei	Univ	1965(L)	N	42
SC-2	30	F	N	Cap	Hopei	Hopei	Univ	1962(L)	N	16
SC-3	36	F	YCL	Cap	Hopei	Hopei	Univ	1964(L)	N	10
SC-4	37	M	CCP	Os-Ll	K	K	Univ	1968	Y	8

Total: 22 students.

CADRES:

	1	2	3	4	5	6	7	8	9	10
C-1	32	M	YCL	Os	Os-K	K	UP+	1963	N	12
C-2	33	M	N	Os	Os-Fukien	Hopei	Univ	1963(L)	N	10
C-3	35	M	CCP	Mp	K	K	LM	1968	Y	3
C-4	32	M	YCL	Ll	K	K	Univ−	1964	N	1
C-5	24	M	N	Rp	Kiangsi	K	UM	1965	N	1
C-6	23	F	N	Cap	K	K	UM+	1968	Y	4
C-7	39	M	N	Pet	K	K	UM	1968	N	1
C-8	28	M	YCL	Pp	K	K	Univ−	1965	N	2
C-9	30	M	N	Ll(Con)	K	K	UM	1967	Y	2
C-10	28	M	YCL	Os-Mp	K	K	Univ	1968	N	2
C-11	36	M	N	Os-Ll	K	K	UM−	1965	N	3
C-12	42	M	N	Os-Pet	K	K	Univ	1968	Y	4
C-13	31	F	N	Os-Rp	K	K	UM	1967	N	1
C-14	28	M	N	Rp	K	K	UM	1969	Y	2
C-15	37	M	YCL	Mp	K	K	Univ	1968	Y	5
C-16	40	M	YCL	Pp	K	K	Univ−	1962(L)	N	1
C-17	28	M	N	Ll	K	K	UM	1968	Y	2
CP-1	29	M	YCL	Pp	K	K	Univ	1968	Y	1
SC-1	32	F	YCL	Rev	Hopei	Hopei	Univ	1965(L)	N	42
SC-2	30	F	N	Cap	Hopei	Hopei	Univ	1962(L)	N	16
SC-3	36	F	YCL	Cap	Hopei	Hopei	Univ	1964(L)	N	10
SC-4	37	M	CCP	Os-Ll	K	K	Univ	1968	Y	8

Total: 22 cadres.

PEASANTS:

	1	2	3	4	5	6	7	8	9	10
P-1	26	M	YCL	Mp	K	K	UP	1969	Y	6
P-2	48	M	N	Pp	K	K	UM—	1968	Y	2
P-3	22	M	N	Pp	K	K	LP	1968	Y	4
P-4	37	M	N	Os-Rp	K	K	LM	1967	Y	2
P-5	35	M	N	Pp	K	K	na	1967	Y	1
P-6	27	M	N	Ll	K	K	LP	1967	N	1
P-7	26	M	N	Mp	K	K	LM	1966	N	2
P-8	23	M	N	Pp	K	K	LM	1968	N	1
P-9	29	M	N	Ll	K	K	UP	1967	Y	1
P-10	29	M	N	Ll	K	K	LP	1968	N	1
P-11	28	M	N	Mp	K	K	LM	1967	N	1
P-12	23	M	N	Pet	K	K	Univ—	1967	Y	2
P-13	23	M	N	Cap	K	K	UM	1969	Y	1
P-14	26	M	N	Ll	K	K	Univ—	1968	N	2
P-15	26	M	N	Ll	K	K	UP	1968	N	1
P-16	19	M	N	Pet	K	K	LM—	na	N	1
P-17	24	M	N	Rp	K	K	LM—	1967	Y	1
P-18	20	M	N	Os	Os-K	K	UM	1969	Y	1
P-19	na	F	N	Ll	K	K	UP	1969	N	1
P-20	33	F	N	Pp	K	K	LM	1964	N	2
PM-1	29	M	CCP(Ex)	Mp	K	K	LM	1964	N	2
SP-1	23	M	N	Rp	K	K	UM	1967	Y	5
CP-1	29	M	YCL	Pp	K	K	Univ	1968	Y	1

Total: 23 peasants.

WORKERS:

	1	2	3	4	5	6	7	8	9	10
W-1	28	M	N	Cap	K	K	LM	1968	N	1
W-2	20	M	YCL	Wor	Kiangsu	K	LM—	1967	Y	3
W-3	28	M	N	Os	Os-K	K	LM—	1962(L)	N	1
W-4	26	M	N	Cap	K	K	UM—	1968	N	1
W-5	28	M	N	Rp	K	K	Univ—	1965	N	2
W-6	26	M	YCL	Ll(Con)	K	K	LM	1968	N	2
W-7	29	M	N	Cap	K	K	LM	1967	N	1
W-8	29	M	N	Ll	K	K	UM	1967	Y	1
W-9	27	M	N	Ll	K	K	UM	1967	Y	1
W-10	29	M	N	Pet	K	Sinkiang	UM—	1964	N	1
W-11	37	M	CCP	Pet	K	K	UM+	1969	Y	2
W-12	23	M	N	Ll(Con)	Kwangsi	K	LM	1968	Y	1
W-13	32	M	N	Ll	K	K	LM	1962	N	1
W-14	26	M	N	Rp	K	K	LM	1968	Y	1
SW-1	25	M	N	Ll	Kwangsi	K	UM	1965	N	2

Total: 15 workers.

LABOR CAMP INMATES:

	1	2	3	4	5	6	7	8	9	10
I-1	43	M	N	Cap	K	K	UM	1969	Y	3
I-2	32	M	N	Ll-Cap	K	K	UM—	1968	N	2
I-3	40	M	N	Mp	K	Heilung-kiang	UP	1965	N	1
I-4	25	M	N	Rp	Kwangsi	K	Univ—	1967	N	2
I-5	32	M	N	Ll(Con)	K	K	UM+	1962	N	2
I-6	47	M	N	Ll	K	K	Univ	1969	N	1
I-7	34	M	N	Ll	K	K	UP	1965	N	1
I-8	54	M	N	Ll	K	Inner Mong.	Univ	1966	N	2
I-9	28	M	N	Ll	K	K	UM	1967	N	1
I-10	34	M	YCL(Ex)	Ll	K	K	UM+	1962	N	1
I-11	28	M	N	Mp	K	K	LM	1963	N	2
I-12	25	M	N	Cap	K	K	Univ—	1962	N	1
I-13	56	M	N	Ll	K	K	Univ	1965	N	1
I-14	49	M	N	Wor	K	K	UM	1966	N	1

Total: 14 labor camp inmates.

OTHER MISCELLANEOUS:

URBAN RESIDENTS:

	1	2	3	4	5	6	7	8	9	10
R-1	27	M	N	Pet	K	K	Univ—	1967	N	1
R-2	22	M	N	Ll	K	K	UM+	1969	Y	1
R-3	23	M	N	Cap	K	K	LM	1967	Y	1

MILITARY:

	1	2	3	4	5	6	7	8	9	10
M-1	29	M	N	Mp	K	K	UM	1964	N	2
PM-1	29	M	CCP(Ex)	Mp	K	K	LM	1964	N	2

Total: 5 other.

Total number of persons interviewed	101
Total number of interviews	260
Total hours of interviews	780
Total number of informants used	93
Number of interviews used	252
Hours of interviewing used	756

INDEX